ROSEY

My Life in
Somerset Cricket

Brian Rose

with Anthony Gibson

foreword by Vic Marks

FAIRFIELD BOOKS

Fairfield Books
17 George's Road, Bath BA1 6EY
Tel 01225-335813

Text © Brian Rose
Foreword © Vic Marks
Introduction © Anthony Gibson

The photographs in this book come from a number of sources,
principally Brian Rose himself, Somerset Cricket Museum, Somerset
County Cricket Club, Somerset County Gazette, Ivan Ponting and
Alain Lockyer. We are very grateful to them all for their help.

The following images appear by permission of their copyright holders:

Pages 33, 35, 39, 52, 53, 56, 73, 84, 94 & front cover – Getty Archive
Page 110 – PA Images

Thanks are especially due to Steve Pittard and John Winnifrith for
their invaluable scrutinising of the factual details in the text.

First published 2019

ISBN: 978 1 9996558 5 3

Printed and bound in Great Britain by
CPI Antony Rowe, Bumpers Way, Chippenham SN14 6LH

Contents

Foreword

by Vic Marks

It dismays me that Brian Rose is still the most successful Somerset captain of all time. Not just because I would have quite liked that accolade myself. The real reason for my distress is that Somerset CCC has endured so many near misses in the last decade or two. They should have won more trophies after Rosey's time as captain. I know that this dismays Brian just as much since in more recent times he was often the club's cricket director agonising in the pavilion as another trophy slipped from the club's grasp.

The sad fact is that Somerset, for all their recent excellence, have been unable to replicate that golden period of four decades ago when they collected five cups in swift succession. Now you can read all about those adventures from the man who was in charge at the time.

With the help of Anthony Gibson, Brian has recalled those heady days when Somerset finally won something. Here is the inside view on the legendary Brian Close, our first captain and our most unforgettable one, the emergence of Viv Richards and Joel Garner, plus some interesting local talent: a certain Ian Botham from Yeovil, Pete Denning, the other blond from Weston, and the rest of us from all corners of the county, whom Brian was eager to hurry into the first team when he took over in 1978. There is triumph, despair and bewilderment along the way, whether Brian is captaining the side, chairing the cricket committee, which he soon disbanded, or taking on the role of cricket director.

For almost half a century Brian has been wedded to the club – as well as to the ever-smiling, long-suffering Stevie. That remained the case even when he was doing a 'proper job' in the paper industry. Now Brian is the club's president, and how fitting it would be if the current team contrived to honour that overdue appointment by finally delivering the elusive Championship pennant.

You may be surprised how much I looked forward to reading this – given that I was around Brian for most of his time at the club. I'll tell you why: whether it was 1977 or 2007 Rosey did not give too much away. It was always hard to work out what he was thinking – just occasionally one wondered whether he was thinking at all. He always preferred to keep his cards close to his chest. Now he has opened up, and we can all have a clearer idea of what has been churning around inside his head over the last half-century.

With hindsight Brian was the natural choice to take over from Brian Close as Somerset captain in 1978. This was less obvious at the time, partly because as a youngster eager to establish himself in the team he gave so little away in the dressing room. In this instance – and not for the last time – the cricket chairman, Roy Kerslake, knew best. It turned out that Brian was easily best man for the job.

We soon came to realise that he was tough, clear-thinking and desperate for the club to win something. He recognised that he had some good young players alongside the three extraordinary ones, and he was bold enough to get them in the team as soon as he could. Close, a wonderfully maverick tactician, had been replaced by a surprisingly ruthless strategist, who was prepared to take the difficult decisions. At the same time the captaincy enhanced Brian as a cricketer; he started to play his shots again, and suddenly he became one of the most dominant batsmen in the county game.

As a leader he was seldom Churchillian in his oratory. As the seasons of 1978 and 1979 gained momentum, he would say something at 10.57 each morning and it was usually, "This is the most important day in the club's history." And off we went. Team meetings were rare; they usually took place only before cup finals when the club would pay for a grand meal, washed down with wine and the odd glass of port. The occasion would often end up in a (relatively) friendly argument about something ridiculous, with Rosey eventually raising his eyebrows and making an exasperated exit. Yet all this seemed to relax everyone before a big day out at Lord's.

Beyond the merriment Rosey planned meticulously and agonised over the pursuit of some long-awaited silverware, and he had a sure hand on the tiller with Kerslake alongside to offer guidance. Deep down, Brian knew the odds were in our favour, such was the talent in the team, provided he could keep a disparate bunch of cricketers heading in the same direction. Somehow he managed that.

The same qualities resurfaced when he returned to the club as cricket director. He rebuilt the team, plotted a path back to the top and came so close to overseeing a Championship victory in 2010. On the disappointing days there was sympathy for his loyal labrador, which was destined for interminable walks among the dunes as Brian sought another solution to the latest setback. He could still be impenetrable, but once again he commanded the respect of a Somerset dressing room. It was so obvious to everyone how much he cared. It still is, and you will be rapidly reminded of that in the story of Somerset's greatest captain.

'Mr Somerset'

by Anthony Gibson

> Rosey came to be seen as the soul of Somerset cricket. He was the embodiment of its best qualities. He was entertaining – the smack of his square cut on the County Ground on a May morning was as fresh as the Quantock wind; yet he was not prodigal and never placed the advertisement of himself above the team cause.
>
> **Scyld Berry**

For a lifelong Somerset cricket follower, being asked to help Brian Rose with his autobiography was a commission made in heaven. I first saw him at Clarence Park in August 1969, batting with Peter Denning. The two young blond left-handers, both Somerset to the core, seemed to me even at the time to be signalling a new, brighter era for Somerset cricket, as they took the attack to Tom Cartwright, David Brown and the rest of the Warwickshire bowlers for a glorious hour or so before lunch on the second day. From that moment on, he was a cricketing hero and, when he went on to captain that magnificent Somerset team to five trophies in five years, he became a hero in excelsis.

I did not really know him until we started work on this book in the summer of 2018. He had always struck me as shrewd, thoughtful and a bit reserved; there was clear evidence of steel beneath the amiable exterior, not only in the way he had captained Somerset but in some of the decisions – initially unpopular but proved correct – which he made as Director of Cricket. I think I expected him to be modest about his own achievements, and so it has proved. Even to those who know him well, Brian is an understated man, whose instinct is to play down his own achievements and to play up those of team-mates and colleagues. And whilst that may be a most desirable quality in a human being, it is perhaps not ideal for someone telling their life story.

Since our first meeting, I have spent many hours with him, sometimes at the County Ground, mostly in the Feathers Bar in the Royal Hotel at Weston, going through his drafts, asking him questions and recording his answers for subsequent transcription. I have tried to keep the words on the page as true as possible to the voice and personality of Brian Charles Rose, something which does mean, of course, that there is not much blowing of the Rosey trumpet in the chapters that follow, something which could easily leave his legions of faithful followers feeling that he might have undersold himself and his role in what were, unarguably, Somerset cricket's greatest years – to date!

So, to balance the Rose modesty, I decided to ask a selection of people with whom he has worked closely for their assessment of our man, in the confident expectation that they would prove rather more effusive than Brian himself. They did not disappoint.

Roy Kerslake, who has known Brian since his Somerset 2nds days in the late 1960s, remembers him as "a very fine left-handed opening batsman with a wide array of shots all round the wicket," as anyone who saw Brian bat will confirm. But he also stresses his courage as a batsman, particularly when faced with "the ferocious pace attack of the West Indies tourists in 1980". In that context, it is worth remembering that Brian topped the English batting averages in that series, against Roberts, Holding, Garner and Marshall at their peak. Goodness knows how many more Test runs he might have scored, had it not been for that eye injury which surfaced in the West Indies.

Roy became Chairman of Somerset CCC in 1979, shortly after Brian had taken over as captain. He was there in the dressing room at Worcester when the fateful decision was made to declare, and he was there at Lord's and Trent Bridge to share in the triumphs that would follow later that season. This is his assessment of Brian as a captain:

> Brian was his own man and led by example. When he took over the captaincy in 1978 from Brian Close, he inherited an exciting squad into whom his predecessor had injected a steely resolve to win. It was always going to be a challenge for any new captain with a dressing room comprising headline-making international stars supported by a very talented bunch of largely unsung heroes. Brian's answer was to have no favourites and to play his cards close to his chest – but always to make it clear what he expected of his team. Brian was not unduly demonstrative on the field, but he had a very keen tactical brain which made him a good reader of the state of the game. He never lost his nerve in close encounters.

Vic Marks, in his foreword, surely speaks for all of Brian's team-mates in his appreciation of him as a leader and his affection for him as a man. It is worth recalling as well what Peter Roebuck, who was not always the most generous in his praise of team-mates, had to say about Brian's captaincy in his autobiography *Sometimes I Forgot to Laugh*:

> Rose deserves considerable credit for the successes of his team. Captaincy is not as straightforward an occupation as it seems.

Admittedly, he was leading a highly motivated young team containing great players and numerous intelligent and powerful characters. But he was also presiding over a change in the club that involved the gradual replacing of older players. Moreover, he had to keep his side together for five months while surviving the inevitable setbacks, insecurities and differences and still performing upon the field, for a struggling captain swiftly loses his authority.

As a captain, Brian was nothing if not inscrutable, something with which some of the younger players found it hard to come to terms when they first came into the side. But there was invariably a breakthrough moment when BCR showed his true colours, as Nigel Popplewell discovered on one of his first appearances for Somerset:

> I remember to this day the enormous smile and congratulatory expression that he bestowed on me when, playing in a low-scoring Sunday game against Middlesex in August 1979, I dived forward and caught a blinder of a catch (though I say it myself) to dismiss Graham Barlow. I came up clutching the ball to find Rosey, who was fielding not far away at mid-on, charging towards me with a huge smile on his face. It was then that I thought that it might be worth carrying on with the first-class cricket lark!

Dr David English, the former manager of the Bee Gees, who has done such great service to English cricket as the founder of the Bunbury ESCA Under-15 Festival, now in its 33rd year, captures the atmosphere of that Somerset dressing room of extraordinary talents and personalities, as he recalls the time he was invited down to Taunton by Ian Botham, shortly after one of their triumphs at Lord's:

> The boys had just finished practising as I was met by the mighty Beefy at the dressing room door. To my right, Peter Roebuck and Vic Marks, the boffins, were absorbed in the *Times* crossword. Nigel Popplewell, full of vim and vigour, greeted me with a warm handshake: "So you're The Loon that Beefy's been telling us all about. Pleasure to meet you!" Suddenly, I found myself surrounded by Dennis 'Breakers' Breakwell, wicket-keeper Derek Taylor, Phil Slocombe, Colin Dredge, Peter 'Dasher' Denning ...
> Whilst all this was going on, a magnificent solitary figure stood in front of the mirror, banging his hair down with a book!

"Nice to meet you, Loony," laughed Viv with an enormous smile and never once taking his eye off his book-to-hair motion. "It's the only way I can keep my curls down," explained the West Indian genius, as his soul-mate Joel Garner looked on, smiling and slowly shaking his head in disbelief.

Suddenly amongst all the chaos and laughter of the dressing room, a young voice piped up. "'Ere Beefy, I've got this ticket for a dance in town tonight. 7 for 7.30, black tie ... 10 bob ... Blimey, Beef, 10 shillings for half an hour is a bit steep, isn't it?" Gary 'Peddler' Palmer's complaint was greeted by an avalanche of riotous laughter and leg pulling ... even the boffins, Marks and Roebuck, looked up from their crossword with a wry smile. And there, seated in the corner, witnessing all this mayhem, was Skipper, Brian Rose, drinking a cup of tea and enjoying the cabaret.

"Loony, I want you to meet our leader, Rosey," announced the Beef. We shook hands, a very special handshake which was to start an adventure and friendship still going strong after forty years.

He was a brilliant visionary and an inspirational captain.

What did Somerset's opponents make of the team's enigmatic, understated, cigar-puffing skipper? Geoff Miller, who played against Brian many times for Derbyshire (and several times with him for England), offers these thoughts:

> When Brian was due to open the batting there was always a bit of debate in the Derbyshire changing room as to whether we should appeal for lbw if he missed a straight one, just in case the finger went up and Brian's departure brought Viv Richards to the crease!
>
> On a more serious note, as a team-mate for England, his attitude, focus, humour and conduct in the team room kept the spirit positive, whilst his dedication to Somerset CCC, and to cricket, has been exemplary.

On into the 1990s and Brian's years as Chairman of the Cricket Committee, when one of the first decisions he made was typically hard-nosed: to bid farewell to the prolific Jimmy Cook and replace him with the top-quality fast bowler that Somerset needed if they were to win more matches, a certain Andrew Caddick. The two of them have been close ever since, their friendship even surviving the difficult decision that Brian had to make in ushering Caddy into retirement in 2009, as his endorsement of Brian's Somerset Presidency illustrates:

> In all my years associated with Somerset, there has been no other person more passionate about the club than Brian Rose. Whenever Brian has been involved with the club, it has prospered, and I believe it will happen again due to the passion for success shown by Brian and which players and supporters alike have come to appreciate over the years.
>
> In his time as Director of Cricket, the partnership that he formed with Andy Hurry saw the emergence of a team that won one-day trophies, coming so close to winning the ultimate prize, the county championship.

The man who gave Brian Rose the job as Director of Cricket in 2005 was Giles Clarke, at the time Chairman of Somerset CCC, subsequently Chairman of the ECB. He acknowledges the role that Roy Kerslake, by then President of the club, had to play in what turned out to be a hugely successful appointment:

> We were entrusted with rescuing the county's fortunes on the field, and Brian was the only man Roy Kerslake, another great Somerset man, even contemplated. Nobody else would fit the bill, and fit it Rosey did.
>
> His passion for the county is absolute, with a determination to ensure happiness, good results and tremendous prospects in looking after the future. He is a man of the highest integrity, respected throughout the game worldwide. His ability to talent-spot is legendary: from the time he as Cricket Chairman dropped the captain and insisted upon an unproven youth opening the batting in his place, a certain Marcus Trescothick, to the signing of Alfonso Thomas on the basis of watching him bowl two overs in an unimportant game in South Africa.
>
> He is beloved in Taunton as a man without ego, with Somerset engraved on his heart, and integrity and great cricket knowledge in every fibre of this being.

Brian's fellow Westonian, Peter Trego, has more reason to thank him than most, as he looks back on the day at Lord's when, bowling for Middlesex, his Somerset career seemingly over, he spotted what he thought was a familiar figure in the crowd:

> I thought to myself, while waiting for the umpire to call 'Play', "Why in the world would Robert Redford be watching Somerset

play cricket?" It took me about two overs to realise that the man intently studying my bowling was my fellow Westonian, Brian Rose.

Later that day he sent a message to the home dressing room for me to meet him in the bar next to the Grace Gates. It was there that he uttered the words that literally both saved and kick-started my career: "It's time for you to come home." To a young man, trying to make his way in cricket, having a man who, I believe, is one of sport's great man-managers show that sort of faith in you has endless power.

Whether it's me, Sir Viv or Jos Buttler, we all have one thing in common, and that's a friendship with BCR that's hard to put into words. At times he's been hard, told us things we don't want to hear, but the funny thing is, it's OK coming from Rosey because with all of us at some time, he's gone out of his way to protect us, stand up for us and, in my case, dig me out of the shit so many times. I have nothing but total trust in what he says.

The man who Brian appointed as head coach when Mark Garaway left for the England set-up in 2006 was Andy Hurry, now Somerset's Director of Cricket. Together with captain Justin Langer, the three of them developed what Andy calls "an identity – a style of play, a method to support developing players. We were exciting to watch."

Through that whole period, Brian was there, mentoring me, giving me the freedom to learn from the successful and unsuccessful decisions I made. He gave me confidence, and together we formed a very strong partnership. I will for ever be grateful for the support and opportunity that BCR gave me.

A sign of the respect in which Brian Rose was and is regarded throughout the world of English cricket was his appointment to the Schofield Review, set up in 2007 in the wake of World Cup failure and Ashes humiliation, to chart the way forward for the England team. Glamorgan's Hugh Morris was the ECB's man on the review and refers to Brian's "insightful contributions" to the process. However, the man that Brian worked most closely with was Surrey and England's Micky Stewart:

Because most of the other members of the group, like Nasser Hussain, Nick Knight and Angus Fraser, were heavily committed elsewhere, Brian and I ended up doing a lot of the donkey work. I took to him immediately. He is personable, with a great sense of humour, and I soon found out that we shared many ideas about the game. He had a very structured approach to the job in hand, and his time in the paper industry meant that he understood business as well as cricket. I think we were both happy with the way the report came out – less happy that some of its most important recommendations, on strengthening four-day county cricket, have not been implemented.

One of the strongest themes of Brian's career has been his determination to create a pathway for identifying and developing young home-grown cricketers. One such was Somerset's latest cricketing super-star, Jos Buttler, who was taken into the Somerset Academy at almost the same time that Brian became Director of Cricket:

> Right from the start of his tenure it was clear that he had a clear strategy for Somerset, and a huge part of that was the development of home-grown players and the emphasis on the Academy producing first class cricketers for Somerset. This was hugely exciting to hear and be a part of and gave me a clear and realistic goal that I now felt was very attainable.
>
> You would often see Brian at age-group matches, scouting talent and keeping his eye on players on the Academy and players he thought had the potential to be a part of it. He would always be present at 2nd XI fixtures too, keeping close attention to this and the production line of cricketers and creating clear pathways from 2nd XI to 1st XI. He had already made some shrewd signings who had an impact on the first team immediately and got the club heading in the right direction, but his attention to young players really made you feel that he wanted to future-proof the club with local talent.
>
> This was a fantastic time to be involved with Somerset as it made you believe that with hard work and dedication you could become a part of something special. I owe a great deal to Brian for his philosophy as Director of Cricket at Somerset. He was a huge influence in the development of my cricket and giving me opportunities to fulfil my potential and my ambitions.

While I was researching this chapter of tribute, I took a call from Alec Stewart, who had heard from his father Micky what was afoot. I asked him what he thought of when he heard the name Brian Rose.

"Brian Rose?" he said. "That's simple – Mr Somerset!"

1

Growing up in a services family

I'm proud to call myself a Somerset man, but I was actually born in Kent, at Horton Kirby Hospital on 4 June 1950. But that was only because my parents, Charlie and Jean, happened to be visiting my grandparents on my mother's side, who had retired to Swanley, and I popped out unexpectedly early. But apart from those first couple of weeks, and three-and-a-half years in Singapore in the late 1950s and early 1960s, I'm happy to say that I've lived all my life either in or very near Weston-super-Mare. If I was a stick of rock, you would find 'Weston-super-Mare' stamped right the way through me!

The Roses were a services family. My mother's father, Peter Buchanan, served in the RAF; my father's father, Chuck Rose, was in the army, based for many years at Norton Barracks, just outside Worcester, something which has given me a strong affinity with the city ever since. My father, Charles Llewellyn Rose, was a gifted footballer and cricketer, who had trials with West Bromwich Albion and whose ambition was to become a professional sportsman. The outbreak of war in 1939 put a stop to all of that, and he enlisted in the RAF, spending part of the war in India and Burma on ground crew duties. He was due to be demobilised when the war ended, but service life suited him, not least because of the opportunities it provided to play cricket and football, and he decided to stay on.

He had met my mother through the RAF, whilst he was posted to Westonzoyland, a few miles from Bridgwater, which is why he started playing football for Bridgwater Town. They had married in 1947 and, shortly afterwards, he was posted to RAF Locking, a technical services training base, three miles from Weston-super-Mare. This worked out in a way that could not have been more fortunate. Besides his sporting abilities, my father's other great skill was with plants and animals, something he had learned from his father, who had set up a smallholding at the back of his house next to Norton Barracks. One of the senior officers at RAF Locking got to hear of this and promoted Sergeant Rose to become manager of the camp's pig farm. Quite why an RAF station should need a pig farm, I have never entirely understood, but my father was in his element.

Wessex saddleback pigs on the farm at RAF Locking

As well as the pigs, he had a decent-sized garden, in which he grew a bewildering variety of beautiful roses and dahlias. When I was old enough, I used to help him with the pigs and in the garden after school and at the weekends. These were formative experiences, whether watching him killing rats with a shovel, or taking the finished pigs to Weston abattoir, or learning the skills of growing roses and tomatoes. By the age of about six, I could prune roses or take dahlia cuttings like a veteran, and it gave me a love of gardening which I have kept to the present day. It also gave me my cricketing nickname – 'Harry', after the famous rose-grower Harry Wheatcroft.

I had a very happy childhood. Some of my earliest memories are of being taken by my father to cricket matches or football games that he was playing in and, as soon as I was old enough to play a variety of games myself, I knew that I had a natural talent for ball games of all sorts. RAF Locking was also the perfect environment for a sports-mad youngster to be brought up in. The base was expanding as the technology developed. It attracted a lot of servicemen from overseas, mainly the Commonwealth, so the sporting facilities were excellent. Right outside our house there was a great expanse of playing fields. The cricket club was there with its little wooden pavilion (not dissimilar to the one in Clarence Park in which I would later get changed as a Somerset cricketer), where the RAF team played, and the nets were available in the summer, while in the winter we had complete access to the sports hall after school and you didn't even have to ask; you could just go, provided there was space available, and play basketball or five-a-side football, tennis or badminton.

I didn't need much encouragement from my father to play whatever game was available and, in any case, he was usually playing sport himself – cricket for Weston-super-Mare CC or for various RAF sides; football for Bridgwater Town. He was a wicket-keeper, with a great pair of hands, who batted at six or seven, and on the football field, where he wasn't the quickest, an artful left-half. His sporting achievements were all the more remarkable, given that he had contracted malaria during the war (something that he kept from me and my sister Jennifer) and was taking quinine tablets and regularly had the shakes. He was an inspiration to me, not only in the sheer volume of sport that he played but in his modesty about his achievements. He would never boast that he was off to play for the Singapore Combined Services side; he was just "off to the cricket". For such a fine sportsman, he also had a remarkably calm temperament, taking good or bad fortune in his stride. That is something I'm afraid I didn't inherit from him, fiercely competitive as I have always been!

My mother Jean was sporty, as well. Her father had been posted with the RAF to Malta when she was growing up, and that was where she'd learnt to swim. Unlike my father, who was strong and wiry but no more than about 5' 9", my mother was tall, lithe and athletic, and she became a great long-distance swimmer. She was quiet and placid and didn't seem to mind my father's frequent absences for his football or his cricket. She was a wonderful mother to me, my elder sister Jenny and my younger brother Chris. Our house on the base – which is still there – wasn't exactly luxurious. There was no central heating, the electric fires were so unreliable as to be positively dangerous, and in the winter I would have to scrape the ice off the inside of the single-glazed, metal-framed windows in my bedroom. But we were well looked after. As a child, I suffered badly from bouts of bronchitis and whooping cough, and I didn't realise until much later how lucky I was not to have suffered any long-term ill effects or worse, as so many children of that generation did. My mother's remedies included putting my head over a bowl of water in which she'd dissolved half a jar of Vicks, covering my head with a towel to make sure I breathed in all the vapours, before rubbing the other half of the jar into my chest!

The other great thing about growing up on an RAF base was the aircraft! An Avro Lancaster and De Haviland 98 Mosquito were parked up outside B Block, presumably used for apprentice training but also available for the primary school children to view in company with a designated NCO. I remember sitting in the pilot's seat in the cramped cockpit of the Lancaster and clambering down the fuselage past the radio operator's seat, the bomb bay, and the mid-turret and then sitting in the rear-gunner's turret and being able to rotate it manually. We were not old enough at the time to comprehend that over 55,000 aircrew in Bomber Command were lost between 1939 and 1945 out of a total of 125,000 (44.4%), one seventh of the entire British service casualties during the whole of the war. Boys and girls in my generation, born shortly after the war, owe a huge debt to the servicemen and women who fought to keep this country free.

Sitting in the pilot's seat of the twin-engined DH Mosquito was especially exciting, and we were told by the NCO that this version flew in operations with the newly-formed PFF squadron (Pathfinder Finding Force), an elite unit that was to be equipped with OBOE, a revolutionary radio navigation and bombing aid. It was nicknamed the 'Wooden Wonder' as the airframe was constructed mainly of wood, partly because metal was in short supply during the war, but also because it gave the aircraft a spectacularly good power-to-weight ratio. This meant it could be developed as a multi-role aircraft: night fighter, photo-reconnaissance, low-level ground attack bomber and pathfinder. It also played an important role in the Second Tactical Air Force, set up in early 1944 prior to Operation Overlord, to hit vital targets. One of their more famous missions was to hit Amiens prison to release the resistance fighters held there. Years later, when I was playing for Somerset, I discovered that the legendary Eric Hill, who wrote for the *Western Daily Press* and was the father of the Taunton press box for so many years, had been a navigator in a Mosquito during the war. There was a runway at RAF Weston, just up the road, so I presume that both the Lancaster and the Mosquito had finished the war there and then been towed to Locking.

Weston Airport had been developed in the mid-1930s as a commercial airport but was taken over in 1940 by the RAF and a factory built in nearby Oldmixon, manufacturing the Bristol Beaufighter. In October 1942 No. 286 Squadron, flying Hurricanes, moved to Weston, to be joined in November 1943 by No. 116 Squadron, a technical services unit specialising in anti-aircraft radar. Post-war the western end of the site was used by Westland Helicopters for development and manufacturing, and a glider training school continued to use the airfield until 1993. A helicopter museum and helipad are based on the south-eastern corner of the field, and the old control tower still exists and was refurbished in 2009. Although most of the airfield has been sold for commercial and housing development, a very large open area still exists and is a great spot to walk the dogs and remember those early days when we walked across the fields from RAF Locking to watch the planes, helicopters and gliders land.

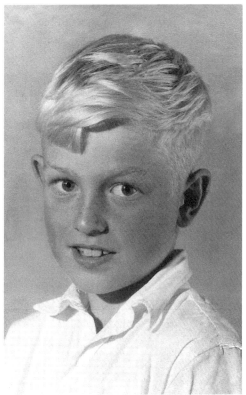

My father, Sergeant Charles Rose; my athletic mother Jean; and me, aged about seven

In 1958 news came that my father was to be posted to Germany, taking us with him. Then, at the very last moment, there was a change. It wasn't to be Germany; instead, we would be setting off for RAF Tengah, in Singapore, for what proved to be a memorable and fascinating three-and-a-half years. I've never been able to establish why there was this last-minute change of plan, but it wouldn't entirely surprise me if it was down to the fact that the RAF cricket team in Singapore were short of a wicket-keeper! At any event, barely a week after packing our bags for Germany, we found ourselves boarding a Bristol Britannia at Stansted Airport. It turned out to be a proving flight, involving stopovers at Istanbul, Karachi, Bombay and Singapore Changi, to allow ground crew to check engines and airframe and passengers to do a spot of sight-seeing. It was a fascinating experience for an eight-year-old, even if the air-sickness bags were in fairly regular demand.

Singapore was hot, usually about the 85°F mark, very rainy and incredibly humid. Our house on the base was still being built, so we were put into a small hotel just outside the city for three weeks, and then moved to a house near the airbase. I remember being fascinated by the huge storm drains alongside the road when we moved to our temporary accommodation, built to carry the torrents of rain produced by Singapore's frequent downpours safely out to sea. The storm drains were also the scene of another moment I will never forget. I was playing tennis with my sister Jenny and the ball went into a drain, and disappeared into a culvert. I jumped down and crawled into the tunnel, only to be confronted by the biggest, hairiest spider you have ever seen. It was bigger than one of my hands, and my hands are big. I've never crawled so fast backwards in my life!

There was one incident, though, which would come back to haunt me many times over the years that followed. I was playing in the street with some other boys from the base, when we were set upon by some of the local lads who started throwing rocks and stones at us. One caught me smack in the mouth, breaking two of my front teeth. Dental technology was still pretty primitive in those days, and for some reason they wouldn't put a proper crown on the broken teeth; until I was about 19, I had to be content with a series of temporary ones. It was an issue all through my teens, and the start of what has proved to be a long history of problems with my teeth.

Despite the heat and the rain, we enjoyed our time in Singapore. I was amazed at the difference in diet and at breakfast revelled in the availability of tropical fruits such as pineapples, lychees, mangos and melons – all of them still very rare in Britain in the fifties. Singapore also gave me a lifelong taste for Indian and Chinese food, something that my old friend Peter 'Dasher' Denning couldn't abide. His diet on away trips consisted almost entirely of rump steak and chips, and he always carried a bottle of tomato ketchup with him wherever we went!

I was at an age when I was starting to understand what was going on around me, and this was a fascinating period for Singapore, in the transition period running up to independence. The future constitution was agreed in 1958 and on 5 June 1959, the day after my ninth birthday, Lee Kuan Yew was installed as the first Prime Minister. He was to govern for three decades and oversaw a huge transformation in both the economy and the fabric of the city, as Singapore grew into one of the 'tiger economies' of the Far East.

To me Singapore City at the time was one big 'China Town' with Singapore Cricket Club, Orchard St shopping, the Botanical Gardens and the Raffles Hotel as stand-out attractions. Later in life, I read *The Virgin Soldiers* by Leslie Thomas, set during the conflict in Malaya and describing in fairly vivid terms what the young soldiers used to get up to in Bougie St. It resonates with me because Leslie lived for a time near Somerton and was a regular at Taunton to watch us play. We had several conversations about his time in National Service in Singapore and my time at Tengah.

In 1958 the island was still affected by the Malayan emergency, and security was still very tight. The South-East Asia Treaty Organisation (SEATO) was created, and RAF Tengah became host to squadrons from the Royal Australian Air Force and the Royal New Zealand Air Force. My father was attached to RAF 45 squadron, flying English Electric Canberra B2 bombers mainly used for photo reconnaissance missions over Malaya and Indonesia. Work also started on a massive extension to the runway at Tengah to accommodate Victor and Vulcan V bombers flown in conjunction with RAF Butterworth in Malaya. More recently, since the Official Secrets Act embargo expired, I've learned that Tengah was also home to 43 Red Beard tactical nuclear weapons. No wonder my father never talked much about what he did in his service years!

We travelled into Singapore city by 'pickup' taxis, which would stop to pick people up if they had vacant space, a bit like miniature buses. It was a great way to get to know what was a very diverse population.

I passed the Singaporean version of the 11+ and went to Alexander Grammar School, the army school, which was built on just about the highest point of the island, overlooking the harbour. It also took boys and girls from the schools at the various RAF bases on the island, and to get there, we had the excitement of travelling in sheeted-down army lorries, each with a machine-gun mounted at the back, just in case one of the various warring factions of that time attempted an abduction. I was only there for a couple of terms before, in November 1961, we were posted back to England, arriving on a freezing-cold night amidst the huts which were the only buildings then at what is now Stansted Airport. My father was given a month or so's leave before reporting back to RAF Locking, which he and I spent living in his best friend's pub, the Ashcombe in Weston, helping out behind the bar, whilst my mother stayed with her parents in Kent.

January 1962 was when I started at Weston Grammar, and it was the beginning of a new chapter.

A love of gardening since the age of six

2

Into cricket

When it came to playing organised cricket, I was a relatively late starter. I had been knocking a ball about, or bowling to my father in the garden or the nets at RAF Locking, for virtually as long as I could remember but, being an RAF school, we didn't have any other schools nearby to play against, so we didn't have sports teams as such. What we did have were those superb facilities in the sports hall and the playing fields, where the PT instructors would bowl at me and provide some rudimentary coaching.

The first cricket teams I played for would have been at the primary school in Singapore, where we played on matting over concrete. After passing the 11+, I went to Alexander Grammar School, which was the army school, and they used to play matches against school teams from the other bases, and I once even played at Singapore Cricket Club. When we came back from Singapore, it was straight into grammar school cricket and Weston Cricket Club. By the time I was 14 or so, I was playing in the school 1st XI for cricket and made the 1st XV for rugby when I reached the sixth form, although I had discovered by then that being good at all ball sports could be a bit of a mixed blessing. It could cause resentment among the other boys and leave you standing out, a bit isolated. It couldn't be helped. I was naturally very competitive, and I knew that, if a game involved a bat, a racket or a club, I would be good at it. There was no arrogance or ego about it; I just knew.

I started playing cricket for Weston-super-Mare in my early teens – my first game for the first team was against a Keynsham side that included Marcus Trescothick's father! – and soon found myself in the Somerset Under-15s, where I first encountered Dasher Denning and had the great good fortune to be coached by Bill Andrews. Bill was one of Somerset cricket's great characters: tall, angular and, when in a temper, with a pronounced stammer. He was both voluble and uncompromising in his opinions, having played for Somerset from 1930 until 1947 and coached them intermittently thereafter. His two great claims to fame were that he had been sacked by Somerset four times, twice as a player, twice as coach, and that he had once taken the wicket of the great Don Bradman. "Shake the hand that bowled Bradman," he would boom on first acquaintance, the invitation which became the title of his autobiography. Bill came from Weston and took me under his considerable wing almost from the start.

From the age of 12 or 13, when I started playing for Somerset Under-15s, Bill was like a second father to me. He had a sports shop at Uphill, just south of Weston, which was where we moved to in 1964, and, because my father was always playing, it was Bill who would take me down to the nets at Taunton or to Under-15s fixtures. By the time I was 14 or 15, he was telling me that I could make a career out of cricket, something I wasn't entirely sure about, as Bernard Spanner, the pro at Weston-super-Mare Golf Club, which was just over the road from the grammar school, was telling me at the same time that I could make a career out of golf – and I quite fancied football!

I can honestly say that I learned more about life from Bill than I did about cricket. "Keep the top hand in," was one his favourite pieces of advice, and I never did understand quite what he meant by it! But he was a larger-than-life figure and, a bit like Brian Close later on, he used to do some extraordinary things. When I was about 15, he took me with him to a Somerset 2nd XI

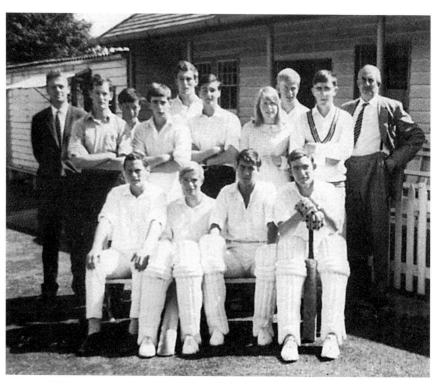

A Somerset youth team, with Bill Andrews standing on the right.
I am two to his left; Peter Denning is sitting second left.
Bill's daughter Sarah, our scorer, is just in front of me.

match against Wiltshire at Devizes, to carry the drinks and pick up some useful experience. It was a hot day and, after a good lunch, Bill fell asleep in a deck-chair, a knotted handkerchief covering his head. He woke up just before the tea interval, to discover that we weren't doing too well, so he decided to give his players a piece of his mind. Back in the dressing room, he went round them, one by one, berating them for their performance. He came to Johnny Martin, a quick bowler who had played for Oxford University and was a regular in Somerset 2nds at that time, his stammer to the fore in the heat of the moment. "And as for you, Martin, you're just a f-f-f-f-fucking waste of f-f-f-", at which point he was interrupted by Johnny. "Hang on a minute, Bill. I've not even been playing. I'm twelfth man." We all collapsed.

Then there was a trip to Folkestone, to play Kent 2nds, who had Derek Underwood and Alan Knott playing for them. It was rained off – not a ball bowled – so we set off in good time for the long drive back to Weston. There were no motorways in those days, of course, and Bill stopped at at least six pubs, to break the journey. Eventually, at about 10.30 at night, we reached the Ship and Castle at Congresbury, and by this stage I was starving. So Bill offered to get me a pie, whilst he had yet another pint. Eventually he came out, pipe going full blast, and gave me the pie, which turned out to have nothing in it. "Bloody hell, Bill," I complained. "This pie's rubbish. There's no meat in it. It's just pastry."

At this, he got into a right strop, and we took off down the A370 towards Weston, Bill more concerned with his pipe than his driving. When we reached the corner where the road bends sharp right, Bill went straight on into the hedge. The pipe went flying, the burning tobacco caught his trousers alight, and there was Bill frantically pouring my Coke all over his crotch and the seat to put out the flames!

Dear old Bill. He never really talked to me about his sacking as coach at the end of the 1969 season, although I knew it hurt him. Somerset were an ageing side and had had a poor season, and by that time Bill's 'coaching' amounted to little more than cheer-leading. But I'll always be grateful for the way he used to drive me, as a young lad learning the game, down to Taunton on a Monday evening all through the winter for sessions in the damp, dingy and often downright dangerous indoor nets.

Later on, when I was playing for Somerset, I was able to return the favour, driving him to matches at the out-grounds and, on one occasion, to a speaking engagement. This was at Timsbury CC, just south of Bath. Bill was due to make a short speech, then I would present the club trophies. He was a great one for his home-made wine and, when I arrived at his home at Worlebury to pick him up, he was already getting stuck into some particularly good elderberry.

He insisted that I have some as well, and his wife Enid and I exchanged meaningful glances as I surreptitiously poured mine into a potted plant. On the way to Timsbury, he insisted on stopping at a couple of his mates' pubs, then had a few more pints in the bar when we got there. By the time we sat down for dinner, he was gone, could barely stand up. So I said to the bloke who was organising it that I would do both, the speech and the trophies, which I did, before driving the by now comatose Bill back to Worlebury and carrying him into the house, where Enid, as you would expect, went berserk. She did have a lot to put up with. She was with him at Bath in 1977, when we beat the Australians, a victory that Bill celebrated with even more than his usual enthusiasm. He was driving that day, with Enid cowering in the back seat, just in case. They came home to Weston via Shepton Mallet and Wells and were within half a mile of making it when Bill drove into a lamp-post, throwing Enid forward onto the handbrake, breaking her arm.

The Weston Festival, in early August, was the great event for anyone in the town who was remotely interested in cricket. All of my mates from school would go, and we got to see some of the truly great players, like Colin Cowdrey and Tom Graveney. Bill Andrews played a big part in organising the festivals and, because I knew him through his coaching, he got me all sorts of jobs, like working the scoreboard or helping out with the covers. He also introduced me to the players whenever he got the chance, so that I got to know Bill Alley and the Palmer brothers. That was a great help when Dasher and I started playing for the Somerset 2nds, because there were no other cricketers of our age who were remotely good enough to play cricket professionally and our new team-mates would otherwise have been completely unknown quantities.

Bill died in 1989, and Enid, Mark and Sarah asked me to take charge of his ashes and have them spread over the outfield at the County Ground. Which I did, except that there was no wind on that particular day so Bill just stayed where I'd put him and I got a terrible bollocking from the groundsman, Phil Frost, because the ashes burnt the grass. So, right to the end, Bill was a thorn in the side of the Somerset cricket authorities. But what a character, and what a cricketer!

My earliest memories of watching cricket are of being taken to matches in the Weston Festival at Clarence Park by my father, when I would have been about eight. Among many great names, I particularly remember watching Peter May batting for Surrey. What a player he was! But it was in the '60s that I started to follow cricket seriously, and no one fired my imagination more than Garry Sobers. It wasn't just the skill and grace with which he batted, bowled and fielded, it was his whole approach to the game, which had

Three Somerset heroes
Arthur Wellard, Harold Gimblett and Bill Andrews at Weston

a sense of real joy about it. I have seen and played with many great cricketers in my time, but no one will ever shake me in my belief that Garry Sobers was the greatest all-round cricketer of them all.

In the England teams of those years, the men I most admired were Tom Graveney for his elegant strokeplay and Basil D'Oliveira, again, not just for his cricket but for the way in which he had overcome so many difficulties in his home country before coming to England, thanks to a lot of help from John Arlott. The 158 that he scored in the Oval Test against Australia in 1968 was a magnificent effort, under huge pressure. It should have guaranteed his place on that winter's tour to South Africa, although of course it didn't, for reasons that have never satisfactorily been explained. A few years later, I tried talking to Tom Cartwright about it and, in particular, his decision to pull out of the tour, citing 'injury' as the reason, when the strong suspicion was that it was down to his hatred of apartheid – something which I shared. But he was always very reticent about it, unlike Dolly, who'd happily sound off about it all for hours, over more than a few pints at the Anchor, over the bridge from New Road, after close of play!

Among the Somerset players of that era, my real hero was Harold Gimblett. I don't remember seeing him playing for Somerset, but after his retirement he carried on playing for teams like the MCC for many years, and I used to see him at Millfield sometimes, and even played against him for Weston in what

I think may well have been his last game for the MCC. Even in his fifties, you could see that he was a great player, and he was easy to talk to as well.

Brian Langford, who was captain of Somerset in my debut season of 1969, was another wonderful cricketer. It is extraordinary to think that he took 1,390 wickets for Somerset over his career, at less than 25 apiece, and yet never got a look-in at Test level.

At the end of June 1968, while I was still at Weston-super-Mare Grammar School waiting for my 'A' level results, I had a call from Colin Atkinson, the headmaster of Millfield, the immediate past captain of Somerset and by then Chairman of its Cricket Committee, inviting me to play for his Invitation XI against the English Schools Cricket Association (ESCA), which was effectively the England Under-19 team. The game would be played at Millfield in July as a warm-up for their fixtures against Scotland, Wales, Holland and ending with the traditional game against the Public Schools XI at Lord's. The ESCA squad that year included future county players such as Richard Lumb from Yorkshire, Graham Barlow from Middlesex, Alan Hill from Derby and John Spencer from Sussex. No one in Somerset to my knowledge had been asked to any of the ESCA trials so I didn't know any of their team.

I was asked by the headmaster to open the batting with my old friend Dasher, who by now was captain of Millfield. At that time Millfield, which had been founded by another remarkable Somerset cricketer, the brilliant but erratic Jack 'Boss' Meyer, was not part of the Headmasters' Conference and was thus outside the official public school system, with the result that no one from the school represented the Public Schools at Lord's. I did more than OK, scoring an unbeaten 98, and two days later found myself on a train travelling to Newcastle, having been invited to join up with the ESCA squad. It turned out that the ESCA selectors had assumed I was from Millfield, until someone at the ground told them that I was from Weston Grammar.

The tour went well, and I ended up playing against the Public Schools at Lord's, top-scoring in the first innings with 36. Rain on the second day denied us the win, but at lunchtime Colin Atkinson came into the ESCA dressing room to ask me if I would play for Somerset the following year. I made an instant decision to go for it, despite the fact that I had already applied to go to Goldsmiths College, but I did add that I would give it a year to see how it went. A two-year contract was duly signed, at £450 per season. This was paid between April and September so I had to find winter jobs wherever I could. Fortunately I got a job at Sanders Garden and Wholesale Vegetable business at Lympsham, which had the added benefit of increasing my knowledge of flower and mushroom growing.

If I hadn't gone into cricket, I would probably have been a teacher, although I was sorely tempted by football. I used to score a lot of goals for Worle OBs and later for Bridgwater Town and was invited over to Cardiff for a trial. I was there for a couple of weeks but, at the end of it, Mel Charles – brother of the great John – told me that, although I had got all the skills, I wasn't quite quick enough, which was probably fair.

I made my debut for Somerset the following April in a Sunday League game against Leicestershire at, of all places, Weston-super-Mare CC's home ground at Devonshire Road. What with my father as groundsman and my mother looking after the bar, it was quite a Rose family occasion! It was Somerset's first-game in the Sunday League– and one of only two limited-overs games that we played at Devonshire Road rather than Clarence Park. Other than that, it was not a memorable occasion. I scored 2, bowled by Terry Spencer, and we lost by five wickets.

My baptism of fire came a couple of weeks later, in a first round Gillette Cup game against Derbyshire at Taunton. What an eye-opener that was! Fred Rumsey, who had just joined Derbyshire from Somerset to play one-day cricket, opened the bowling, with Harold Rhodes and Alan Ward to follow. All three of them were England fast bowlers and, if Fred and Harold were past their prime, they could still be seriously quick in short bursts. I had never faced anything like this pace before, and there I was, a towel for a thigh-guard, a pair of pads dating back to my school-days and gloves from the previous year. No helmets, of course, in those days – nor sponsorship. If I wanted new kit, I had to buy it myself.

I went out to bat at 80 for seven, kitted out like a club cricketer. What Bob Taylor, the Derby and England wicket-keeper, must have thought about this yokel coming to the wicket, I dread to think. It didn't take me long to realise that a fibre-glass thigh pad and a decent pair of gloves might be a wise investment, when Fred's first delivery hit me on the inside thigh and I'd fended off a throat ball from Harold Rhodes. My old headmaster at Weston Grammar, Dr Whimster, had written in my fifth form, pre-'O' level report that 'Five O-Levels are worth more than 500 runs.' Suddenly his words had the ring of truth! Somehow or other I managed to survive long enough to score 28 and to help the skipper, Brian Langford, add 44 for the ninth wicket. It wasn't enough to save the game, but at least I'd shown that I could play when the chips were down.

That was not a great season, to be honest, either for me or for Somerset. We had what looked like a decent side on paper, with a young Greg Chappell the star attraction, but we won only one of 24 championship matches, to finish bottom of the heap. Our record in the John Player's County League, as it was known, was not much better, winning five games and finishing second to last, although it did produce two remarkable performances. The first was at Brislington, where we played Surrey. Greg Chappell, who had joined Somerset the previous summer as a promising 19-year-old learning the game, scored a quite remarkable 128 in an hour and three-quarters. He was a lovely player to watch, particularly his shots through the leg-side, and he had the same sort of inner steel as Steve Waugh showed later on, albeit allied to a lot more natural talent. He was a good friend to me as well, saying that I should be opening the innings, not going in at seven or eight.

The other highlight of what was the first season of Sunday League cricket came at Yeovil, where we played Essex. Brian Langford, who was captaining, put Essex in and brought himself on to bowl when the second wicket fell. He then proceeded to bowl his full allocation of eight overs without conceding a run! The wicket was low and slow, and the ball was gripping so that, if you tried to hit the spinner, the chances are it would go straight up in the air. Langie bowled mostly at Brian Ward, who had evidently decided to see him off, but even the hard-hitting West Indian all-rounder Keith Boyce could not get him away when he came in. There was just one anxious moment, when the ball ran away down to fine-leg off what might have been a glove, but it was signalled a leg bye. I would like to be able to say that a wave of relief went around the side when that happened, knowing that an unbeatable achievement remained within our captain's grasp. But, in all honesty, I don't think any of us realised that anything particularly special was happening. Even Langie only knew about it when the umpire, John Langridge, said something to him at the start of his last over. But it was a remarkable achievement, a record that can never be broken. (And, by the way, I was out first ball!)

Dasher came into the side on a summer contract in June, and Eric Hill, in his *Wisden* notes, was kind enough to write that 'two of the 19-year-old newcomers, Rose and Denning, thrust into the deep end, did enough to give hope for the future.' But the fact is that I scored only 344 runs in 25 championship innings, at a miserable average of 15.63, and 60 runs in ten innings in the Sunday League, at an average of 8. Highlights were few and far between. Two were in the Sunday League: a painstaking 35 not out – in 24 overs! – to take us home against Notts at Glastonbury, and a match-winning partnership of 38 with Pete Robinson when we played Sussex at Torquay. In the championship my top score was 46 against Northants in May, although I did pretty well in the Weston Festival at the beginning of August. That was followed all too swiftly by the season's low point: successive pairs against Essex and Gloucestershire, which cost me my place in the team.

Trying to look cheerful at the end of 1969, my first season

This was taken during a Sunday League game at Southampton where I was bowled for 0 – in the middle of a seven-day period in which I also recorded two pairs in the County Championship

If you look through the names of the bowlers who got me out in championship cricket that season, it's not hard to tell what my problem was: Peter Sainsbury, John Mortimore, Mushtaq Mohammad, Pat Pocock, Don Shepherd, Geoff Cope, Ray East, Mike Bissex ... spinners all. I could just about cope with the quicker stuff but, against the many top-class spinners of the time, operating on uncovered pitches, frequently on out-grounds, I really didn't have much of a clue, and it showed.

My 1970 season was not much better, not helped by a major crisis at home. Early in the New Year, my father had suddenly left, running off with the girl who kept horses in the field next to Weston Cricket Club. He had retired from the RAF about six years earlier and had been working as groundsman and bar manager for the club, as well as looking after the ground in Clarence Park during the winter. It was a bolt from the blue. I got home from work one evening to find my mother in a heap. "What's happened?" I asked her. "He's gone," was all she said, and he had. I did not see him again or have any contact with him until years later, when I was captaining Somerset and he started to show up, almost secretively, at some of our games. He had been working at various farms in the area and spent some time delivering Cheddar cheese to smart London hotels. We made it up in the end, but at the time I was completely shocked and very angry. My mother was so distraught that she had a nervous breakdown, which led to her spending three months in hospital. My elder sister Jennifer had left home some time before, so I suddenly found myself head of the family at the age of 19.

My father had stopped paying the mortgage when he left, and we were in real danger of losing our family home. Fortunately one of the blokes I'd been playing with at Weston was an estate agent and, when he learned about the trouble we were in, he took me along to see his manager at the Midland Bank in Weston. "How much is the mortgage costing you?" he asked me. I said £33 a month. Did I think that I could find that sort of money? Well, I had worked out that, with my £450 summer contract with Somerset, plus some expenses, plus what I could earn at Sanders Garden Centre in the winter, I just about could and said so. So he said, "Sign there," and the mortgage was transferred into my name. It was the first financial transaction I was ever involved in, and it worked out well. When we decided to convert a house in Neva Road near Weston Station for my mother, the profit on the sale of the house at Uphill paid for the work.

Even so, that was one of my lowest points, with my father gone, my mother in hospital and my cricket career in jeopardy. That I got through it was down to Stevie, my girlfriend as she was then, my wife as she eventually became.

Somerset in May 1970

*standing: Me, Tom Cartwright, Roy Palmer, Allan Jones,
Graham Burgess, Maurice Hill, Derek Taylor, Peter Robinson
sitting: Tony Clarkson, Merv Kitchen, Brian Langford, Roy Virgin*

We had met at the Monk's Rest Café, just down the hill from Worlebury Golf Club, when I was 18 and she was 17, and she was my first and only girlfriend. I don't know how I would have coped that year if it hadn't been for her unfailing support and common sense.

Come the cricket season, and I was spending most of my time either playing in the 2nd XI under Roy Kerslake or carrying the drinks. Roy was a good sort, who acted as a sort of bridge between the players and the old-fashioned committee set-up which ran the club. Peter Robinson was another who was a great help to me in the early days. We had a bit of an affinity, as he came from Worcester, just as my father's family did. He was a more-than-useful cricketer and a fine coach, who had one peculiarity: his hands sweated when he bowled, so much so that when he tossed the ball to one of the seamers at the end of an over, it would be soaking wet. Kenny Palmer used to go berserk!

I played in only six games in the championship in 1970 – scoring the grand total of 73 runs, top score 16 – and two games in the John Player League, scoring two against Leicestershire and not getting the chance to bat at Hampshire. It came as no great surprise when a letter arrived from the

The County Ground in 1970

Somerset Secretary, Jimmy James, at the end of the season, baldly informing me that my contract would not be renewed. He did not, of course, bother to ring me up to explain exactly why, or say whether I should hold out any hope for the future. That was not the Somerset way in those days.

By then I had already decided that I needed to get myself another career option, in case the cricket came to nothing. Teaching seemed the obvious choice, maybe with some sport thrown in. I might have done my training at St Luke's at Exeter, which is what Dasher had chosen, but I had had just a hint that Middlesex might be interested in me if I was playing in the Middlesex League so decided to try my luck in Osterley, London: not Goldsmiths this time but Borough Road College, of which I'd heard many good things.

So I applied, was accepted to start in the autumn of 1971 and got a full grant. In the meantime I earned and saved some money working for Sanders Garden Centre and digging ditches for electricity cables in Weston for Kent Baker Ltd. I played most of my cricket for Weston, who had a good side that summer and won the Somerset Cup.

Borough Road turned out to be an inspired choice. The facilities were exceptional, and it was packed with great athletes like Alan Lerwill, the long-jumper, the Tancred brothers, of shot-putt and discus fame, and Brian Green, at that time the fastest man in Britain. We studied hard, and we trained hard.

I didn't have five minutes to myself, what with lectures and classes during the day, and then training in the afternoons and evenings. For me, it was the perfect routine for helping me to put the troubles at home in perspective and get back on an even keel, as well as teaching me a lesson which I carried with me throughout my cricket career about the importance of genuine fitness. The regime at Borough Road, and the levels of fitness you were expected to achieve, made our out-of-season training at Somerset seem like a joke.

There was plenty of good-standard cricket as well. We played other colleges on a Wednesday and strong club sides on a Saturday, and we won a lot more games than we lost. Besides myself, we had two other players who went on to play first-class cricket: Nigel Briers, who captained Leicestershire for several years, and Paul Roberts, who looked to have a decent career ahead of him at Worcestershire when he was tragically killed in a climbing accident in the Lake District. But it was what Borough Road taught me about what it means to be a professional athlete that was the most important aspect of my time there, plus, of course, the teaching qualification that I obtained and which I followed up almost immediately with three months' teaching experience at Broadoak School, the comprehensive which my old grammar school had now become. At the end of that I got the certificate which meant I was a fully-qualified teacher, with all that that meant in terms of career options.

So I have a lot to thank Borough Road for. When I had applied to go there, my family life was in turmoil, my cricket career was in jeopardy and my confidence was pretty much shot. When I left there, in the summer of 1974, I was fit, happy, self-confident, qualified and being offered a new contract by Somerset. It was quite a transformation.

What with that, and Brian Close taking over as captain of Somerset in 1972, my life was taking a significant turn for the better.

3

Closey

Brian Close was a one-off, as a cricketer and as a man. He had come to Somerset for the start of the 1971 season after one bust-up too many with the Yorkshire committee, to spend the twilight years of his career turning a bunch of southern softies into a tough and competitive cricket team. And although we didn't actually win anything with Close as captain, he certainly laid the foundations for the successes that followed, not least in his influence on what became my style of captaincy.

Closey was genuinely a hard man. He had a filthy temper and could be physically intimidating, especially if he sensed any weakness, usually on the part of the opposition, but sometimes in members of his own team. He despised any show of pain or vulnerability and had no patience with injuries, his own or his team-mates'.

The battering that he took from the West Indies fast bowlers at Old Trafford in 1976 was sickening to behold, yet he never flinched and wore his many bruises as badges of pride. So he did not have much sympathy with me after the inside of my thighs had taken a fearful battering from Alan Ward

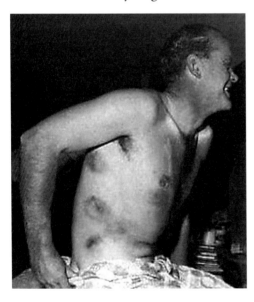

Closey displays his bruises

on a dodgy wicket at Chesterfield, a few days after that Test. We were playing Warwickshire in the Gillette Cup at Edgbaston the next day, which I fully intended to spend having my injuries tended by Bernard Thomas, the England physiotherapist, who was based at Birmingham. But not a bit of it. Closey virtually hauled me off the treatment table: "Come on, Rosey lad. There's nowt wrong with you. Get your pads on. You're opening the innings." I was soon coming back off the pitch, having been hit straight between the eyes by a lifter off a length from Steve Rouse in the second over. A stone had somehow been rolled into the pitch!

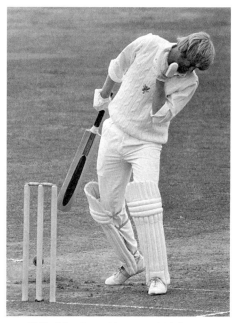

Felled by Steve Rouse at Edgbaston

In the field, he was virtually a permanent fixture at short-leg, especially if Tom Cartwright was bowling, and you could see some batsmen almost shrink from this glowering presence just a few feet away. He was immensely strong, with the most powerful upper-body strength I've ever seen, and he could hit the ball very hard, especially with his own version of the slog-sweep, carting the ball away through straight mid-wicket. It may have looked a bit agricultural, but technically it was an incredibly difficult shot to play, requiring great hand-eye co-ordination and a really strong bottom hand. His approach was always to try to intimidate the bowler, or get under his skin, and some bowlers could not handle it. They would lose it – start bowling too short, which is probably what he wanted. Mind you, he did take a lot of hard knocks from the real quicks, not all of them necessary or justified. But it was his way of making a statement. He was the one who was dictating terms, not the bowler. I was a pretty good player of fast bowling, and sometimes I would be batting with him, swaying out of the way of the short stuff, and he would be taking it on the chest. I doubt there has ever been a tougher cricketer.

He could be tough with his own players, as well. When he arrived, persuaded to come south by my old coach, the inimitable Bill Andrews, Somerset were rebuilding after the crisis of 1969, when they had won only one championship game and the chairman, secretary and treasurer had all either been sacked or resigned. An ageing team had been strengthened by the signings of Derek Taylor from Surrey, Allan Jones from Sussex and, most importantly, Tom Cartwright from Warwickshire, but under Brian Langford – a great off-spinner but by no means a natural captain – we performed only fitfully in 1970 and finished 13th. Close was happy enough to return to the ranks for his first season in 1971, but no one was surprised when he was persuaded to take over as captain in 1972. His mission was twofold: to get his side playing consistently good, hard cricket, and to bring on the youngsters, like myself and Dasher. In both he succeeded, but not without a few upsets along the way.

I was playing for Somerset only occasionally when Closey arrived, as Borough Road College was taking up most of my time, and my batting was still very much a work in progress. One of my early encounters with him was when I was summoned from a 2nd XI match against Devon at the County Ground and told that I would be opening the batting the next day at Bournemouth, against a Hampshire side that included a certain Andy Roberts, then in his prime. Given that he had already broken several arms that season, I was more than a touch apprehensive!

The away dressing room at Dean Park was split into two separate rooms and I was in the back, having a cup of tea, when the 15-minute bell went, so I strapped on my pads, nervously. In strides Closey, come for his tea. "You can take that fooking lot off, lad. You're twelfth man. I've played the extra bowler." And with that, he walked out, having forgotten to tell me when he tossed up!

The mention of tea in the dressing room reminds me of the time at Taunton, when Closey was in a foul mood and came dashing out of the shower, stark naked, to claim his mug of tea. Ethel the tea lady had, as usual, taken the urn off the gas fire, which heated it up, and retreated, leaving a tray of mugs and the fire still lit. Closey, desperate for his tea as usual, leant over to claim his mug, managing in the process to fry the end of his still wet knob on the fire! The sizzling noise and his agonized shriek, I will never forget! Goodness knows what his wife, Vivienne, made of the resulting injury – if, that is, he ever told her!

But for some reason Closey took a bit of a shine to this tall, fair-haired, quiet young man from Weston – 'Dozey Rosey', as they liked to call me in the dressing room. In my first game for Somerset with Close as captain in 1972, I made 38 against a Gloucestershire attack led by Mike Procter, surprising even myself with how easy it seemed, and put on 77 for the third wicket with the skipper. He didn't exactly shower me with compliments afterwards, although I gathered he had said to someone else that 'this lad will get a hundred in his next match.' Which was exactly what I did – 125 at the Morlands ground at Glastonbury against Kent, the first of my 25 first-class centuries. He took

Brian Close

to insisting that I changed next to him, and I was one of the few players he would take into his confidence if things weren't working out exactly as he had planned. Not that that saved me from a Close bollocking if I dropped a catch or gave my wicket away. In one of my first games for Somerset with Closey as captain, at Edgbaston, I dropped a sitter at mid-off early in the Warwickshire innings. "Bloody hell, Rosey," he bellowed at me. "I could have caught that between the cheeks of my arse." Rohan Kanhai and John Jameson then went on to add 247 together. I had been out for a duck!

A few days later we were playing Gloucestershire in front of a big crowd at the Imperial Ground in Bristol in the John Player League. The Gloucestershire openers, Sadiq and Roger Knight, had made a good start when Close decided to bring himself on, bowling his ancient off-spinners. His first ball was nothing more than a schoolboy donkey drop. Sadiq was clearly baffled, unsure which part of Bristol to despatch it to, and ended up smashing it, baseball style, back towards the bowler. There was a tremendous kerfuffle as non-striker and umpire dived for cover, leaving Closey unsighted. The ball hit him amidships and got tangled up in his trousers where it stuck for long enough for him to retrieve it from somewhere between his legs and triumphantly claim the catch. Out! He came straight over to me, laughing his big bald head off. "There you are, Rosey. Cheeks of my arse! I fooking told you!"

Or there was the occasion at Chesterfield against Derby in 1972, when we were chasing 127 to win, with Mike Hendrick causing all kinds of trouble by bowling off-cutters into a wet wicket. I was going well, with 32 out of 104/7, just 23 more needed, when I went to turn a length ball through mid-wicket, got a leading edge and was caught at extra cover. Closey was waiting for me as I came off the pitch. In fact, he had come all the way down the pavilion steps onto the outfield to tell me exactly what he thought of me, in front of all the Derbyshire members, who thought it a great laugh. He was still chuntering on about how I had cost us the effing match whilst I was in the shower, and it was only when Kerry O'Keeffe came into the changing room to say that we had actually won by two wickets that he started to calm down.

Episodes like that are funny mainly in retrospect. At the time it could be genuinely frightening. But he could also have us in stitches with some of his antics. You always knew that there would be an explosion if he was given out and there was any doubt about the decision. The dressing room would clear, ahead of his furious return, except maybe for Dasher and me. I remember a time at Bath, when we were playing Middlesex in 1976. I was already out, treading on my stumps against AA Jones, who had joined them from us that season, when Closey was given out for a duck. Sure enough, everyone within earshot melted away, leaving just me, still with my pads on, sitting there,

awaiting the explosion to come. He slammed the door open with a huge oath, and the next thing I saw was his bat, sailing through the air, to end up sticking in the double-skinned changing-room wall like a spear! We lost that game by an innings, with Jones taking 7/68, something which did nothing at all to improve the captain's humour.

He liked a smoke, did Closey – so much so that, as Allan Jones was running in to bowl the first ball of a match at Taunton, I noticed a plume of smoke heading skywards from the slip cordon, as the skipper took a final drag from his pre-match cigarette! He liked a drink as well: gallons of tea during the day, a few pints of lager and a drop of whisky in the evening. When it came to 'walking the bottles', or drinking a pint from the top of his head without using his hands, he was world class. For the pint trick, he would stand up against a wall, with the beer on his head, then gently slide the glass towards the wall, before trapping it and gradually easing it down between his face and the wall, until it reached mouth level, whereupon he would grip the rim with his teeth and lips and, sip by sip, up-end the contents into his mouth. His skill at walking the bottles was just as remarkable. The contest involved taking a bottle in each hand, and supporting yourself just on those and your feet – as if you were about to do press-ups – and then seeing how far you could stretch out one or other of the bottles without collapsing in a heap, before bringing them back again. Closey, with his incredible upper-body strength, could get one of the bottles out almost to the full length of his arm, his body stretched out like a plank. Viv Richards and Beefy, both immensely strong men, tried it and could not get anywhere near him. If there had been a world championship for walking the bottles, I guarantee you that Brian Close would have won it!

Which is more than could be said for his driving. In the 1970s the idea of giving high-profile players sponsored cars was just catching on and, on the day before we were due to play Surrey at Guildford in 1976, Closey took delivery of a brand-new three-litre Ford Capri, sponsored by Ford UK. Dasher and I were sitting in the bar at the Hog's Back Hotel that night, when Closey came in, late and unusually flustered. He took me to one side and quietly asked if I could give him a lift to the ground the next morning. "OK, Skip," I said, "we'll leave at 8.30." The next morning, three lots of kit – mine, Dasher's and Closey's – had to be crammed into my little Mazda, with not a word about what had happened to the new Capri. When we got to the ground, an obviously grumpy skipper got out of the car and headed straight for the changing room. As Dasher and I were unloading, a Ford van arrived, complete with trailer, on which was a brand new Ford Capri. "What's this all about?" we asked the driver. "Oh," he replied, "it's Mr Close's new Capri. He wrapped the first one around a tree yesterday evening!"

Richard Lumb, with whom I had played for England Under-19s, had a fund of stories about Closey's driving exploits during his time at Yorkshire: being pulled over by the police for towing a caravan up the A1 at 90 mph, for example, or the time when he decided to ignore the bollards at a set of road works and ended up in a big hole recently excavated by a JCB! None of us much enjoyed being his passenger when he was driving at 90 up the M5 with the *Racing Post* spread out on the steering wheel, as he checked out the runners and riders. In fact, very often the only volunteer would be Hallam Moseley, who shared Closey's fondness for the horses and who could double up as navigator and form-book consultant.

As a captain, whilst he was always aggressive, he could also be unorthodox to the point of eccentricity, especially in one-day cricket, where he might, for example, post two short-legs when the situation cried out for run-saving. Often his policy of all-out attack succeeded triumphantly. Sometimes it didn't. One such occasion was a second-round Gillette Cup match in 1973 at Taunton. We had made 212 and all was going well until, midway through the Leicestershire innings, our keeper Jim Parks injured a finger and had to go off. There was never any doubt as to who would take the gloves. "I've kept in a Test match, you know," announced Closey to all and sundry, putting on Parks' gloves but not bothering with any pads. At first, he didn't do too badly, even taking a catch to get rid of Garth McKenzie, and the required rate gradually climbed. With two overs left, a powerful Leicestershire side had it all to do with 15 or so still needed, which in those days, with no fielding restrictions, was a big ask. The unpredictable Allan Jones, who had more than a few run-ins with Closey and who had already dropped a sitter off Leicestershire's century-maker, Chris Balderstone, stepped up to bowl the penultimate over.

Sure enough, the first ball was fast and short, Ken Higgs played and missed, and Closey dropped it. The next ball was even quicker but wide down the leg side. Close didn't get anywhere near it, and it ran away for four byes – whereupon the skipper shouted up the pitch to his bowler, telling him exactly what he thought of the delivery, then handed the gloves to the umpire, saying that they were too small for him. So there you had it: the captain of Somerset, keeping wicket in the penultimate over of a big Gillette Cup match in his bare hands! Dasher and I looked first at each other, then at the notoriously fiery Jones. He had steam coming out of his ears. I wish I could say that the story had a happy ending, but it didn't. With the help of yet more bouncers and byes, Chris Balderstone and Ken Higgs knocked off the last 11 runs in the space of Jones' remaining four balls, to take their county across the line with an over to spare.

Eccentric, dictatorial and sometimes grumpy he may have been, but Brian Close did Somerset cricket a power of good. I had been brought back from the wilderness to play a few games at the tail-end of the 1972 season, in the summer break from Borough Road College, and had done pretty well, scoring that century against Kent at Glastonbury and making some useful contributions in the Sunday League. I could see immediately how things had changed under his leadership. The entire side, even the old stagers, were playing for each other, rather than for themselves or just not bothering at all. The only real exception was Roy Virgin, who had been so dominant in 1971 but who never really saw eye to eye with Closey. He had a nightmare of a season on and off the pitch and left at the end of it for Northants, where he finished his career in fine style.

By the end of the 1972 season I was a much better player than I had been when I had been shown the door after the 1970 season. The key difference, thanks to the coaching I received at Borough Road College from the old Middlesex and England batsman and off-spinner Jack Robertson, was that I had learned to play spin – something that was absolutely essential on the uncovered wickets of the time, when virtually every county had at least one international-class spin bowler. Jack was a real gentleman of the game, tremendously knowledgeable, and one of the things he said that I was doing was thrusting my hands out too hard at the turning ball so that, if it took the edge or a glove, the chances are it would carry to slip or short-leg. He taught me how to play spin later and with much softer hands, especially on English wickets where you know that the ball is not going to turn that quickly.

I played a few more games in 1973 and got my first shot at opening the innings when we played Glamorgan in August, without in any way setting the Tone on fire. It was not a great summer. Quite apart from snatching defeat from the jaws of victory in that game against Leicestershire in the Gillette Cup, we won only seven out of 20 championship matches, to finish 10th, failed to qualify for the Benson & Hedges quarter-finals, and finished in the bottom half of the Sunday League table – although I did have the personal satisfaction of making an unbeaten 65 in the game against Derbyshire, when Graham Burgess and I added 98, to take us home with more than 11 overs to spare.

Our one saving grace was a quite outstanding season from Tom Cartwright. Since joining Somerset, he had taken 86 championship wickets in 1970, 96 in 1971 (104 in all first-class cricket), 93 in 1972 and 88 in 1973, to top the national bowling averages at the age of 37. But there was much more to Tom Cartwright than that metronomic medium-pace, hitting the perfect line and length ball after ball, over after over. For a start, he was a more than useful lower-order batsman, at his best in a crisis, and had the safest pair of hands at second slip. But beyond all of that was his wider influence on the team, as player-coach, the role to which he had shrewdly been appointed in 1973, and as mentor and friend. He was a very different character from his bombastic, bludgeoning, somewhere-to-the-right-of-Attila-the-Hun skipper, of course. Tom was understated, as upright in his standards as in his bowling action, decidedly leftish in his politics, without being a firebrand, and, unlike Closey, he was always happy to talk and to listen.

Tom Cartwright

They did not always get on, especially when it came to field placings, but for a young cricketer, trying his hardest to learn the game, they were the perfect partnership. And we should not forget the third member of the triumvirate who were reviving Somerset's cricketing fortunes in the early 1970s – Derek Taylor. He was another quiet but hugely determined man, a great thinker about the game, who seemed to know just about every player on the circuit and chatted to most of them, picking up an incredible amount of useful information in the process. I learned a lot from Derek when I opened the innings with him from 1975 to 1977, and his quiet words of suggestion and advice were so important to me when I came to captain the side in 1978. The three of them were the heart of that Somerset team in the mid-1970s, and one can only imagine what it must have felt like for the opposing batsmen, with the immaculate Cartwright running in to bowl, Derek Taylor standing up menacingly to the stumps, and the looming, intimidating bulk of Close glowering at short-leg.

1974 was my last year at Borough Road, with finals at the end of June, meaning that I did not get back to Somerset until July. I was soon playing 2nd XI cricket and did well enough to be called up for a couple of games at the tail-end of the season, one in the championship and the other in the Sunday League. More importantly, Closey had seen enough to convince him that I should be offered a full-time, two-year contract, which I duly signed that August. Meanwhile, Vivian Richards and Ian Botham were giving notice of the greatness to come, Peter Roebuck played his first two championship games and Vic Marks and Phil Slocombe were waiting in the wings. The future for Somerset cricket was looking brighter.

I spent that winter partly playing Grade cricket for Claremont-Cottesloe in Westerrn Australia and partly teaching PE and Geography at Broadoak School. The Australian trip, which was arranged thanks largely to Greg Chappell and Graham McKenzie, was a great experience. The game was changing fast at that time, with the emergence of a remarkable crop of fast bowlers: Lillee and Thomson for Australia; Roberts, Holding, Daniel and later Marshall, Garner and Croft for the West Indies. Batting against genuinely fast bowling and learning to cope with high-bouncing wrist-spin on hard, fast pitches involved a very steep learning curve but did wonders for my confidence and technique. It also gave me the chance to go to the second Test of England's tour at the WACA and wince as I watched David 'Bumble' Lloyd and the 41-year-old Colin Cowdrey trying to fend off Lillee and Thomson on a lightning-fast pitch, to the highly vocal accompaniment of Ian Chappell and Rod Marsh. Test match batting had suddenly become very painful and difficult.

I embarked on my first full season in county cricket in April 1975. The fitness, self-confidence and technical skills that I had acquired at Borough Road all paid off, as I played in 20 out of 22 championship matches, opening the innings with Derek Taylor and scoring over 1,000 runs in all first-class cricket. There was only one century, a distinctly painstaking 115 not out in a high scoring draw against Nottinghamshire, but I was generally fairly happy with my form, in a summer which started wet and then turned hot and when batting was never particularly easy. One thing I learned that year was what you might call a more professional approach to my batting. Early in my career, I had a tendency to get out for low scores, two or three innings on the trot. With Close as captain, that put your place in jeopardy so, if I wasn't completely on song or if the pitch was tricky, I started trying to put together a scrappy 20 or 30, rather than going for the big shots and getting out early on. It may not have been particularly pretty, but the runs I scored and the confidence they gave me laid the foundations for the free-scoring fluency which I developed from 1976 onwards.

Somerset's performance looked disappointing on the face of it: 12th in the championship, quarter-finalists in the B&H, second-round losers in the Gillette and a lowly 14th in the Sunday League. But beneath the surface there was real progress, with Vivian Richards laying claim to be the most exciting young batsman in world cricket, Ian Botham confirming his boundless all-round talents and both Phil Slocombe and Peter Roebuck scoring important runs for the county for the first time.

Funnily enough, some of my happiest memories of that season were of my bowling. Closey had decided that I could do a job for the team in Sunday League cricket with my left-arm medium pace. My stock ball was the inswinger to a right-hander although, thanks to Tom Cartwright's advice, I also learned to hold my fingers across the seam so that it went straight on. Unsurprisingly, given the Cartwright influence, I had a nice easy approach, a high action and, on Tom's advice, I didn't try to bowl too fast. I got my first chance at Bath, taking 1/16 in four overs, and that obviously encouraged Closey to give me another go against Lancashire, up at Old Trafford. My figures that day were 6-0-25-3. My three victims?

FC Hayes	c Close	b Rose	23
CH Lloyd		b Rose	15
J Sullivan		b Rose	5

Not a bad trio!

I was in the wickets again with 2/37 against Northants at Torquay, and I also performed respectably at Weston, conceding 22 in my four overs, as compared with Beefy, who went for 61 in his eight! Over that season in the

John Player I took 6/100, at an average of 16.66 and an economy rate of 4.54, which wasn't half bad, though I say it myself. Yet that was virtually it for Rosey the bowler. Closey hardly used me again, and I only rarely felt the need to give myself a go when I became captain. In the whole of the rest of my one-day cricket career, I bowled 14 more overs, without taking a wicket.

My other abiding memory of the John Player that year is of the match at the Westlands ground in Yeovil, against Leicestershire. In front of the biggest crowd that ground had ever seen, we had made a modest 150 in our 40 overs, on a slow pitch. When Leicestershire batted, tight bowling and keen fielding saw them fall further and further behind the asking rate so that, with just one over to be bowled, they needed 16. The mercurial AA Jones, with whom Closey always had something of a love-hate relationship, stepped up to bowl, with two tail-enders, McVicker and Booth, at the crease. His first four balls were all there or thereabouts, conceding just six runs. So 10 were needed off the last two balls, McVicker on strike. Jonesey bowled a length ball on off stump, and McVicker, expecting it, was already moving outside leg to smash the ball over the shortish off-side boundary. I was at deep extra cover, Budgie Burgess was at long-off. The shot went more or less straight to Budgie, travelling like a tracer bullet, just over head height. His hands never moved. I looked at him, as if to say, "Why didn't you try to catch it?" The next ball sailed over the off-side boundary again, and that was that. Closey was incandescent. I don't think I have ever seen anyone quite so angry on a cricket field.

We did not do ourselves justice in the Sunday League that year, winning only five games and finishing a lowly 14th, which was poor when you consider the strength of our batting in particular. I think the explanation was partly that we never had a settled batting order. Closey was forever experimenting. Sometimes Dasher would be at three, sometimes Viv, while Beefy could find himself anywhere between six and eight. It was a lesson I learned for when I became captain, trying to keep as settled a batting order as possible, so that everyone knew their place and what was expected of them.

It was 1976 that was really my breakthrough season and, oh so nearly, Somerset's as well.

Most of my memories of that glorious summer are golden ones. Playing with much greater freedom than the previous season, on hard, dry pitches, I scored over 1,500 runs in the championship, with four centuries, whilst the opening partnerships that I put together with Dasher in the Sunday League – me driving straight and through the off-side and whipping the ball away through mid-wicket, Dasher chopping and carving like, well, like the son of a Chewton Mendip butcher! – were a key part of our challenge for the title. Somerset were without Richards – he was scoring mountains of runs for the West Indies – but Botham continued his irresistible advance with bat and ball, Closey played well enough (and bravely enough, when the West Indies came to Taunton in May) to earn an England call-up, Merv Kitchen returned from a year off to bolster the middle order, Dasher had his best season yet, Hallam Moseley bowled his socks off as usual and yet another promising local youngster was uncovered in the slightly ungainly but usually highly effective shape of Colin Dredge, from Frome.

We did not start too well, and we suffered a gut-wrenching defeat against Gloucestershire in early June, after they had followed on 254 runs behind. It was a good match for me: 104 in the first innings, 48 out of 110 all out in the second, this against Procter mixing off-breaks with high pace, sometimes in the same over! The outcome might have been different had Tom Cartwright been in the side, but he had cracked his shoulder-blade, tripping over a fielder whilst taking a single in early May, the latest of a sad series of injuries and the one that would eventually, after some acrimonious exchanges, end his Somerset career, both as player and as coach. Somerset's self-inflicted loss became Glamorgan and Wales's gain, when he made the short trip across the Bristol Channel to coach there.

During that summer of 1976 I scored four championship centuries, the biggest of them, 177, against Leicestershire at Taunton in early September. They were a strong side, county champions the previous year, captained uncompromisingly by Ray Illingworth. Besides him, they had a young David Gower to open the batting, alongside Brian Davison, John Steele, Chris Balderstone and Jackie Birkenshaw, whom I knew quite well. He and my father shared a common great friend in Paddy Ireland, who kept the Red Cow at Brent Knoll. I would often stop there for a pint and chicken in the basket on my way back from Taunton to Weston, and Jackie would always stay there whenever Leicestershire were in Somerset, so we had quite a few beers together over the years. Anyway, after he had got me out, caught and bowled, he had a real old go at me, saying that I had only needed to stay in for another half an hour or so, and I would have scored a double century.

By that stage in the season I was batting well, possibly as well as I have ever done. The wickets were pretty good throughout that amazing summer and, as the season went on, there was more and more turn on offer. But by that time I had overcome the worst of my problems against spin, and the longer the season went on, the more confident I became, to the extent that I began to feel that I was one of the better openers around the country – an impression reinforced by Beefy Botham, who would tell me that he couldn't understand why I wasn't playing for England!

Batting with greater freedom in 1976

Dasher's Chewton Chop

I had a pretty good season in the Sunday League, as well, opening with Dasher and more often than not getting the innings off to a good start. By September, after a series of narrow, thrilling victories, we needed only to tie with Glamorgan at Cardiff, and Somerset would win its first trophy, after 85 years of trying. Expectations were sky-high. Glamorgan had lost their previous six games and were struggling. Of the 7,000 spectators who turned up at Sophia Gardens that day, most were from Somerset, the cider had been flowing and the atmosphere was electric. Glamorgan made 191/7 in their 39 overs, and it would probably have been fewer, had Closey not dropped Alan Jones on 29, only for him to top-score with 70. It was a straightforward chance to backward square leg. The ball went into his big hands, and then, with Jones already on his way back to the pavilion, out again.

Even so, and despite losing three early wickets, we should have knocked off the runs. I have always blamed myself for what happened. Merv Kitchen and I had been rebuilding the innings, in a partnership of 70 for the fourth wicket, but we were falling behind the scoring rate. So I said to Merv that I had better have a go, and I got myself out swishing. What I should have done was to anchor the innings and allow the others to bat around me. As it was, despite a gallant 48 not out by Graham Burgess, we needed three off the last ball for the tie and the title, and Colin Dredge was run out – by inches –

going for the third. It was a dreadful moment. Some of the older players felt that their last chance of winning anything with Somerset had gone. Closey was distraught, blaming himself for putting Glamorgan in, dropping that catch and not keeping a cooler head. But they say you learn more from defeat than victory, and what happened that day taught me lessons about how to win cricket matches that I would never forget.

I have always thought that I played just as well in 1977 as in 1976, without the same weight of runs: 1,193 in all first-class cricket, as against 1,624 the previous season. It was a wet summer, there were a lot of green wickets and batting became much more difficult. When I got my 205 at Weston in August, against a Northamptonshire side featuring the brilliant Indian slow left-arm spinner Bishan Bedi, every other ball seemed either to grip or to turn, but it didn't matter because I was in such good nick. A call-up to the England side for the Headingley Test, as cover for a struggling Bob Woolmer, followed almost immediately, although I didn't play. Once the news came through that the TCCB – under pressure from the Packer business – had suddenly increased the Test match fee from £100 to £1,000, Woolmer staged a remarkable recovery!

If that was one highlight of the 1977 season, then the other was the match against the Australians at Bath in May. It nearly wasn't played, because a few days before the game was due to start the outfield was under floodwater. But the ground staff, led by Don Price, did a fantastic job in getting the ground fit, the sun came out just in time, and I have never seen the Rec so packed

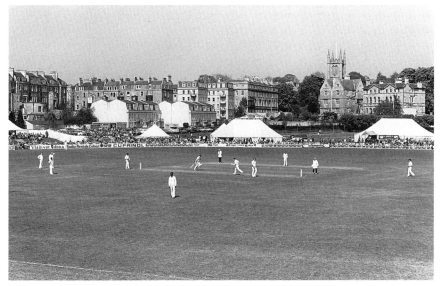

Somerset v The Australians, Bath, May 1977

as it was on that first morning. The Australians were a good side, led by Greg Chappell, with McCosker, Walters and Hookes to score runs, and Jeff Thomson and Somerset old-boy Kerry O'Keeffe to take wickets.

This was the Somerset debut of a certain Joel Garner. We had heard exciting things about the young Barbadian giant, who was contracted to Littleborough in the Lancashire League, and the reality did not disappoint. His first delivery, on a soft wicket, was just short of a length, took off past McCosker's nose and thwacked into Derek Taylor's gloves, head high. Dasher and I looked at each other. Hallelujah! We had got ourselves a fast bowler, who could frighten the life out of any batting line-up in the world. Four balls later, McCosker was on his way back to the pavilion.

They ended up making 232, thanks largely to a brilliant century by Greg Chappell, which left us well in the game. I then made a cautious, painstaking 100, while Dasher, Botham and Phil Slocombe played their shots at the other end. We had reached 340, with me 110 not out, when Closey suddenly declared. I could not believe it. It was one of the rare moments when I lost my rag with him and demanded to know what he thought he was on about. "I had to declare," he insisted, "so that we can get on and bowl them out a second time" – although I have always wondered whether the committee's desire for a remunerative third day's cricket might not have played a part, given that, if we had batted on, we might have skittled them and won by an innings.

At any rate, it worked out well enough. Botham took 4/98 as they were bowled out for 289, leaving us to score 182 for victory in three and three-quarter hours. We got there with a good hour to spare. Dasher and I led the way with 50 for the first wicket, before Richards scored a rapid 53, leaving his great mate Beefy to knock off the winning runs. It was a great day, one of the greatest in Somerset cricket history. We had beaten the Australians for the first time, at the 22nd time of asking, and we had beaten them fair and square.

That game was memorable off the field as well, thanks inevitably to Closey. To mark the occasion, Bath City Council gave a civic reception for both teams. There were speeches by the Lord Mayor and the Somerset Chairman, Len Creed, after which we were all invited to have a dip in the Roman Baths. Now, one of Brian Close's many natural talents was the ability to hold his breath for several minutes at a time. And as he had enjoyed a glass or two at the reception, he thought it would be a great laugh to dive to the bottom of the pool and stay there, to give the lifeguards the fright of their lives. Well, it worked well enough. They were just about to press the panic button when Close emerged from the depths, laughing his head off. Sadly, they didn't see the joke. "Out," they shouted at Closey, and they meant it. Out he had to go, much to the amusement of the rest of us!

The other game etched on my memory from that 1977 season was the championship match against Lancashire at Southport at the end of July. This time the wicket was hard and fast, with a ridge just short of a fast bowler's length at one end. Closey won the toss, and it was at the ridge end that I found myself opening the innings against a young West Indian fast bowler, eager to impress, called Colin Croft. His first ball took off from just short of a length and would have hit me in the middle of the forehead if I had not somehow instinctively managed to get the handle of the bat in front of my face. The ball ricocheted off the very top of the handle, flew over the top of the wicket-keeper and ended up hitting the sight-screen first bounce. To say that this unnerved one or two of the waiting Somerset batsmen would be putting it mildly. Merv Kitchen promptly removed his false teeth! Dasher was out soon afterwards, which brought in Vivian Richards, who proceeded to play what I still regard as one of his greatest innings for Somerset. By lunch on that first day, on this bouncy, unpredictable pitch, he had scored 117. The ferocity of his strokeplay had to be seen to be believed. The faster Croft bowled, the farther the ball travelled, and the Lancashire spinners, David Hughes and Jack Simmons, were treated with a similar fierce disdain. Richards was eventually out for 189, scored out of 267/5! It was the innings of a master. But it was not enough to win the game. In the second innings we were bowled out for 83, not by Croft but by Peter 'Leapy' Lee, and Lancashire knocked off the 79 they needed, to win by eight wickets inside two days.

This was one of Richards' greatest seasons for Somerset, scoring 2,874 runs in all competitions for us, including three double centuries and four centuries in the championship. The 241 not out that he scored at Bristol in June, to save the game for us after we'd been bowled out first time around for 133, was the greatest match-saving innings I have ever seen.

1977 turned out to be Closey's final season. He had missed the start of the season with a shoulder injury, then went down with a chest infection followed by gastric flu. He was well enough to captain us in that famous win over the Australians at Bath, but he then contrived to walk through a glass door in a Chelmsford hotel, which kept him out for another week. All of this meant that he had played only two championship games by the end of June, and in the Sunday League he appeared in only two matches all season. At 46, and unable to throw because of that shoulder, he was becoming a distinct disadvantage in the field. In Closey's absence, Derek Taylor took over as captain and did the job well.

Because of his contract with Littleborough in the Lancashire League, Joel could only play midweek for us, which meant only four championship appearances. But he showed what a potent weapon he would be in one-day

Last days with Closey – our team at Ilkeston for the Gillette Cup match
standing: Phil Slocombe, Dennis Breakwell, me, Joel Garner,
Colin Dredge, Ian Botham, Keith Jennings   sitting: Peter Denning,
Mervyn Kitchen, Brian Close, Derek Taylor, Viv Richards

cricket in our Gillette Cup campaign. After a few nasty moments in our second round match against Northumberland, we had beaten Derbyshire comfortably at Ilkeston, where I had made a man-of-the-match century.

We set off for Lord's, for the semi-final against Middlesex full of confidence, knowing that we had developed into probably the best one-day side in the country. What followed was a mixture of farce, ill-fortune and bitter disappointment. For the three days that had been set-aside for the semi-final, it rained unrelentingly. There were no 'bowl-outs' in indoor cricket schools to settle things in those days, so we headed off to play Kent in a three-day game, the authorities having decided to postpone our championship match against Middlesex, which was due to follow, to give us another crack at settling the semi. Well, we got one day's play in at Canterbury before the rains came, and it was still raining when we got back to Lord's on the Wednesday morning. After two more days, the rain eventually stopped, leaving a saturated outfield and a mud-heap of a pitch. Conditions were really not fit for play, but the powers that be insisted on a 15-over game. Almost inevitably, Closey lost the toss, we were put in against Wayne Daniel and co; we panicked and were bowled out for 59. Joel took four wickets when Middlesex batted, but even he could not prevent them cruising to victory by six wickets with three overs to spare. It felt like we had been cheated out of a place in the final, and that left its mark.

I do have one happy memory of that episode, which concerns Brian Close the golfer. He was a good golfer, who could play to a low single-figure handicap either right or left-handed but, rather like his fellow Yorkshire Test cricketer FS Trueman, he was not beyond bending the rules of the game when it suited him. In FS's case, I became aware of this when we were playing in a pro-am at El Pariso in Spain. It was during the off-season, which meant that 'winter rules' applied – players could lift, clean and replace the ball within six inches, not nearer the hole. Fred was not the greatest golfer, and at the third hole his drive finished three inches the wrong side of the white line indicating 'out of bounds', which meant he would have to go back to the tee, hit another one and take a one-shot penalty. But Fred wasn't having any of that. He picked up his ball, moved it six inches back over the out of bounds line, and prepared to play. 'What do you think you're doing?' I asked. "It's winter rules," he explained indignantly. "I am entirely within my rights, young man." And that was that.

The Closey example happened at Finchley Golf Club, on one of the many days we spent in London, waiting for the pitch to dry at Lord's. He and I were playing a match with Merv Kitchen, and we came to the last with him needing a par to win. For once his swing failed him, and the ball sailed away to the right, burying itself in a great thicket of bushes. As Closey fought his way in, I decided it was best to leave him to it. The noise was unbelievable: crack, snap, creak, rustle, swear. Then suddenly, out came the ball, clean as a whistle, to finish on the green, followed eventually by a dishevelled Closey, trying not to look guilty. Merv and I looked on in amazement!

Close polarised opinion when it came to how he handled the younger players. Eric Hill, who was never Closey's greatest fan, writing in his review of the 1975 season for *Wisden*, suggested that 'not for the first time, his demands for maximum efficiency sometimes seemed too tough for the present day.' That also seemed to be the opinion of some in the Somerset cricketing establishment, with Roy Kerslake, the highly-respected chairman of the Cricket Committee, at one stage taking Close aside to accuse him of being, in Close's words, "too hard on the young players" – this in the wake of the public 'rollicking' which the skipper had given Botham after he, Botham, had lost his temper and shouted at his team-mates in a Sunday League defeat up in Yorkshire. It was an accusation that Close deeply resented, to the point of threatening his early retirement. 'It was a ridiculous charge,' he asserted in his autobiography *I Don't Bruise Easily*. 'If anything, I was too lenient with them ... God! If some of them had had to make their way into the Yorkshire side of the '40s and '50s ...'

Eric Hill and Roy Kerslake may have had a point. Brian Close's style of captaincy was distinctly abrasive, besides being at times distinctly eccentric, and he was, as Peter Roebuck has written, sometimes more popular with his players off the field than on it. Some of the less strong characters in the side would almost certainly have responded better to some gentle encouragement and sound advice, as opposed to the intimidating barrage of invective which Closey would deliver whenever one of his players fell short of his demanding standards. I was a bit nervous of him at first because he was such a powerful presence, but I soon learned to take him with a large pinch of salt; to laugh at his rages and eccentricities, rather than being upset by them, and the same went for Dasher. As for Botham and Richards, for all the shouting matches that they had with him, they loved the man. It was Closey who taught the pair of them what I would call a 'Test match mentality'. He told them to go out and dominate, and they did.

Two things, above all, I learned from Brian Close: the first technical, the second to do with captaincy. The technical issue cropped up during a match at Worcester, when Closey and I were batting together against an attack which featured the West Indian Test bowler, Vanburn Holder. I was struggling. Three times in an over, he nipped it back into my pads, producing three huge appeals for lbw. Somehow I survived. At the end of the over, Closey came striding up the pitch. "For Christ's sake, Rosey lad, what do you think you're playing at? You're letting your head fall over to the off-side. Keep it upright." So I did, and I was a different player. Head position is vital in both batting and bowling.

As for captaincy, what I learned from Closey was to be my own man. Not in the belligerent style that he adopted, but more quietly, albeit with the same determination. Somerset were a very talented side in the mid-1970s, but also a potentially explosive mix, with all of those strong characters. So I decided, right from the outset really, that I would not ask everyone in sight what we ought to do, or how we ought to play, because the chances were that I would get ten different answers. Yes, I would sometimes have a quiet word with Dasher or Derek Taylor but when it came to it, like Closey, I would make the decisions. I would take responsibility, and I would carry the can if things went wrong. It might sound old-fashioned today, but it worked.

I will finish this chapter with one final Brian Close story, one which shows not just how tough a man he was, but also how proud a man, who never wanted to reveal the slightest trace of weakness.

It was in the match against the West Indies at Taunton in 1976, the game which earned Closey his recall to the England side at the age of 45. Their opening bowlers were Andy Roberts and a young Wayne Daniel, who was as fast as any of the West Indies quicks and nastier than most. There was rain about, and the pitch was playing tricks. I had been battling it out, ducking and weaving, taking the knocks, and was still there when Close came in, at number four, about half an hour before the close. He had been taking the short stuff on his body as per usual, when Daniel hit him somewhere amidships, there was what sounded like a sharp crack and, most unusually for Closey, he sank to his knees, obviously in severe pain. Of course, he waved away those of us who came to see if he was OK, struggled back to his feet and somehow carried on. But I could see he was in agony and could barely walk, let alone run, so there were no quick singles.

Eventually, the umpires called time, took off the bails, and we could go in. Fortunately the changing room was deserted. I was about to go off for a shower when he said, " Rosey lad, you've got to help me." He started to take his trousers down, still with his pads on. I had the delightful task of taking his jockstrap off and, as I did so, I realised that he had a club cricketer's box on, one of those pink plastic jobs. And it had split, and then shut, so that one large testicle was hanging out, trapped by the crack in the box. I knew that the team doctor, a wonderful bloke called Dr David Challacombe, was in the pavilion, so I went to get him, complete with his black bag, but he was at a loss as to what to do. Then I thought, "I know", and I dashed round to the groundsman's hut to see Don Price and borrowed the big screwdriver with a wide flat blade that he used for adjusting the mower.

Back in the dressing room, I showed it to Closey. He went even whiter. "Fucking hell, Rosey lad, what are you going to do with that?!" But I put it in the crack of the box, twisted it to open the crack, and whipped his bollock back in, with a huge great wheal on it. I could see the relief on his face, but there was no word of thanks. Instead, he said, "You're not going to tell anybody, are you?" I didn't, or at least not until he had retired. I think it was what led him to recommend me as captain!

4

Pakistan and New Zealand

I knew that I was very much in the selectors' minds for the winter tour to Pakistan and New Zealand from the fact of my call-up to Headingley. But it would be naïve to suggest that my path into the England side was not considerably smoothed by the ramifications of the Packer controversy, which had broken that August. The six English players contracted to Packer's World Series Cricket – Tony Greig, Dennis Amiss, John Snow, Alan Knott, Derek Underwood and Bob Woolmer – were all effectively banned from playing for England, as were Majid, Imran, Mushtaq and Zaheer for Pakistan. The situation made for a lot of politics and a lot of legal arguments. Even when we had got out to Pakistan, as late as the eve of the first Test, we still weren't entirely sure whether the series would go ahead or not, as there was talk of Pakistan allowing their Packer players to take part after all.

Sweet sorrow – Stevie waving me off to Pakistan at Weston station

In Greig's absence, Mike Brearley had been appointed captain, and he and Boycott would open the innings, with me coming in at number three. I started well enough, with a century in one of the warm-up matches before the first Test, against a United Bank XI. But when it came to the Tests, I had no luck at all. In the first, at Lahore, I was batting against Sarfraz when he got one to bounce and cut back, hitting me on the inside of my right thigh. He appealed, of course. In fact, he didn't just appeal. He engaged the umpire in a discussion which must have gone on for the best part of two minutes, in Urdu or Punjabi, at the end of which the umpire gave me out. Even Boycott, at the other end, was nonplussed. When I'd dragged myself off and got back to the pavilion, I took my trousers down and showed Brearley and the rest of them the mark left by the ball. It was somewhere up near my crotch. But that was the standard of umpiring you had to put up with in Pakistan in those days.

I didn't get a second chance in that game, which was memorable – apart from my lbw decision – for two things: the slowest century of all time, by Mudassar Nazar, who took nine hours and 51 minutes to score 114, helping to keep us out in the field in the broiling heat for the best part of two and a half days and through not one but two riots! The first happened towards the end of the second day, when one or two spectators ran onto the ground in premature celebration of Mudassar's 100. The military beat one of them up, and the crowd decided to take revenge, chasing the soldiers all the way to our dressing room, where they took refuge. The second, on the following day, was more serious, prompted by the arrival at the ground of Benazir Bhutto, daughter of the ex-Prime Minister Zulfiqar Ali Bhutto, who had been arrested and imprisoned by the military a few months earlier. The military responded by lobbing tear-gas grenades into the crowd, forcing spectators out onto the pitch. When play resumed after the rest day, we managed to bat out time without too much trouble, thanks mainly to Geoff Miller, but the atmosphere was very subdued.

The second Test, at Hyderabad, was not much better. After Pakistan had made a painfully slow 275, Boycott and I were trying to bat out time on the second day against Abdul Qadir and his leg breaks. We had survived until the very last ball, which Qadir pitched in the bowlers' footmarks outside my off-stump, I left it, and it turned violently, flicked my pads and fell on the leg stump. Boycott's 100 in the second innings closed the door on whatever slim chance of victory Wasim Bari's over-cautious declaration had left his side.

So that was 1 and 27 in my first two Test innings, but I still felt that I was playing pretty well, and I reinforced that confidence by making 72 in the drawn game against a Punjab XI in an opening partnership of 137 with Derek Randall. By that stage of the tour, rumours were rife that three of the 'Packerstanis', as they'd been called, were on their way back from Australia to play in the third Test. We weren't too happy at this prospect, to put it mildly. A team meeting was called in a private room at our hotel, at which it was the younger players – myself and Beefy included – who were most hostile to the idea of the Packerites being allowed back into the fold. It all got fairly heated, but there was also a strong feeling that it shouldn't be left to the players to make a stand; it was the England cricketing authorities who ought to be making the running. Telephone conversations were indeed held with Lord's, and a statement was eventually put together, setting out our opposition, albeit still in the name of the team, rather than of the TCCB. In the event, the Pakistan Cricket Board backed off at the last minute, and the three Packer players weren't chosen. Had they been, I do know that plans were in place to fly us out of the country, as I am fairly sure we would have boycotted the Test.

And boycott, or rather Boycott, was very much the word of the moment. In the midst of all the Packer-related controversy, Mike Brearley had had his arm broken by a lifter from Sikander Bakht in a meaningless one-day game against a Sind XI and had read out the team statement with his arm in plaster, shortly before flying back to England, leaving Boycott to take over as captain. Playing under the pair of them during that tour provided a fascinating contrast in styles. Brearley was a consultative captain. He liked to talk to his players, his bowlers particularly, and explain to them what he was thinking. What I learned most from Brearley was the importance of thinking ahead. He would always be thinking about where he wanted to be in five or ten overs' time, and he would quite often talk to his bowlers about that as well, so that they knew exactly what he wanted from them.

Boycott, on the other hand, was insular, a man apart. He didn't often share his thoughts with his team-mates, so that you were never quite sure what he was thinking. And because he kept himself to himself socially, he had no rapport with his players off the field. He could also be incredibly selfish when it came to his batting, as in the second Test against New Zeland, which I'll come to in a moment. But it wouldn't be fair to be too critical of Boycott as a captain. It was a role for which, because of his character and his approach to the game, he was in my opinion unsuited.

Boycott's spell as England captain started with him winning the toss in the third Test at Karachi, and walking out to open the innings with BC Rose for company. It looked like – and subsequently proved to be – another turgid, low-bouncing pitch, but I felt full of confidence after my runs against the

Punjab XI. I'd scored 10 when I clipped Sarfraz firmly off the middle of the bat into the leg-side, only to be brilliantly caught by Javed Miandad at short-leg. The match finished in the dullest of dull draws, meaning that all three Tests had failed to produce a positive outcome.

Even so, I enjoyed my visit to Pakistan. I was lucky enough to be roomed with another England new boy, Geoff Cope, and we got on really well together. He wasn't at all like the other Yorkshiremen I'd met. He was friendly, very family-orientated, and we talked a lot about the cricket. I was very concerned to hear of his later problems with his eyesight and was delighted to be able to go with him recently to the West of England Cricket Society in Bath, to talk about his autobiography, *In Sunshine and in Shadow*.

I have always believed in making the most of any tour – to get out, experience the local culture and visit places you might never see again. On one day off, I played golf with Ken Barrington at the Gymkhana Club, and we ended up playing an interesting game of snooker on a table, on which the green baize had obviously been ripped and then stitched up. I was with Kenny again, on a trip up towards the Khyber Pass, when we came across a cabinet maker's shop, which specialised in jewellery boxes. Inside, it felt like we were travelling back 300 years, as we watched them using ancient tools to make every box by hand. As usual, we had rupees in our pocket – our tour expenses, which we had to spend, because we weren't allowed to take them out of the country – so I decided to buy one of these boxes for Stevie, with her name inlaid on the top. We agreed the design, and I paid and gave them my address in Weston, Kenny expressing some doubt as to whether anything would ever arrive there. But not long before I got back from New Zealand, I had a message from Stevie to say that a parcel had arrived for me. That box remains one of our most treasured possessions.

One other memento that I bought was rather more bulky, an onyx chess set. I'd picked it up at the same time as Derek Randall invested in a rocking chair, and the pair of us lugged our prizes all over Pakistan and New Zealand, making ourselves very unpopular with our team-mates, who had to wait for the chess set and the rocking chair to be unloaded from aircraft holds before they could be on their way. I'm pleased to say that Derek has still got the rocking chair, and I've still got the chess set, although one of the horses bearing the knights did lose an ear in a lively party at my house during one Weston Festival!

Then there was my visit to a Pakistani dentist. Not long after we arrived in the country one of my front teeth started to give me gyp, and over the following days it got progressively worse. In the end I had no option but to go to our physiotherapist, Bernard Thomas, to ask him to fix up some

Bob Taylor and Kenny Barrington on the look-out for bargains in Pakistan

treatment for it. He arranged for me to see a Pakistani army dentist in a local barracks. Now Pakistan was changing fast at the time of that tour, as the old, slightly chaotic ways of doing things gave way to more modern practices and technologies, but it was still a work in progress, particularly when it came to the electricity supply, which was prone to frequent power cuts. Sure enough, just as I arrived at the barracks, the lights went out, so that the dentist had to use a torch to see what he was doing, as he prodded around in my teeth and gums. It turned out that a root filling had come out and would need to be replaced. "How are you going to manage that, with no electricity for the drill?" I asked. "No problem," he replied, pressing a bell. There then appeared an assistant, who mounted what appeared to be some sort of bicycle, wired up to the drill, and started pedalling away. I couldn't believe it! A bicycle-powered-drill wallah! In fact, it was no worse than any other drill, and the dentist did a great job. But it was certainly a moment I'll never forget.

My run of bad luck with the bat continued when we got to New Zealand, not helped by some poor weather and dodgy practice facilities which made it difficult to find some form in the nets. My confidence was given a boost when I made 107 in the second innings of a rather jet-lagged warm-up game against Auckland, but in the second innings of the first

Test, at Wellington, Richard Hadlee hit me a fearful blow on my right arm. I thought I'd broken it and had to go off, with the team needing 136 to prevent New Zealand from recording their first ever win against England. There followed a horrific collapse against Hadlee and Collinge and, when I came back, last man in, with arm heavily strapped, we were 63/9. I survived, 5 not out, but we were beaten by 72 runs. It was a great moment – if you were a New Zealand cricket follower! We got our revenge at Christchurch, but not before a scare at the start of our first innings, which saw us three down for 26, BC Rose c Howarth b Chatfield 11. How he took that catch, I'll never know. I'd flicked it off my toes, clean as a whistle, and he somehow clung on to it at leg slip.

A happier memory of that game concerns the second innings, and our captain for the match, Geoff Boycott. With a lead of 183 on first innings, we needed quick runs to set up a declaration. So we called an impromptu players' meeting, without the captain present, and decided two things: first, to go for our shots, and second – as he was sure just to accumulate slowly in his usual selfish way – to run out the captain. So, after Randall had been scandalously run out, backing up, by Ewen Chatfield, out marched Ian Botham on a mission to dismiss the captain. He succeeded brilliantly, calling Boycott through for an impossible run, as the rest of his team tried not to laugh too loudly! He was a great Test player, Geoff Boycott, but found it difficult to escape from his own mental bubble, which sometimes led to problems for his team. There was a Sunday League game at Scarborough in 1977 when we quite deliberately didn't try to get him out, because Yorkshire needed 195 to win and we knew that, as long as he was batting, they wouldn't get them. Sure enough, they were bowled out for 110, Boycott, last man out, 45!

As it turned out, the game at Christchurch was the last Test cricket I would play for over two years, as I was dropped for the third Test at Auckland. I've no complaints about that. Whilst I had played well in the run-up to both the Test series and in the one-day internationals against Pakistan, I had averaged only 13.5 in the Tests against Pakistan and 14.67 against New Zealand.

Yes, the gods had been against me for some reason. I didn't feel I had done myself justice and, in all honesty, didn't expect to get back in the side for the return series that summer against Pakistan and New Zealand. It had been a great experience and one, despite all the politics and the riots and the heat and the dust and the umpiring, that I had thoroughly enjoyed, but I knew when I came back that my focus needed to be firmly on captaining Somerset.

5

Captain of Somerset

It was in November 1977 that I got a call from the immediate past Chairman of Somerset, Herbie Hoskins, asking me to meet him at, of all places, Shepton Mallet. By that stage, I'd been picked for the England squad to tour Pakistan and New Zealand that winter, and we were due to leave in just a few days' time. When we met, he explained that the committee had decided to ask me to be captain and wanted to get it settled before the tour, rather than bothering me when I was away. I said that I would think about it for 24 hours, although in reality I had long since decided that, if they offered me the captaincy, I would accept.

Not that that was a certainty, by any means. Dasher was very much in the frame, as was Merv Kitchen, and Somerset had also looked around to see if there was an experienced player from another county who might fancy coming west to take on the job, much as Closey had done. But, in the end, I don't think they had much choice. Dasher had the reputation of being difficult, because he was, naturally, pretty aggressive; Merv was getting on and had already missed a season; the university boys, Marks and Roebuck, were too young; and I think they really wanted to appoint from within. The fact that I didn't say too much may even have helped my cause. I think they looked at me and said, "He's thinking about it; he's going to give himself time to think" – which I generally did.

I had already decided that, much as I admired Closey, there was no point in attempting to follow his verbally aggressive style of captaincy, because, unlike him, I didn't have the physical presence to back it up. Nor was I ever going to confront great players like Richards, Garner and Botham and start questioning their commitment. Instead, I would be my own man, do things my own way and earn their respect for the way that I played and the way that I captained the side. It helped that I was in the form of my life and that, almost as soon as I took over, we started winning. That year's Somerset Cricket Handbook referred to the 'almost instantaneous' transformation in the way the team approached one-day cricket, and it was right. We were young, we were fit, we were aggressive, and we had the winning mentality. John Barclay, who became captain of Sussex soon after, told me that he had never played

Pre-season training

against a side which brought such intensity, and sustained intensity, to their cricket. We frightened people, especially with that wonderful Taunton crowd behind us in a big one-day game.

That is not to say that I never made mistakes as captain. One, which is fondly remembered by my old team-mates to this day, was in a Sunday League game at Taunton, when we were losing wickets in pursuit of a target that we needed to reach to stay in the hunt for the title. I had got out early on and was sitting on the balcony outside our dressing room, smoking a cigar and watching on anxiously. When yet another wicket went down, I noticed that Dennis Breakwell, sitting nearby, had not got his pads on. "For Christ's sake, Dennis, put your effing pads on and get out there," I shouted at him. "But, Skip ...," he'd started to protest, before I shut him up again with "Don't argue, just effing do it!" This time he did manage to get a word in edgeways: "What I was trying to say, Skip, is that you told me three hours ago that I was twelfth man!"

In his notes about the 1978 season for *Wisden*, Eric Hill highlighted one of the biggest changes that I brought to the captaincy. 'Never before,' he wrote, 'had such careful thought and preparation been given to a season.' And that was exactly right.

The first thing I had done when I got back from New Zealand in March was to marry Stevie. We had decided during the long separation that winter that it was time to put our relationship on a more formal basis, and my proposal and her acceptance were actually broadcast live on *BBC Radio Four*, thanks to some careful planning by Don Mosey. It was not the sort of cricketer's wedding you see nowadays, costing tens of thousands of pounds. I held my stag party at the Queen's Arms at Bleadon at lunchtime, where Beefy succeeded in downing the yard of ale, then headed back to the Dolphin in Uphill for a quick one before going to the Registry Office for the ceremony and so up the hill to where we lived for the reception!

The second thing I had done was to start preparing for the new season. We had a lot more discussion pre-season than we ever had with Closey, when we had just gone out onto the pitch and got on with it. We prepared better, we netted better and we trained better. Pete Robinson, who had become coach when Tom Cartwright had gone in 1976, had a big part to play. He may not have been the greatest thinker about the game, but he was non-stop, ever-present and liked to get on with things. Another big factor was that our three biggest players, Viv, Joel and Ian, were maturing as cricketers and were entering their best years.

Eric Hill also referred to the 'team spirit and optimistic spirit' that we showed that year and which he attributed to my captaincy. In fact, I didn't have to do very much. We were such a competitive bunch that the team spirit came naturally. It made captaincy very easy. At the end of every over, I would usually have a chat with Derek Taylor about how the pitch was playing, or what the batsmen were up to, but we never went in for agonised team meetings about what we were trying to do. When it came to the bowlers, I mostly left them to it. You weren't going to tell someone like Joel how he ought to bowl, and with Ian I always believed in letting him get on with doing what he was good at. You knew that some of it might turn out to be hopeless, but you also knew that a lot of it would be brilliant. I didn't see any reason why I should be an overbearing, interfering captain. When it came to field placings, sometimes I would leave it to the bowler, sometimes I would do it myself. I never found it very difficult.

I was probably more tactically aware, especially in one-day cricket, than Closey, with his bull-at-a-gate approach, and strategically I was more defensive. But it was defensiveness with a purpose: to build pressure on the opposition batsmen. It helped that I had Joel and Ian up my sleeve and that I could bring them back on, if we'd had a bad over or two. But the other bowlers all played their part as well, including Viv, who put in some telling spells. I knew that, if I set fields, they would bowl to them, and that made it

The Cidermen – celebrating Taunton Cider's sponsorship
Derek Taylor, a man from Taunton Cider man, Dasher Denning,
Hallam Moseley, Graham Burgess, Ian Botham, me, Viv Richards,
Dennis Breakwell and another man from Taunton Cider

very hard for the opposition batters. It meant that we were usually in control of matches – continually in control. That's why we didn't lose too many. In fact, as the season went on, it became clearer and clearer that a lot of other sides simply didn't want to play us.

The first month of the 1978 season was miserably wet but not unsuccessful. In the 55-over Benson & Hedges group stage we won three out of four games (the other one was abandoned), including an extraordinary finish at Cardiff, where Glamorgan needed to score only four runs from the last nine balls and managed just three, leaving the scores tied and Somerset the winners, by virtue of losing fewer wickets. They panicked; we stuck to our guns. It happened a lot that season. Rain meant that that game stretched over two days, as did the quarter-final against Sussex at Taunton, which we won comfortably, thanks to a brilliant, counter-attacking knock by Ian Botham and good bowling from all the seamers.

The semi-final was against Kent, again at Taunton, this time going into a third day, thanks to the wretched weather. Kent batted first and had the best of a pitch which deteriorated markedly as the game went on. We needed 205 to win and fell 42 runs short, despite what *Wisden* describes as a 'defiant' 48 from me and 44 from Dasher. It was the sort of wicket where you had to fight for every run, and Kent were a strong bowling side, who would go on to win the final and, in September, the county championship. After the form we had shown, it was a huge disappointment, and it hurt. We were never good losers, and our luck with the weather and the pitch was all too reminiscent of what had happened the previous season at Lord's against Middlesex. The feeling was growing that, with all the world apparently against us, we would need to exploit whatever little bit of luck or opportunity that might come our way if we were ever going to win anything.

When it came to the Gillette Cup, a knock-out played over 60 overs, we almost fell at the first hurdle. We played Warwickshire on a cold and windy day at Taunton in early July. Thanks mainly to Geoff Humpage, they made 292, which was the highest one-day score made against Somerset at that time. By the time we went in to try to chase down what was a daunting total, it was gloomier and windier than ever. I was out early on, but then Viv came in and made batting look like the easiest thing in the world. With good support from Dasher, Peter Roebuck and Vic Marks, he carried us home with almost three overs to spare, finishing on 139 not out and winning the game with a straight six. It was a magnificent innings, better even than one or two that he scored in one-day finals, because he didn't yet have the intimidation factor that he later developed, and because conditions were so much against him.

In the next round, against Glamorgan, it was Dasher's turn to star. He and I added 70 for the first wicket, and he went on to make 145 not out to carry us to 330, which proved more than enough. The pair of us were a bowler's nightmare. Having batted together since we were about 13, we had an instinctive understanding in our running between the wickets, and we used it to rotate the strike as much as possible. This meant that the bowlers were constantly having to change their lengths. They knew they couldn't pitch it up to me, or I would drive them, so they tended to bowl short. And they knew that they daren't drop it short to Dasher, as he would carve and pull them for a pastime, so they would end up bowling half-volleys, which he would still cut for four! If you look at Dasher's career averages – 26.68 in first-class cricket and 28.06 in the one-day stuff – you might not think he was anything special. But, as with that 145, he made some fantastically telling contributions, not just with his batting but with his sheer physical presence on the pitch. He was so aggressive, growling at fielders and so on, that he intimidated people, and it was that same fighting spirit that made him such a popular member of the dressing room.

Dredgie

Another of our local lads stepped up in the quarter-final against Kent, Colin Dredge, the 'Demon of Frome' as he was christened by Alan Gibson in *The Times*. He took 4/23 to bowl Kent out for just 120 and pave the way for a very satisfying five-wicket victory and some revenge for what had happened in the B&H. I had first noticed him a couple of years earlier when, on debut at Bath, he had bowled the great Worcestershire and New Zealand opening batsman, Glenn Turner, all ends up with one of his nip-backers, before calmly batting out time with Derek Taylor on the third day to save the game. His progress was a key factor in our eventual successes. He had a knack of getting out really good batsmen – Procter and Zaheer Abbas, for example – and I knew that if, say, Beefy was having a bad time, I could chuck the ball to Dredgie and he wouldn't let me down. He was also, despite looking a bit ungainly, a superb out-fielder, who would eat up the ground with those great long strides of his and had a wonderful pair of hands. He may not have been the most famous or glamorous member of that side, but he was one of the keys to our success.

I did have my doubts though when, in the semi-final, with Essex needing seven off the last three balls, he produced a no-ball which, with overthrows, went for three runs. I nearly died. He made partial amends with only a single off the next two balls, meaning that John Lever needed three off the last ball. I was fielding at deepish cover on the Coal Orchard side of the ground, with the crowd going mad behind me. I was praying that the ball wouldn't come to me. Well, it did, of course. Lever played a scruffy sort of cut shot, about 10 yards to my left and slightly behind me. As I set off to field it, I knew that the one thing I must not do was fumble it. Derek Taylor said to me afterwards that he had never seen a fielder take so much time and trouble over picking the ball up cleanly. But I managed it, sent in a skimming throw just to the right of the stumps and Derek did the rest. It was a great moment, probably the best of that entire summer. It had been another tremendous innings by Richards, 116 out of 287, which had set us up for the victory, but everyone had played their part. In a way, that performance epitomised our one-day cricket over the next few years, with star performances from a young, fit, and highly competitive side, playing aggressive cricket, and with a huge crowd, hungry for success, behind us.

Celebrating victory over Essex in the Gillette semi-final
Me, Beefy and Derek Taylor

The semi-final against Essex at Taunton – Viv on 49, me on 16

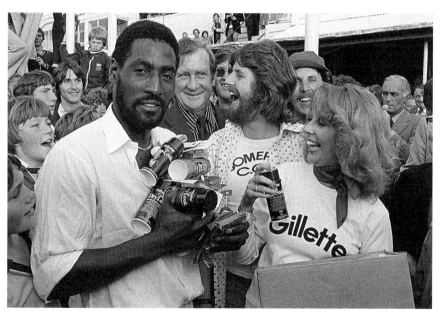

Jim Laker, lost in the crowd, chooses Viv as Man of the Match

The final at Lord's, on September 2, was an anti-climax. I lost the toss, we were put in on an autumnal morning, and hopes were high when I took 14 off the first over from Imran. But, after that, we never really got going. For once, Viv seemed to be overawed by the occasion, rather than inspired by it, and only Botham, of our main batsmen, contributed significantly, carrying the total past 200 with some typically big hitting. I didn't think that 207 would be enough but, when Joel got Javed Miandad and Beefy caught and bowled Imran after hitting him on the head with a venomous bouncer, to leave them at 110/4, I thought we were right back in it. At that stage, I took off our two main strike bowlers and was criticised for it afterwards. But it stemmed partly from my confidence in our support bowlers, Dredge, Keith Jennings and Budgie Burgess, and partly from the need to keep a few overs from Joel and Beefy up my sleeve. In the event, although they were economical, they couldn't break a very solid partnership between Paul Parker and Paul Phillipson and, when I did bring Beefy back, he bowled far too short. We lost by five wickets, and it was a bitterly disappointed group of players who made their way back to Taunton for the climax of the John Player League on the following day.

Even so, we were pretty confident: four points ahead at the top of the table and having lost only three games all season. Two partnerships I remember in particular: 109 with Dasher against Yorkshire at the Imperial Ground in Bristol – runs and wins against Yorkshire were always especially enjoyable! – and 107 with Viv against Warwickshire at Weston, of which I contributed just 28. In the penultimate game I made 49 not out as we hammered Gloucestershire at Bristol by eight wickets and, despite the disappointment of Lord's, hopes and expectations of a first trophy were sky high.

This time, in front of another packed house at Taunton, I won the toss and put Essex in. We soon had them 29/3, and it would have been 29/4 if Derek Taylor hadn't missed Keith Fletcher off Budgie Burgess before he had scored. It was a very rare mistake by Derek. I always rated him as one of the best wicket-keepers I ever played with or against. He was big for a wicket-keeper, but he had brilliant timing with his feet and his hands, and his ability to take down the leg-side was outstanding. But that miss cost us. Fletcher went on to make 76 not out, and we were left to score 190 for the tie – and the title.

Dasher and I were out early, but Viv, Beefy, Roebuck and Phil Slocombe all got going, then got out. In the end, we needed 33 off the last five overs with three wickets standing. Jennings and Dredge took the score on to 177, before Dredgie was bowled by John Lever, and it came down to 11 off the last over. I still believed that we could do it, especially when an Essex overthrow allowed Keith Jennings to steal three off the first ball. Two singles followed, but then Derek Taylor was run out, going for a second run, to leave the new batsman, Hallam Moseley, on strike, with five wanted from two balls. They ran a leg bye off the fifth ball, but Keith Jennings was never really a big hitter, and two was the most they could muster before Hallam was run out. It was a cruel blow, especially after what had happened the day before. I don't think I have ever felt quite so devastated on a cricket field as I did then. To have got so close to winning two trophies in a weekend, and ending up with neither, was heart-breaking. The critics had a field day: 'same old Somerset', 'the nearly men', 'often the bridesmaid, never the bride' and so on.

But we learnt a lot from those two defeats. Thinking about them afterwards, I came to the conclusion that we had been too desperate for success, that we had tried almost too hard, that we had got too tight. The other thing was our preparation for the Gillette final. We had stayed at the Europa Hotel in Kensington, where we had never stayed before, and, instead of relaxing on the night before our big day, we had had a team meeting – something that I never normally called – which went on far too long and in which various people got rather over-excited and uptight. It did us no good at all when the time came. Our mind-set and our preparations were very different a year later.

Meanwhile, in the championship, we had had a good season: played 24, won 9, lost 4, drawn 11. It was a wet summer, by and large, and the pitches were often tricky, but I had batted well, scoring four centuries and a 99. The fact that I was making plenty of runs was a big factor in the success of my captaincy. It meant that, automatically, the team had confidence in me, so there was never any real pressure. Viv had a great season as well, with over 1,500 runs in the championship, and this was Phil Slocombe's best year: second in the averages with 1,172 runs at 40.4. It was a success that he never really recovered from. By the following year, he seemed to have lost all confidence in facing genuinely fast bowling, and his star gradually faded. It was a shame, because he was a seriously talented player.

For two or three days after the Essex defeat, I was sunk in gloom and misery. As I've said before, I have never been a good loser. But then I began to see things in perspective. Taken all in all, we'd had a great season: fifth in the championship, semi-finalists in the B&H and runners-up in the Gillette and the John Player League. Besides all that was the wonderful support we had received from the Somerset supporters, in defeat as well as in victory. When you look back across all the years in between, it is that, more than anything, that stays with me.

6

Zero to hero

I had had a quiet winter. Stevie was pregnant with our first child, and I spent my time helping out around the house, pottering in the garden and playing golf. On 19 March, to the joy of family and friends, Stevie produced a fine, healthy, bouncing baby boy, Stuart. It made for the perfect run-up to what I was determined would be an even better season than 1978.

May that year was horribly wet. Of 37 county championship matches during the month, only three reached a definite conclusion. We had had no comings or goings during the off-season, the only significant development being Joel Garner signing a full-time contract, which meant that, apart from a break for the World Cup, he would be available for all of Somerset's games. We were a settled side, and a very determined side, with perhaps an extra touch of aggression born of the disappointments of the previous autumn.

After a bizarre game in freezing conditions at Worcester, where a new pitch had to be cut after the groundsman had inadvertently rolled the starting handle for the heavy roller into the original wicket, we'd notched up a comfortable win against Glamorgan in the B&H, beaten Northants in the championship at Taunton, despite losing an entire day to the weather, before thrashing Gloucestershire in the B&H on a green wicket at Bristol. A routine win against Minor Counties South gave us a three-point lead over both Glamorgan and the fifth county in our group, Worcestershire, going into the last round of qualifying matches. We were due to play Worcester at New Road and, needless to say, the weather was foul. The first of the three days set aside for the match was rained off and after the sort of spring we'd endured, we knew that conditions on the second available day, 24 May, could be such as to make the outcome a lottery. Memories of how we had been diddled out of a Gillette Cup semi-final at Lord's in 1977, by being forced to play a farce of a game on a mud-heap of a pitch, came flooding back.

The enforced day off also gave us time to think about our situation. Two sides from each group would go through to the quarter-finals, and B&H regulations stated that, if two or more teams were level on points at the end of the qualifying games, the tie-breaker would be 'strike-rate' – the number

Away from it all on the golf course at Worlebury, watched by Bill Andrews,
who lived just down the road, with his pipe on the go as ever

of wickets per 100 balls – the idea being to reward attacking bowling. Technicalities like this were very much on our minds, having twice lost at the last gasp in the Sunday League, in 1976 on away wins and in 1978 on run-rate. We weren't going to be victims of the small print again.

Our strike rate was the best in the group – 33.32 to Worcestershire's 36.92. I think it was in a conversation between Peter Roebuck and Phil Slocombe on the morning of the second day, with the rain still falling, that the idea first surfaced that, if we denied Worcestershire the chance to improve their strike rate, they couldn't overtake us in the qualifying positions, even if they were to win the game. As we sat in the changing room, watching the rain come down and fearing the worst, the initial idea was shaped into a firm plan. If I won the toss, I would bat first, and declare after one over, so conceding defeat but ensuring qualification. After all, there was no law against declarations in one-day cricket. It was just that no one had ever done it before. That said, we knew perfectly well that it would bring a storm of criticism down on our heads. But it was very much a collective decision. Only Derek Taylor spoke out against it. Even Roy Kerslake, our Chairman and a solicitor, was cautiously in favour. Just to be on the safe side, it was agreed that I should phone Lord's, to clear it with Donald Carr, the Secretary of the TCCB. I rang him from the Worcestershire Secretary's office in the New Road pavilion.

The conversation was matter of fact. I told him what, mathematically, the situation was and what I proposed to do. I asked him if there was anything in the regulations which might prevent me from doing it, and he said no, there wasn't, although he did add that, if I went ahead, it might have repercussions for the regulations, as of course it did eventually, with the banning of declarations in the one-day game. What he didn't do was to caution me against it. To be fair to Donald Carr, whom I came to know very well when we worked together on various committees later in my career, I think I took him rather by surprise. He was a calm, considered cricket administrator, who liked to think things through rather than rushing to judgement. If he had said to me, "For Christ sake, Rosey, don't be such an effing idiot, there's no way I'm letting you do that," I would have backed off. But that wasn't Donald Carr's style. As far as I was concerned, I had been told that yes we could do it and yes it was legal. There was no warning as to what the consequences might be, beyond that change to the regulations. He subsequently claimed to have warned me that if I went ahead "there would probably be severe repercussions", which was true, and that my action "would be viewed with disgust", which was not. The fact that Roy Kerslake, the Somerset Chairman, had been in the dressing room when the decision was made and had supported it provided further reassurance – though it is only fair to add that Roy soon had second thoughts and offered his resignation to Somerset's President, Colin Atkinson, who declined to accept it.

It was a bleak scene as Dasher and I walked to the wicket after lunch on the second day, a Thursday, when the umpires finally decided that the ground was fit for play: grey overhead, green underfoot, with just a handful of members in the pavilion and around 100 other spectators. I played out a maiden from Vanburn Holder, which included a no ball and at the end of it said to the umpire Terry Spencer what he already knew, that I was declaring, and walked off. The Worcestershire fielders just stood there, stunned rather than angry. I put Dredgie on to bowl when Glenn Turner and Alan Ormrod came out to bat and, after an over from him and four balls from Keith Jennings, they scored the two runs that they needed to win, and we all trooped off to a few jeers and catcalls from the spectators, such as they were. Nothing much was said after that. We got changed and left.

My initial feelings were ones of defiance. As I said to the press outside the New Road pavilion, "In the prevailing weather conditions I had no alternative. My first duty is to Somerset County Cricket Club." What I meant by that was that rain-affected one-day games in those pre-Duckworth/Lewis days were a lottery. If I could see a way, within the rules, by which I could protect my team from the vagaries of the weather and ensure that we qualified, I was duty bound to take it. What I had done was within the rules, as had been confirmed by Lord's. What was there to be ashamed of? Somerset, so often the victims of technicalities, had used the rules to our advantage for a change. Poetic justice had been served, along with notice that perhaps we weren't such a bunch of country bumpkins after all.

It was not a view shared by our President, Colin Atkinson. No sooner did he get wind of what had happened than he was on the phone, apologising profusely to his Worcestershire opposite number and offering to get the game replayed. This proved to be impossible, so congested was the fixture list, and I suppose he cannot be blamed for trying. Even so, his grovelling apologies, then and even more so when, at Glamorgan's behest, a special meeting of the TCCB was held on 1 June, didn't go down at all well with the players. He did acknowledge that I had done what I thought was right for my side, and that it was within the rules, but went on to describe the declaration as "wholly indefensible", which certainly wasn't true, and "deeply regretted by the Somerset committee and captain", which was only half true. That hurt at the time, especially as I was beginning to have second thoughts myself about what had taken place, but it is only fair to add that it did help to defuse the situation. By 17 votes to one (good old Derbyshire!), Somerset were ejected from the B&H, their place in the quarter-finals being taken by Glamorgan. Declarations in one-day cricket were subsequently banned but, in terms of sanctions, that was it. I have no doubt that there were those on the committee who were arguing that I should be sacked. But, given that it was a team decision, endorsed by the chairman no less, they found little support.

In the midst of all this, with press, photographers and television reporters quite literally banging on my door at Weston, I gave an impromptu press conference. I had an anxious and upset Stevie and two-month-old baby son to consider, and it felt like we were under siege. Perhaps if I gave them what they wanted, they would go away and leave us alone. So I decided to confront them, and I wasn't in any mood to apologise! I said that, if I were to be faced with the same situation, with the rules as they stood, I would do the same thing again and that it was my team that mattered to me, not what the rest of the world might think of what I'd done. I was probably a bit over the top, but it did at least do the trick of keeping the press off our backs!

It took only a few days' reflection for me to realise that what I had done was wrong, certainly in the context of the spirit of the game, and the barrage of criticism hurt. But the experience did have its positive side, thanks mainly to the wonderful support that we received from the Somerset supporters. Our next fixture after Worcester was a Sunday League game against Hampshire at Taunton. The ground was packed. You could almost feel the emotion in the air. As I led the side out into the field, we were given a standing ovation. And when I walked back to the pavilion some while later, run out for 25 after an opening partnership of 46 with Dasher, they stood for me again. I am not a particularly emotional man, and I tend to keep my feelings to myself but, when I got back to the changing room, there were indeed a few tears, after all that I'd gone through over the previous three days.

People often ask me whether I now regret the declaration, or whether I would do it again if the circumstances were the same. The answer is a bit of both. Looking back, it is something that I would not want to do again, because it was against the spirit of cricket. But equally, I remember to this day the feeling of the troops at the time. I was their general, and I wasn't going to abandon them or let them down. If I had cut them off at the knees, I doubt very much if we would have performed for the rest of that season and beyond as we did.

If the episode united the Somerset faithful behind their team, so it also united the team. It made us even more determined to prove ourselves as what we believed in our hearts we were, the best team in the country – so that, ironically, what was an unquestionably traumatic few days served as a spur rather than a distraction, and not just for the team as a whole but for my form as well. After a rain-ruined draw at Edgbaston, where proceedings were enlivened when a particularly colourful Warwickshire supporter known as 'Loopy Lugs' produced a banner proclaiming 'IT'S ROSE, I DO DECLARE!!', I made two fifties in our championship game against Hampshire at Taunton and followed that with a hard-hitting, deeply satisfying 78 out of 135 to win our Sunday League game against the old enemy, Gloucestershire, at the Imperial Ground at Bristol.

By this stage, we had lost Richards, Garner and Botham to the World Cup, but two of our older stalwarts, Merv Kitchen and Hallam Moseley, stepped into the breach, while Vic Marks really came of age that summer, scoring almost 800 runs and taking 50 wickets in the championship and being consistently one of our very best one-day performers. I always thought that the key to his success as a one-day bowler was pace, or the lack of it. Batsmen couldn't use the pace on the ball to pick up easy runs behind square, which meant that I could set the field for hitting down the ground, with a straight mid-wicket and me at straight extra-cover, plus one man out deep at long on. Vic was brilliant at bowling to his field, on an off-stump line, which meant that if batsmen tried to go aerial against that field they were taking big risks, so they tended to play it along the ground, which meant ones and twos, not boundaries. Mind you, he did sometimes bowl remarkably slowly. In championship cricket, I tended to field close-in at silly mid-off to Vic's bowling and, if he looped up what was obviously going to be a full-toss on off-stump, he'd shout down the pitch at me, with ball in mid-air, "Watch it!!"

He was a more than useful batsman as well. His 93 in the second innings against Essex at Bath that June turned the match on its head. At 63 for five, only 38 ahead, we were looking down the barrel. But Vic and a stone-walling Colin Dredge added 140 for the sixth wicket, allowing me to declare in time for Hallam Moseley to pick up five quick wickets and nearly bowl us to victory.

That was one of a number of close-run things in the championship, games that we might have won but didn't quite. In fact, our very next game, against Glamorgan, also at Bath, was one of those, as the Glamorgan number 11, Andy Mack, somehow survived Hallam Moseley's last five balls to save the game. We lost only one championship match all season, and that was the last one, against Sussex at Hove when, with the Gillette final coming up, we fielded a weakened side. There were five wins, undoubtedly the most dramatic being an extraordinary game against Sussex in the Weston Festival that August. As usual in the summer of 1979, we lost more than a day to rain, and our first innings, in reply to Sussex's 154, didn't finish until an hour after lunch on the third and final day. But then Garner, with good support from Breakwell and Marks, tore through the Sussex batting, to bowl them out for 64, which left us to get 69 in 9 overs against Imran and Geoff Arnold. I got us off to a steady start, but then Richards and Botham were both run out for not many, and it was left to Dennis Breakwell to smash a six and two fours to take us home with three balls to spare. It's a game that they talk of in Weston to this day!

But 15 draws out of 21 championship matches was at least half a dozen too many, and we finished eighth. A lot of that was down to the weather, of course, with our home games bearing the brunt of all the depressions rolling in from the Atlantic. Essex topped the table by a street – their first championship triumph and richly deserved – but you could not help but notice that four out of the top five counties that season – Essex, Surrey, Sussex and Kent – were in the south-east of England, which tends to miss the worst of the weather in a wet summer. If you are looking for explanations as to why Somerset have yet to win the county championship, the prevailing weather pattern has got to be in there.

Another factor in 1979 was that we didn't quite have the spin bowlers to finish sides off in the third or fourth innings. Vic Marks was wonderfully effective in one-day cricket and picked up wickets regularly in the championship, but he lacked the ability of someone like Derek Underwood or Pat Pocock to run through sides on uncovered pitches; while Dennis Breakwell's bowling style meant that he tended to undercut the ball, so that it skidded, rather than putting a lot of revolutions on it to generate sharp sideways movement. To get the most out of those pitches as a spinner you needed to have a high arm, so that the ball would bite and turn, and that was something which, fine cricketers though they both were, neither of ours had.

Test calls and the World Cup also had an impact. Botham missed almost half of our championship matches that season and, without him and Joel, we had a decent but not devastating seam attack: Colin Dredge and Hallam Moseley to open, with Budgie Burgess and Keith Jennings as back-up.

The other point to make about our relative lack of success in the county championship in those years was the sheer pressure generated by our success in the three one-day competitions. Cricket was virtually non-stop in those days, and hardly a week seemed to go by without a big game of one sort or another looming. It meant that the pressure was on us all the time, and something had to give.

Joel Garner played 14 championship matches that season, topping the Somerset bowling averages with 55 wickets at 13.83. That was terrific, and in the Gillette Cup he was simply magnificent. In four matches he took 19 wickets for 79 runs in 43 overs, which works out at a 'strike rate' of a wicket every 13.6 balls and an 'economy rate' of 1.8 runs per over! We had a bye in the first round, so our first game was against Derbyshire at Taunton in mid-July. On a decent pitch, we restricted them to 224 in their 60 overs, and then knocked off the runs with almost four overs to spare, BC Rose 88 not out! I'd set out to anchor the innings, against a strong attack led by Mike Hendrick, and shared partnerships of 85 with Phil Slocombe for the first wicket, and 112 with Viv for the second, in which both of us played just about as well as we could, and the crowd loved it.

The quarter-final, against Kent, one of the best one-day sides in the country, was also at Taunton. That was a stupendous game. The ground was absolutely rammed, to the extent that dozens of people were perched in the trees on the Coal Orchard side of the ground and the atmosphere was electric. It was a cloudy day, and the Kent seamers, Jarvis, Dilley and Woolmer, soon had us four down for 45. Botham and Richards added a quick 50, but it was really Budgie Burgess who saved us, making 50 not out with the tail. Even so, our 190 didn't look like a cast-iron winning score – until Kent started to bat! Garner and Botham operating at full speed, with that crowd behind them! I don't think I have ever known anything like it. The ground was so full that, to reach the pitch, each incoming Kent batsman had almost to fight his way through the massed ranks of Somerset supporters in front of the old pavilion, and as the wickets went down, you could see the fear in the eyes of each incoming batsman. They were out almost before they'd reached the middle. One of our lot had supposedly told Joel that the Kent captain, Alan Ealham, had been heard to say that he didn't rate Garner because he wasn't really quick! Whether that was true or not, I don't know, but on that day he was frighteningly fast. They were taking off from just short of a length like Jumbo jets! Kent didn't know what had hit them and folded for just 64, Garner 11.4–2–11–5. That was a great day.

For the semi-final, we were back at Lord's, where we had been robbed by the weather three years earlier. This time, with the ball swinging all over the place, it was Budgie Burgess who did the initial damage for us, with 3/25, before Garner swept away the tail. We were left to score 186, and Dasher made sure that was never in doubt, cutting and carving his way to 90 not out, before Beefy finished things off with a six off Mike Selvey, with the best part of ten overs in hand. It was a win which confirmed our reputation as the best one-day side in the country and meant that we were firm favourites for the final against Northants on 8 September.

For that weekend, the scenario was remarkably similar to a year previously: Gillette Cup final on the Saturday; a chance to clinch the John Player League on the Sunday, although this time we needed Kent to lose, as well as winning ourselves at Trent Bridge. I and all the team were utterly determined that history should not be allowed to repeat itself.

A few weeks earlier, John Cleese has been at Clarence Park, in his home town, to watch us in the Weston Festival. As usual, he was in a deckchair, glasses and sun hat in place, collar turned up to minimise the risk of being recognised. After play one day, we got chatting, with the possibility of a Gillette Cup final at Lord's the main focus of conversation. He asked me what we were planning to do the night before, assuming we won our semi-final against Middlesex. I said, truthfully, that I hadn't really thought about it, except that we weren't going to use up all our mental energy in an intense team meeting in the hotel. "Why don't you all come over and have dinner with me at my place in Holland Park?" he asked. I said thank you very much, we will!

It worked out perfectly. We dined at an enormous table, which he had bought at an auction from Holloway Prison, as we could tell from the initials which had been carved in the wood. He'd had it dressed up in what looked like a big Arab tent, and it was more than big enough to accommodate the entire team as well as John, his wife and one or two other guests. We had a lovely, funny, relaxing evening, went back to the hotel and fell fast asleep. It was the perfect preparation.

So I could not have been in a much better mood the following morning, especially when, under a clear blue sky with the sun beating down, Jim Watts, the Northants captain, won the toss and put us in. I couldn't believe my luck! We lost Dasher quite early on, which brought Viv in with me. I had been batting well, setting out my stall again to be the pivot of the innings for as long as possible, knowing that I could always open up if we fell behind a decent run-rate. I enjoyed batting with Viv, and vice versa. "Keep going, Skip," he used to say to me, "keep going and get us over the bridge." That was exactly what I was trying to do when,

Batting in the Lord's final

with the score on 95, Jim Watts bowled me a short, wide one, which I would normally have marmalised through square cover. But this time, I got an inside edge, and the ball trickled back onto the stumps. I thought at the time I'd been unlucky, but maybe it was a poor shot. Anyway, the responsibility for anchoring the innings now fell on Viv's shoulders, and how determinedly he accepted it. This wasn't a typical Richards one-day innings by any means. He took care to play himself in but, as the innings went on, he became more and more dominant. With a rapid 27 from Beefy and a hugely entertaining 24 not out from Joel, we reached 269/8 in our 60 overs, which might not sound many these days but which we knew, with our fire-power, ought to be plenty enough.

And so it proved. The only real threat came from Allan Lamb, but after Garner had made early inroads, I stuck to my game plan of using the medium-pacers, and in the end it was Richards who got Lamb, brilliantly stumped down the leg-side by Derek Taylor, leaving Joel to mop up the tail. So we had won, at long last. We had almost to fight our way off the field, as delirious Somerset supporters came charging onto the playing area. When we got to the dressing room, it was mayhem; everyone was going mad, there were champagne corks popping everywhere as all sorts of Somerset officials came to congratulate the players. As for myself, I sat in a corner for five minutes, utterly drained, both physically and emotionally. I had captained Somerset County Cricket Club to its first trophy in its 104-year history. I needed time for it to sink in. Then came the cheers, the champagne and the presentation. For all that we finished up winning five trophies under my captaincy, this was the greatest moment of my cricketing life.

Not that we were able to celebrate too raucously at Lord's. More champagne was sprayed than was actually drunk. These were the days before team coaches. We had a brief spell at the Westmorland Hotel to say goodbye to wives and friends before climbing into our cars to drive to Nottingham, for the final, crucial Sunday League game the following day. I had Dasher with me, and we decided to stop at the Watford Gap services on the M1 for some food. We ordered bacon, eggs, chips and baked beans and were tucking into it when a coachload of Somerset supporters turned up. They couldn't believe it. Somerset's captain and his fellow opening batter, eating egg and chips in a motorway service station, just after winning the biggest game in the club's history! But that was how it was in those days. Besides, egg, bacon, chips and baked beans, with plenty of tomato ketchup, was Dasher's second favourite meal!

There were a few drinks when we got to our hotel, but most people were too exhausted to stay up late, and everyone was in good form the following morning, for our second big game of the weekend. We had made a tremendous start in the Sunday League, and had won all of our games, barring a wash-out at Worcester, up until mid-July, when we lost narrowly to Leicester. I had been batting pretty well, opening the innings with Dasher, and, if there were relatively few stand-out performances, everyone in the team had contributed. With Garner, Botham, Dredge and Marks to bowl, and myself, Dasher, Richards, Botham and Roebuck with the bat, plus our excellence in the field, we were a match for anyone and by mid-season were everyone's favourites to take the title. But after that defeat at Leicester we faltered, losing heavily at Old Trafford and then, even more damagingly, going down to fellow front-runners Kent at Taunton. When it came to the final round of games, it meant that we had to beat Notts and hope that Middlesex could get the better of Kent at Canterbury.

Our spirits were, of course, sky high, and they rose even further when news began to filter through of Middlesex's progress at Canterbury. I was out early at Trent Bridge, but useful contributions from the middle-order – Pete Roebuck's 50 being crucial – saw us to 185. With our bowling attack against a side with nothing really to play for, we were pretty confident that would be enough. We were held up for a time by a partnership between Tim

Nothing for 104 years, then two trophies in a weekend
Gillette Cup on Saturday at Lords
John Player League on Sunday at Trent Bridge

Robinson and Clive Rice but, once they had been removed, the rest of the batting quickly subsided. As gleeful shouts and cheers went up from Somerset supporters around the ground following events at Canterbury on their transistors, we knew that a second trophy was within our grasp. Receiving it was another great moment, for it meant that all of the disappointment of 12 months previously had been swept away. Then we had lost two trophies in a single weekend. This time we had won two trophies.

Although we would go on to win three more trophies under my captaincy, I will always look back upon 1979 as our greatest year of that era. We played outstanding cricket in all four competitions, scoring our runs in the championship at a faster rate (55.14 per 100 balls) than any other county and bowling nearly 20 overs per hour; we had won two trophies (and might well have won the B&H as well, but for that declaration and its aftermath) and achieved the longest unbeaten run in the championship (23 games) in Somerset's history. Our supporters had been magnificent, sticking with us through the bad times and putting the wind in our sails through the good; my form with the bat had been as good as it ever was – over 2,000 runs in all competitions, at an average of better than 40, this in a wet summer when batting was never easy; and my captaincy had evolved to the extent that, in his review of the season for *Wisden*, Eric Hill wrote of how my 'composed, calculating captaincy' had knitted the many outstanding elements in that Somerset side 'in admirable style'. Yes, there had been the trauma of Worcester and its aftermath, but not the least satisfying aspect of that summer was the way in which the team had harnessed all of the emotion of that episode and used it to drive us forward, with our wonderful supporters behind us every step of the way, to Somerset's first trophies.

And I had become a father for the first time. Packing up my cricket bag at the end of that season, I wasn't sure that life could get much better. But it did, in the New Year, when I discovered that I had been named as one of *Wisden*'s five 'Cricketers of the Year'. When you consider some of the things I had been called by members of the cricket establishment just a few months previously, it represented a stunning transformation. Eric Hill – who else? – did the write-up for *Wisden*. Referring to the challenges ahead in 1980, when the West Indies would be touring and Somerset would be without its Test stars, he wrote of me: 'Everything that has happened to him over the past two years of heavy and continuing pressure suggests that he will cope quietly and admirably, not least because, as one Somerset observer commented recently, "his players, for some reason I can't fathom, would walk under a bus for Rosey."' It is a tribute that I cherish to this day.

7

Making the best of it

In some ways, you could almost argue that 1980 was an even better year than 1979 had been for Somerset County Cricket Club. The West Indies tour, Test calls for Beefy and myself, and Vic Marks being selected for the England one-day side, meant we were without our best players for large chunks of the season. Yet, despite all of that, we came joint fourth in the championship and nearly won the John Player League for a second year, thanks to a late run of victories.

The year had started in controversy, although this time very much off the field. Roy Kerslake had fallen out with Somerset's ridiculously over-populated General Committee and had resigned. That in turn had prompted a furious response from Roy's supporters, demanding his re-instatement. The furore meant that I had to cut short my second spell in Australia with Claremont-Cottesloe in Perth in order to try to sort things out back at Taunton. I had known Roy since my very early days at Somerset, when he had captained me in the seconds, he had been my solicitor since the family troubles of 1973, and I had always respected his quiet but intelligent approach. In many ways, the relationship that he and I had, as captain and chairman, foreshadowed the sort of management structure which I would recommend to the ECB and which is common practice today. But at that time, there was an element on the committee who resented what they saw as 'player power' – not least when we formed our own marketing company, which we'll come to later, and Roy was seen as endorsing it. 'Too close to the players' was the accusation. He was eventually persuaded to continue as cricket chairman, but the root cause of the problem – a completely unwieldy committee structure – was not addressed for several years, and played a big part in the internal strife that would eventually engulf the club.

We had signed Sunil Gavaskar and a left-arm seamer from Antigua, Hugh Gore, as our overseas players to replace Richards and Garner. Gavaskar was widely regarded as being up there alongside Richards as the best batsman in world cricket, and recruiting him – using Colin Atkinson's Millfield connections with the upper reaches of Indian cricket – represented a real coup. Sadly for us and for Sunil, it turned out to be a wet summer, and he didn't score quite the runs we were hoping for.

Sunil Gavaskar

But he started brilliantly. His didn't arrive until early May and his first game for us was a B&H qualifier against Kent at Canterbury. Roy Kerslake suggested that, as we would be opening the batting together, it would be a sensible idea to share a room together, so as to get to know each other. We hit it off straight away. They batted first and made a respectable 242 after I'd put them in on a typically damp early season pitch. Then Sunil and I put on a record opening partnership of 241, Sunny batting beautifully for 90. He was caught at leg-slip, after Alan Ealham had brought all his fielders up in a vain attempt to stop the winning runs. In came Phil Slocombe, who slogged his first ball for four, and that was that.

Batting with Sunny was a real joy. I had met him before, when the Indians played Somerset at Taunton in 1979, but I had certainly never batted with him. Yet within just a few overs, we had established a complete understanding and were running between the wickets like I'd always done with Dasher. There was no need to call. We knew instinctively if a run was there. It was quite different from batting with Viv, when I always felt that my job was to stay in with him for as long as possible and be ready to sprint a single off the last two balls of an over if he was on strike! Sunny, by contrast, was careful and always had a game plan. Being relatively short, he was a tremendous cutter and puller, but one of his greatest qualities was knowing when to leave a ball. He was the finest judge of the line of a ball on off-stump that I've ever seen. He would leave balls that missed the off-stump by about half an inch! There were times when I could not believe what I was watching.

Another miserably wet May made for a low-key start to the season, with our first four championship matches ending in rain-affected draws, followed by two defeats. In the B&H we started well, but then Beefy hurt his arm which meant he couldn't bowl, I went down with an attack of the bronchitis which had plagued me since childhood, and we missed out on qualifying for the quarter-finals.

Gavaskar was also very good at analysing his batting partners' techniques and passing on tips and hints. In fact, it was partly down to Sunny's advice that I got back into the England side for the third Test against the West Indies. He'd told me that, with extreme pace, the key was to wait for as long as possible before committing yourself to the shot. It was advice that I put into practice when the West Indians came to Taunton. After Richards had hit a blistering century, in a memorable partnership with Clive Lloyd, Sunny and I went in to face Roberts, Croft and Marshall on a wet wicket, with most of the crowd expecting the worst. In the event, by playing late and leaving well, we added 77 without being separated, before rain brought a premature end to proceedings. I made 41 not out, and it was one of the best 41s I ever scored! I will always remember Peter Roebuck, as I came off at the end, coming up to me and saying, "Bloody hell, skip. You're a damn good player now!" Coming from Roebuck, that was a high compliment. That was the day the England selectors were meeting to pick the side for the third Test at Old Trafford, and I suspect that I was already pencilled in. Even so, it was reassuring – for them as well as for me – to know that I could handle the West Indies quicks.

In any case, I had been in good form, averaging over 50 in the championship, and making hundreds in both innings against Worcestershire at New Road in early June. I scored a pretty slow 124 in the first innings, but in the second, after we'd been set a target of 291 in around 60 overs, I went into overdrive, sharing partnerships of 153 with Pete Roebuck and 119 in 59 minutes with Dasher, to finish with 150 not out. I always enjoyed going to Worcester, not least because of my family connections with the city. I often think that, if I had ever played for a county other than Somerset, it would have been Worcestershire. They were captained at the time by Norman Gifford, one of the great characters, and I think it was in this game that I had him grovelling in mid-pitch, after driving him through extra cover for four for the umpteenth time!

My England recall, for the third Test at Old Trafford in early July, was not entirely unexpected. Before the start of the season there had been speculation that I might even be named as captain, after Mike Brearley had stepped down at the end of the winter. An Australian journalist, Murray Hedgcock, quoted Ian Botham as saying of me: "I believe the luck will turn his way if he gets an extended chance as an England player – and as captain, he just seems to have the knack of getting the best out of you. I think he has an excellent chance of succeeding Mike Brearley as England captain."

They were generous words, but in the end the Somerset cricketer chosen to captain England was Beefy, not Rosey. I was not particularly disappointed, as my focus was far more on getting back into the team. The captaincy could look after itself. When the call came, I felt I'd done more than enough in county cricket to deserve it, and I was also helped by the fact that the Chairman of Selectors, Alec Bedser, had fixed on a theory that the best way to counter the West Indies' pace attack was to play opening batsmen at one to four. So Wayne Larkins and I were drafted in as back-up to Boycott and Gooch.

In a statement to the press, Bedser said that I had been picked because of my ability not just to play pace but to take the attack back to the West Indies fast bowlers! It was certainly true that if they pitched it up, I would look to drive, or work it through mid-wicket. But against the short stuff, my technique was to sway out of the way or duck, and wait for something playable to come along. There really wasn't much future in trying to hook and pull the likes of Roberts, Holding and Marshall!

There were butterflies, of course, but I felt pretty confident as I walked out to bat under gloomy skies at Old Trafford on July 10, Clive Lloyd having put us in and Graham Gooch having fallen lbw to Roberts in just the fifth over. After my experience at Taunton, I felt I could handle even an attack as strong as Roberts, Holding, Garner and Marshall, and, taking my cue from Alec Bedser, decided to play my natural, free-flowing game. How I survived the first ball I received from Michael Holding, though, I'll never know as it cut back from off stump and missed the top of leg stump by a whisker.

Boycott was out soon afterwards, followed fairly quickly by Wayne Larkins but, after Mike Gatting had come out to join me, the clouds began to lift, the sun appeared and the runs flowed. The 70 that I scored that day was not only my highest Test innings, it was also my best Test innings, driving Holding and co off the back foot through the covers when they bowled short, tucking them away through the leg side when they overpitched. In an hour and a half, we had added 91, taking the score to 126/3, when Gatting was caught in the slips off Marshall, who followed that up by bowling me off my pads with a really quick one that ducked in late. The rest of the innings was a bit of a procession, and we were bundled out for 150.

When the West Indies batted, Viv Richards decided to go after Bob Willis, hitting five of his first seven balls for four in a brutal, calculated assault, which brought him 65 runs before he was bowled by his Somerset team-mate Ian Botham. Much was made of the press of the fact that, in England colours, our Somerset roles would be reversed, with some pundits suggesting that I might have made the better captain. In the event, I never really gave that a thought, because I was so intent on securing my place in the side.

The match ended in a draw, after the whole of Saturday's play was lost to the rain, a scenario which would be repeated in both the remaining Tests against the West Indies. After adding a 32 to my first-innings 70 at Old Trafford, my good form continued at The Oval, with 50 in the first innings and 41 in the second. Once again, I found myself walking out to bat with just a handful of runs on the board, Colin Croft having gone round the wicket to Boycott and put a short ball through the visor of his helmet. It left him with two black eyes, but it could have been so much worse if the ball hadn't glanced off his forearm.

Jumping for joy at The Oval after catching Malcolm Marshall at leg slip off John Emburey – a sharp chance that came at me low and fast

If Sylvester Clarke was the most dangerous of the West Indies' fast bowlers, Colin Croft was probably the nastiest, the only one who seemed to take positive pleasure in hitting batsmen. In the final Test of that series, at Headingley, I came in at number five in the second innings, after tearing a muscle in my thigh in the field, as we were fighting to save the game. We were walking off the field at tea on the last day when Croft came up to me and said, "Whitey, I'm going to kill you after tea." Peter Willey, who had been acting as my runner, was right behind me and heard the exchange. As tough as they come, he went straight up to Croft, to invite him round to the back of the pavilion to sort things out there! Even without Willey's intervention, I wasn't that bothered. Like any batsman, I was inevitably slightly apprehensive about facing genuinely fast bowling, but never frightened, and in the event, David Bairstow and I were able to hold out for the draw, me on one leg finishing on 43 not out.

Six men of Somerset in the Headingley Test
Ken Palmer, Viv Richards, me, Joel Garner, Ian Botham and Bill Alley

I felt satisfied with my efforts at the end of that series. To play for your country is the proudest achievement that any cricketer can aspire to. And, after the poor luck and disappointments of Pakistan and New Zealand, this time I had proved myself against the best side in the world, topping the England batting averages, with 243 runs at 48.6. The only disappointment was that my thigh injury did my chances of being selected for the Centenary Test against Australia at the end of August no good at all. It is one of very few regrets in my cricketing career that I never got to play Test cricket against the Aussies, especially as I'd always done pretty well against them for Somerset!

Somerset finished that season strongly. We had been knocked out of the Gillette Cup in the first round, slightly ironically by Worcestershire, whom we beat comfortably in the championship both at New Road in June and at Weston in August. But we finished our Sunday League campaign with six wins in our last seven games, including beating the champions Warwickshire in the final game, to finish runners-up. Oddly enough, that last game struck one of the few discordant notes of what was generally a very happy season. Richards and Garner had come back to Taunton when the West Indies tour finished with the Headingley Test, while Gavaskar had been called back to Bombay for selection duties. Once those had been concluded, he flew back to England so as to be available for our final Sunday game, with second place on the line. But the West Indians objected to him playing. In his book *Sunny Days*, published shortly after India's tour of the Caribbean in 1976, he had said some very unwise things about the West Indian crowds, suggesting in one particularly unfortunate passage that they 'still belonged to the jungles and forests'. This had not been forgotten, still less forgiven, by our proud West Indians, and Roy Kerslake, who had encouraged Gavaskar to return from India, was forced to give way. So it was Hugh Gore, a rather overweight and injury-prone seam bowler from Antigua, who played in that last game, rather than Viv's only rival for the title of best batsman in the world.

I didn't actually play in the game. The previous Sunday, against Surrey at Taunton, I had found myself batting against the bowler who, of all the West Indian quicks, always gave me the most trouble, that man Sylvester Clarke. It wasn't just his speed, or his unorthodox action, which made him look as if he was bowling off the wrong foot, rather like Mike Procter. To a left-hander he could bowl a ball that curved at 90 mph from outside leg stump, into your body, and it would bounce, sometimes alarmingly. He hit me several times, and on this occasion he really pinned me. The ball pitched on or just outside leg stump, I went forward to counter the angle across me, and the ball reared off a good length to hit me on the right side of my chest, dropping lifeless in the crease, all of its energy having been absorbed by my torso! I knew straightaway that I'd been hurt, but I decided to carry on, only to nick his next ball. As I walked back, I got halfway to the boundary and then fell on my knees in absolute agony. It turned out that he'd cracked two ribs, and that was me out for the rest of the season.

Looking back on that season, I was happy with what we had achieved. In his *Wisden* notes the following spring, Eric Hill would write that 'there are many signs that Somerset's prospects have seldom been brighter.' Crucially, we had shown that we were not a three-man show. Two young players, Nigel Popplewell and Jeremy Lloyds, had come into the side and shown great potential with both bat and ball. Lloyds took 11 for 95 with his off-breaks in the win against Worcester at Weston, while Popplewell played any number of valuable innings in both the championship and the Sunday League, as well as picking up useful wickets with his lively medium pace.

One of the things I prided myself upon as captain was the ability to bring on young players. This wasn't a question of laying down the law in team meetings, or handing out regular bollockings, as per Closey. Instead, I'd take them aside and have a quiet word, not so much about technique directly but about what we wanted from them that day and what they needed to do to achieve it. With Popplewell, it was usually greater consistency with the ball that we talked out. When he'd arrived with us from Cambridge, he was sharp but a bit erratic. So we talked about building pressure on batsmen by bowling all six balls in an over in the right place, not just four or five. The other thing about Pops was that he was, without question, the scruffiest cricketer I had ever played with. Matters came to a head when we were playing at Worcester the following season. The morning before the game, we were all out training when I spotted Popplewell running round the ground in an old blue plastic mac and the dirtiest pair of gym shoes you'd ever seen. I was always keen that we should be smartly turned out, so the next time he was in batting, I went into the dressing room, collected together all of his training gear, the blue plastic mac included, and put it in the dustbin. When he found out what I'd done, he went ballistic. Not that it made much difference in the end. He will always remain one of the cleverest men I've ever played cricket with – and one of the scruffiest!

Nigel Popplewell, third from left, in that plastic mac

8

Sunshine and shadow

My late-season injuries took time to heal. After tearing that thigh muscle at Headingley, I'd come back into the Somerset side just in time to have my ribs broken by Sylvester Clarke! But as I jogged with the dog along Weston beach that autumn, at least I had the satisfaction of knowing that I would be going on tour to the West Indies after Christmas. Alec Bedser had told me I'd be selected after the Headingley Test and to concentrate on getting myself fully fit in the meantime. And it was the player's responsibility to do just that. There were no pre-tour training camps. You turned up the day before the party was due to leave, had your jab in the bum and then took off!

It was during the run-up to the first game of the tour, that I first began to have trouble with my eyesight. We were playing a practice match on the old Police ground in Antigua, and Bob Willis was flying in at full pelt. I was OK for a few balls, but then suddenly I didn't pick one up at all. It must have missed my head by a whisker. Bob stopped in mid-pitch with his hands in the air in alarm. He told me it had terrified him, because I obviously hadn't seen it at all. Bernard Thomas, our physio, noticed it as well and was equally concerned. It was odd the way it happened so suddenly, given that the injury which, as I discovered later, was at the root of the problem had occurred over a year previously. I suppose it may have been the intense sunshine, which highlighted the little bits that were floating in my dominant right eye. Anyway, it didn't happen again, and for the next few weeks I tried not to think about it too much.

Despite my eye problem, I was selected for the first Test, at Port of Spain. Like much of that unhappy tour, the game was surrounded by controversy. First of all, the West Indies selectors decided to call up the Barbadian, David Murray, to keep wicket ahead of the local Trinidad hero Deryck Murray. This didn't go down at all well with the locals, many of whom boycotted the game in protest. However, it would appear that one or two went rather further and attempted to sabotage the match by spearing holes in the pitch on what they thought was a fast bowler's length. On the day before the game, when we saw how much damage had been caused, we assumed they would cut another strip. But not a bit of it. The groundsman filled the holes in with

Practising in the indoor nets at Taunton, prior to leaving for the Caribbean

A day off on tour – about to take off for Mustique

Geoff Boycott, a West Indian official, Bob Willis, Graham Stevenson, Mike Gatting, me, David Bairstow, Chris Old, Ken Barrington

a mixture of soil and cement and, in fact, the pitch didn't play too badly – certainly as far as the West Indian batsmen were concerned, as they made 426/9 declared after being put in by Beefy! When our turn came, Gooch and Boycott rather flattered to deceive in a fluent opening stand of 45 but, once Croft replaced Roberts and removed Boycott, batting suddenly became very difficult and we were bowled out for 178. I made 10.

Made to follow on, our second innings was no better: bowled out for 169, to leave the West Indies winners by an innings and 79, only Geoff Boycott offering much resistance with a typically stubborn 70. This time, I had made just 5 when I nicked a quick delivery from Holding and was caught behind. However, my main memory of that innings is of Ian Botham. With his side fighting to save the game on the last afternoon, and with rain around to help our cause, he'd aimed a huge slog at one of Viv Richards' off-breaks – no doubt intending to show his old oppo just who was boss – to be caught at deep mid-off. The dressing room emptied as he walked back to the pavilion. Knowing how he must be feeling, I thought I can't let him sit there on his own, so I went in to offer a few friendly words. I've never seen a cricketer so shattered. He was in pieces. All the brashness and the bravado had gone.

There was yet more controversy as the days ticked by before the second Test, due to be played in Guyana. Bob Willis had broken down in the Trinidad Test and been sent home, with Surrey's Robin Jackman being summoned as a replacement. Now Jackman, in common with several other England players, had strong South African connections. He had played for both Western Province and Rhodesia and had a South African wife. Shortly after we arrived at a very wet Georgetown, one of the local politicians started a campaign to have Jackman barred from playing, citing the recently signed Gleneagles agreement, which effectively excluded South Africa from international sport. As far as we were concerned, the Gleneagles Agreement meant that nations would face sanctions if they played sport with South Africa, not individuals, and our tour manager, Alan Smith, made it clear that, if the Guyanese government tried to dictate who could or could not play for England, the Test would be off.

While all this was going on, we had been training and practising indoors in a Guyanese army camp, the incessant rain making it impossible to do anything outside. I was still worried about my eye, after another episode where I'd lost sight of the ball, this time on a practice pitch in Trinidad, batting against Ian Botham, so I was sent to see an army surgeon. He told me that I had lots of floaters, which was probably a sign of something called PVD – posterior vitreous detachment – and the impact on my eyesight had been aggravated by my long-sightedness, which I'd not really been aware of.

He asked me if I had been hit on the head recently. I said I had, batting in Western Australia the previous winter, when a ball had climbed off a length and hit me on the side of the face, breaking my cheekbone and leading to an abscess which would eventually result in my losing four of my lower front teeth. He said that I shouldn't even think about batting until I had been checked out by a specialist, as there was a risk of retinal detachment if I was hit anywhere near the eye again. My heart sank, but there was nothing for it but to head back to Barbados to be seen by an eye surgeon, who confirmed the diagnosis. My tour was over, and quite possibly my entire cricketing career as well. The eventual cancellation of the Guyana Test seemed pretty trivial by comparison.

As I climbed on board the British Airways 747 at Grantley Adams Airport to fly back to England, I felt completely devastated. It was a miserable flight back, but worse was to follow. When we'd taxied to a halt at Heathrow, the pilot sent a message to me to meet him in the cabin. "I'm afraid I've got some terrible news," he said. "Ken Barrington has had a heart attack and has died."

I was shattered. Kenny was one of the good guys. We had played golf – his other passion – together when we'd been on tour in Pakistan and New Zealand and, whenever I played at The Oval, he would make a point of coming up to our dressing room to say hello. Now it was my turn to have my problems put in their proper perspective.

A visit to Bristol to see a consultant provided some reassurance. He confirmed the two diagnoses I'd already had, told me I'd need glasses for my long-sightedness, but said that, provided I was careful and wore a helmet, there was no reason why I should not continue playing cricket. That was a huge relief and, although batting in glasses took some getting used to, especially as they tended to steam up under the helmet, I practised hard that winter and gradually felt some confidence coming back. It was a difficult time, but Stevie was wonderfully supportive and positive, and it was actually nice to be able to spend some time at home with her and Stuart. The club were very good to me as well. Roy Kerslake, our Cricket Chairman, told me that he could see that I was struggling but that, if I gave it time, I would eventually get used to wearing glasses, which is exactly what happened. I was fortunate as well in that it was another pretty wet spring and the pitches tended to be soft and slow, which was just as well given that in our first four championship fixtures, all away from home, I faced Marshall, Holding, Imran, le Roux and Jeff Thomson, who was frighteningly fast at Lord's and hit me so hard I had to retire hurt!

The problems with my eyesight apart, we started that season in great heart and with high hopes. The opening of the new pavilion seemed to signal a new self-confidence in Somerset cricket. There is no denying that the dressing rooms in the dark depths of the Old Pavilion had character. I used to change on the left-hand side of the door leading out to the playing area, with Viv on the right, and Peter Roebuck banished to the far corner, to reduce the risk of him irritating Beefy with his invariably outspoken views on what the issue of the day might be. As for Beefy, he would take great pleasure in winding up the university boys with his distinctly right-wing opinions. Most of us were smokers – cigars for me, Dasher, Viv and Beefy, while Vic chain-smoked his Benson & Hedges. There were times when you could hardly see from one end of the dressing room to the other, especially if it was a John Player or B&H game, when competition for the free smokes on offer was always fierce!

Our new dressing room, on the left-hand side (as you look at it) of what is now the Colin Atkinson Pavilion, could also be a bit smoky, but there the comparison ends. It was smart, light, roomy and provided an excellent view of the cricket from the balcony outside. There had been a plan to install individual shower cubicles, but I insisted on a communal bath where we could all relax together at the end of a long day in the field. The extra cost involved was something like £10,000, and there was a fair amount of grumbling from some members of the committee. But they weren't in a strong position to object, given that I'd shown the way in terms of fund-raising through the success of Wyvern Sports Marketing.

This was the company which I had set up in 1978 to market branded cricket kit, souvenirs and books through a cricket shop on the County Ground and to sell advertising space on the boundary boards and elsewhere. We brought in Mike Taylor to run it, and he did a brilliant job. At the start, when I'd realised the money-making opportunities that were being missed, I had given the club the opportunity to do it themselves, but they were not interested, so I set it up as a company limited by guarantee, with the players as the only share-holders. We were, I think, the first county side to be paid to wear a particular company's logo, when I negotiated a deal with Lyle & Scott to wear their branded shirts in the 1979 Gillette Cup final. Again, officialdom didn't exactly bend over backwards to help. Peter Lush at the TCCB told me that the idea was a non-starter because BBC television wouldn't allow advertising on cricket kit. But I had already taken soundings from a mate at the BBC and been told that shirt advertising was becoming a feature of many different sports and that, provided the logo was no more than about two and a half inches across, they wouldn't have a problem with it. In the end I went to Donald Carr to get clearance, and we duly walked out at Lord's in Lyle & Scott shirts.

The profits that we made were split equally between the player-shareholders. It wasn't a huge amount, maybe a thousand pounds or so a year per head, but that represented a more than useful supplement given the pitiful amounts that professional cricketers were paid in those days. As captain and after winning the Gillette Cup and the John Player League in 1979, my new contract was only worth around £11,000. The big names, Richards and Botham, were paid a bit more, but most of the side were on no more than around £9,000. There was prize-money to go with the various trophies that we won but, after that had been divided up amongst a squad of, say, 13 players, it only amounted to a few hundred pounds per head. In the end, the club decided to buy us out and take over the enterprise themselves, but I like to think that we had shown the way, as well as helping to bind the players together through a shared interest.

The other development in which the players, rather than the hierarchy, took the initiative was the appointment of Dennis Waight as fitness coach. He had been working with the West Indies for some time and had been an important factor in keeping their fast bowling attack fit and firing, and it was at the suggestion of Viv and Joel that the powers-that-be were eventually persuaded to bring him to Somerset. In those days, what you might call the Somerset 'support staff' were distinctly thin on the ground. We were already one of the fittest teams in English cricket, but Dennis took us to another level. He was a nuggety, hard-drinking Aussie ocker, built like the middleweight boxer he once had been, who stood no nonsense from anyone, including Richards and Botham. Besides fitness, he instilled a sense of discipline in the team. Nothing was left to chance. He was a great asset to me as captain, not just because he kept us all fit but because he acted as a foil to Beefy, stopping some of his antics. That meant that I didn't have to confront Beefy, so avoiding what would inevitably have been bust-ups between us, which in turn would have done team spirit no good at all. As with the logos, the marketing company and Roy Kerslake's role as our cricket manager, Somerset were blazing a trail which would eventually be followed throughout county cricket – even if it didn't endear us to some committee-men!

1981 was, of course, Botham's year. Replaced as captain by Mike Brearley, he batted and bowled for England like a giant who had broken his chains. But in Somerset, this was Richards' and Garner's year. Viv scored 1,718 first-class runs at 57.26, plus another 736 in one-day cricket, whilst Joel's statistics were phenomenal: 88 first-class wickets at 15.32 and 44 in our 23 one-day games, at an average of 12.59.

We took a while to get going, what with that succession of away championship matches against tough opposition and me trying to get used to my new glasses. We lost our opening B&H fixture at Chelmsford, but we had a good championship win at Old Trafford, where Jeremy Lloyds made his maiden first-class century before Garner and Botham bowled us to victory as Lancashire, needing 155, were bundled out for 121. It was a taste of things to come. Rain interfered with several of our early season Sunday League games, as well as ruining our match against the Australians at Taunton. But we qualified for the B&H quarter-finals, and we were looking forward to welcoming Gloucestershire to Bath for the Festival in June.

That was an extraordinary game. Zaheer, who was a wonderful batsman, scored 365 runs – 215 in the first innings, 150 in the second – without ever looking like getting out. It enabled Brian Brain, who was captaining Gloucestershire in the absence of Mike Procter, to declare their second innings on 303/4, leaving us to get 349 in 200 minutes. Even with Richards and Botham in the side, that was never remotely on, especially as Peter Roebuck had pulled a hamstring and I had twisted a knee, so that we were both hobbling on one leg and would bat only if the game depended on it. We were soon in trouble as the Gloucestershire seamers, the left-armer Alan Wilkins and Phil Bainbridge, picked up wickets with depressing regularity. When my turn came to go in, at number 10, we were 137/8 with still an hour and a half to survive. The Gloucestershire fielders were all crowded round the bat, so I decided that attack was probably the best form of defence and started whacking the ball through the infield. Hallam Moseley hung on well at the other end as we added 63 in three-quarters of an hour. When he was out, Peter Roebuck limped out. We had a chat. "There's no way I can hit the ball like you've been doing," he said, "so I'll just block the shit out of it, while you carry on the way you've been going and we'll see where we get to." We neither of us bothered with a runner, partly because I was hitting everything for four and partly because with four of us out there the possibilities of a cock-up were limitless. We did hobble the occasional single, but mostly we just took an end each. The Gloster boys got madder and madder, especially Alan Wilkins. Every time he bowled it just outside off-stump, I'd hit him for four through the covers. I finished up with 85 not out, all but nine of them scored in boundaries, while Pete somehow managed to accumulate a gallant 13. We laughed our heads off as we walked off at the end; Gloucestershire were absolutely furious!

We won our B&H quarter-final up at Headingley thanks to some typically steady bowling against a Yorkshire side still struggling to come to terms with the demands of one-day batting. Then, when we batted, Dasher and I put together one of our best opening partnerships in one-day cricket, adding 135 with a mixture of powerful strokes and almost telepathic running between the wickets, which drove the Yorkshire fieldsmen to despair. Viv weighed in with a rapid 47, and we won with plenty to spare. They gave the Gold Award to me, although it might just as easily have gone to Dasher. For the semi-final, it was Kent at home, just as in the Gillette semi back in 1979. The ground was rammed as per usual, and you could tell from the look in the eyes of the Kent boys that the memories of being blown away by Garner and Botham two years previously were still fresh in their minds. They did rather better this time, thanks mainly to a gritty 44 from Chris Tavaré, but a target of 155 in 55 overs didn't seem particularly challenging, even against an attack which included Derek Underwood and John Shepherd. So it proved. After a mid-innings wobble, which saw us reduced to 80/4, with Richards and Botham both back in the pavilion, Roebuck and Popplewell steadied the ship, and we won by five wickets.

For the final against Surrey we prepared much as we had done for the Gillette two years before: a team dinner featuring the usual rallying cries (or growls if it was Dasher Denning!), rather than any serious discussion of tactics or analysis of the opposition. We had played Surrey umpteen times over the previous few years and we were well aware of their strengths and weaknesses. Captained by Roger Knight, with batsmen like Monte Lynch and Geoff Howarth, plus Sylvester Clarke and Robin Jackman to open the bowling, they were a powerful all-round outfit, and we knew would have to be close to our best to win.

I won the toss and had little hesitation in asking Surrey to bat. It wasn't a bright blue morning as in the 1979 final. There were clouds overhead, a heavy atmosphere and a green tinge to the wicket: a day to bowl first, for sure. The Surrey batsmen evidently thought much the same, judging by the tentative, almost fearful start they made to their innings against Botham and Garner. After 17 overs, they only had 17 runs on the board. Roger Knight, whom I always rated and who had often been a thorn in our side, proved to be the main obstacle in more ways than one. We collided with each other when I went to run him out, and he stomped on my hand! But once he had gone for 92, the later batsmen had no answer to Joel's mixture of yorkers and lifters, and I was more than happy with their score of 194/5, Garner 5/14. I wasn't quite so happy when I'd lost my off stump to a nip-backer from Robin Jackman and Dasher had been cleaned up by a ferocious delivery from Sylvester Clarke with just 5 on the board. But I need not have worried. Viv Richards was quite superb, cautious early on but then increasingly assertive as he took the battle back to the Surrey bowlers, Sylvester Clarke in particular. If he pitched up, he would whip him through mid-wicket; if he dropped it

Peter May presents Viv with the Man of the Match award

short, Viv would hook him into the Mound Stand. Peter Roebuck gave him solid and brave support, his 22 in their partnership of 105 being worth at least double that under the circumstances. When Beefy came in, he and Viv took the Surrey attack apart, knocking off the remaining 87 runs in just 13 overs.

That second Lord's win marked the start of the team's best spell in all cricket during my time as captain. In the county championship, we won seven out of our remaining ten games, losing only to Northants at Weston, and then just by two wickets. Had that match gone the other way, as it so easily might with a little more luck in the way of umpiring decisions, we might very well have won the thing for the first time. In the Sunday League, we won five of our last seven games, to finish runners-up for the third time in four seasons.

Everyone in the team contributed to our push for the championship. Viv scored two brilliant 150s, against Yorkshire at the Abbeydale ground in Sheffield and against Worcester on a difficult pitch at Weston, as well as 128 in the drawn game with Essex at Taunton. Garner, who had to miss the Weston Festival through injury, had match figures of 10/64 against Hampshire and 10/80 against Gloucestershire at Bristol, and was a constant threat. Dredge bowled us to victory against Yorkshire, Marks scored 81 not out and took eight wickets in the win up at Edgbaston, Beefy contributed quick runs or vital wickets in virtually every game, while Roebuck, Dasher, Popplewell and Lloyds all scored runs when they were most needed. My own contributions with the bat were relatively modest – up until our final game, a rain-affected affair against Warwickshire at Taunton, where I batted as well as I had done all season for a rapid 75, which got us off to the perfect start as we chased down a target of 376 in four hours.

I did get some runs in the Sunday League – but again it was a team effort which took us so close to a second title. Two memories stand out from that period: the first was the partnership between Viv and Beefy against Hampshire at Taunton. When I was out for a duck, we were 55/4, Richards not out 20-odd. Out strode Beefy, swinging his bat like a gladiator with a battle-axe, as per usual. 21 overs later, we were 234/5, Richards the man out for 93. The cricket in between was carnage as each tried to out-hit the other, this time without giving it away, and the ball was flying everywhere.

The other memory is of our final game, against Warwickshire at Taunton. I made 4, Dasher 1, Beefy 5. Viv scored 101 off 59 balls with six 6s and eight 4s. He took us to 211/6 in our rain-reduced 28 overs, this against a Warwickshire attack led by Bob Willis and Gladstone Small. Admittedly, we knew we couldn't win the league, because Essex were six points ahead at the start of the last round of games, but it lifted us from fourth to second place, which was worth £3,500 in prize money.

Looking back now, I can see that the second half of that 1981 season was when 'my' Somerset team reached its peak. We had won the B&H, come second in the Sunday League and won ten games in the championship to finish a strong third. But beyond the results, it was the way we had played which had been so stunning and the spirit in the team. If my personal career high point was lifting Somerset's first ever trophy at Lord's in 1979, then the team's high point was that 1981 season.

The trouble with high points is that the only way onwards from them is down! Not that it seemed that way at first. I had a quiet winter spent gardening, golfing and looking after Stuart while Stevie was busy bringing Jamie (who we've always known as Joey, after Stevie's father) into the world. Then all was rudely interrupted on the night of December 13 when a huge storm came crashing in from the Bristol Channel, overwhelming the sea defences along the north Somerset coast, flooding homes and farmland up to two miles inland and drowning hundreds of livestock. Stevie had gone into labour that morning and was in Weston General, awaiting another Caesarian; my best mate Harry had come round to help me look after little Stuart. As I was bringing in cups of tea for the pair of us, one of our big bay windows was blown in by a ferocious gust, the glass shattering on the wall behind me. Fortunately, none of us came to any harm, and Harry and I spent the rest of the evening nailing plywood to the window frame to keep out the wind and rain.

The next morning I had Derek Taylor on the phone, from his house on the seafront at Burnham-on-Sea. "Rosey, I need your help," he said. "We've been flooded out." I got down there as quickly as I could and, sure enough, the cellar of his place was full of water. What on earth are we going to do, he wanted to know. Well, it occurred to me that Burnham is built on sand and, if we could rip up a few floorboards, then the water would probably drain away of its own accord. That proved to be easier said than done, but I eventually smashed my way through the floor with a sledgehammer and, sure enough, within a few minutes, the water had gone and Derek and I could have a beer or two to celebrate.

We started the 1982 season as favourites to win all four competitions – surely the only time that can have been the case in the history of Somerset cricket. And with Botham and Richards at the height of their powers, Garner still one of the most potent bowlers in the game and our home-grown talent in the shape of Roebuck, Marks, Denning, Dredge, Popplewell and Lloyds improving with every season, the potential for a truly brilliant summer was certainly there. Yet, in the event, we started rather shakily. Richards and Garner arrived back carrying injuries after a Test series in Australia and a crowded domestic schedule. Viv missed our first few matches, which included a championship defeat at Derby and a loss to Northants in the Sunday League; Joel wouldn't be fit enough to play until towards the end of June. The spirit in the camp was still good, but our early progress in the B&H was anything but assured as we lost heavily at Middlesex and only qualified for the quarter-finals by virtue of narrow wins over Glamorgan and Gloucestershire, the latter thanks largely to a typically aggressive century by Dasher Denning. The 'Chewton chop' was much in evidence against his favourite enemies.

By this stage, in late May, I had decided to try batting down the order. Partly, that was down to injury problems. I was still getting back pains from time to time, and I had torn a calf muscle which would give me trouble for several years. But mainly it was to give Peter Roebuck his chance at the top of the order. After several good seasons, he was now being talked about as a potential England batsman, whereas I was pretty sure that I wouldn't be selected again. So he needed to be up-front, and in Jeremy Lloyds he had an opening partner who was also making a considerable name for himself.

Without Garner, and with me, Botham and Richards firing only fitfully, we lost our first three John Player League games and played catch-up in that competition for the rest of the season. In the championship, we had a good win at New Road, where Jeremy Lloyds took 6/62 with his off-breaks before Pops and I saw us home after a second innings wobble. But, without Joel, we lacked the firepower to turn promising situations into the wins that we needed to challenge at the top. All of which meant that our focus was soon fixed pretty firmly on the B&H. Joel was back for the quarter-final against Kent at Canterbury and contributed a typically miserly 3/22 alongside Beefy's 4/52, as Kent collapsed from 173/4 to 207 all out. It wasn't a comfortable run chase by any means, but Beefy and I got us ahead of the game with a stand of 60 in nine overs and our middle order took us over the line with two balls to spare. The win against Sussex in the semi-final at Taunton was rather more comfortable, after we'd bowled them out for just 110, an opening partnership of 91 between Dasher and Roebuck settling the issue in double-quick time.

Dasher and me, after completing the semi-final victory over Sussex

So that meant another Lord's final, this time against Notts on 24 July. I have to say that, without sounding cocky, I felt as confident as I walked out with Clive Rice for the toss and the pre-match interviews as I ever felt before any big game. Rice, by contrast, was nervous. You could see it in his eyes and read it in the fact that, when I suggested that I should toss, he just said OK. Sure enough, my lucky coin came down the right way up and, on an overcast morning, with Garner and Botham raring to go, the decision to ask them to bat made itself. As the game started, it soon became apparent that it was not just the Notts captain who was suffering from big-match nerves but most of their batsmen. Garner yorked Paul Todd early on and then, after Tim Robinson and Derek Randall were threatening a recovery, Vic Marks bowled Randall, as he tried to cut, and tempted Rice to drive over the top of a typically floated-up off-break.

It would be fair to say that there was some surprise when Tom Graveney gave Vic the Gold Award, given that his figures were 11–4–24–2 as compared with Joel's 8.1–1–13–3, but Vic's were the two crucial wickets. A target of 131, on what was a perfectly decent batting pitch, was never going to stretch us against demoralised opponents, and Richards and Roebuck soon settled the issue. Viv, in a gesture which spoke volumes for the good relationship that the pair of them had at this stage in their Somerset careers, waited for Pete to complete a well-deserved 50 before hitting the winning runs.

So, by half past five, I was once again lifting the B&H Trophy on the balcony of the Lord's pavilion, to the acclaim of the thousands of our faithful Somerset supporters who had made the trip. It may not have been an exciting game, but I felt deeply satisfied with the aggression and dominance of our cricket. Nottinghamshire had simply been swept away. Just as we had done after our win over Surrey the previous year, Beefy, Dasher and I stopped off on the way home at the Woolpack at St George's on the outskirts of Weston, only this time, instead of the pub having to stay open late for us, we were there by half past eight, and a great evening was had by all!

After that, the rest of the season was a bit of an anti-climax. We had high hopes in the NatWest Trophy, as the 60-over competition had now become, especially after a comfortable win against Leicester at Taunton when Vic Marks again showed his value as inventive batsman as well as economical bowler. He thoroughly deserved his call-up for the third Test against Pakistan. The quarter-final was another home game, against Warwickshire. Put in by Bob Willis, we made what I thought was a more than useful 259 in overcast conditions and, with Garner back in the side, and our all-rounders in such great form, I fancied our chances. But a magnificent innings by Alvin

Benson & Hedges Cup 1982

Kallicharran, all five-foot-nothing of him, simply took the game away from us. Against Garner, he kept out the yorkers, while anything even slightly short of a length was either pulled or cut, usually for a boundary. It was like watching Viv batting for us, and there's no comparison more flattering than that! As we came off the field at the end, beaten inside 54 overs, I just said to myself, well there was really nothing we could have done about that. It was sheer brilliance, one of the most outstanding innings I've ever witnessed.

In the championship, the high spots were probably the wins in successive games over Warwickshire and Worcestershire at Taunton in early September. In the first of them, we chased down 309 in 270 minutes for a five-wicket win, thanks to what was probably Ian Botham's most explosive innings for Somerset – 131 not out in 65 minutes, with 10 sixes and 12 fours. His century came up in 52 minutes: not only the fastest of the season but made when his side really needed it. In the next game, on a green pitch against Worcestershire, he produced what was perhaps his supreme all-round performance for Somerset: 98 from 51 balls in our only innings, plus match figures of 8/79 as he and Joel Garner twice swept Worcestershire away. Joel added to the fun with four wickets in four balls at the start of his third over: a run out (Weston) and then Younis Ahmed (broken finger and hit wicket), Alan Ormrod and Phil Neale (both bowled).

Those two wins should have made for an upbeat finish to the season, even though a recurrence of my thigh injury kept me out of our final championship game against Lancashire, again at Taunton, with Botham taking over the captaincy (an interesting sign of things to come, given that Richards had captained the side in my absence earlier in the season). By the close of the second day, Somerset seemed to be cruising to a comfortable seventh win of the season, with Lancashire four down in their second innings and still 62 runs short of making Somerset bat again. Yet on the next day, Garner was allowed by his captain to take the field wearing gym shoes and wasn't called upon to bowl, while Beefy himself sent down only four overs. Against this seemingly lackadaisical cricket, the Lancashire lower order recovered from 66/4 to 275 all out, leaving Somerset 134 to win in plenty of time. The runs should have been knocked off comfortably, instead of which Somerset collapsed against Paul Allott and David Lloyd's occasional slow left-arm, to lose by 14 runs.

In his history of Somerset cricket, *From Sammy to Jimmy*, Peter Roebuck called it 'a profoundly cynical performance'. I don't know about that but, if Peter Roebuck was already harbouring doubts about the commitment and professionalism of some of his more exalted team-mates, as we know now that he was, that episode can have done nothing but inflame them.

9

The Big Three

My first encounter with Viv Richards was in April 1973. Lansdown were playing a warm-up game against Weston 2nds, and Viv was making his debut. Quite by chance, I was at the ground and watched about half an hour of their innings. It was a typical early season pudding of a pitch and, after taking some time to get the measure of conditions which were completely alien to him, he started playing his shots. Hello, I thought, who's this? So I asked the Lansdown boys about him, and they told me the story about Len Creed and the Mendip Acorns. I made a mental note that this was a cricketer to watch.

The next time I came across him was later that same season, when we were both in the Somerset Under-25 side against Gloucestershire Under-25s at Bristol. We batted first on a green, seaming pitch and were three down when I walked out to join him. The next over, he hit straight balls from Julian Shackleton over mid-wicket for four – twice. I decided that a word of advice might be in order, and at the end of the over I went up to him and said, "Be a bit careful, Viv. On this pitch, I should play a bit straighter." And he replied, "Tanks", as if an armoured column was making its way up the Ashley Down road. But that was the last piece of advice I ever gave him about his batting. From then on, it was just words of encouragement.

His talent was obvious, right from the start. It was the same when I first saw Joel bowling against the Australians at Bath. "Bloody hell," you think, as your jaw drops. But, with Viv, there was something extra special about him. My childhood cricketing hero was Garry Sobers, and I was lucky enough to get to know him when he played for Notts, to the extent that he very kindly came and played in a golf tournament at Weston as part of my benefit year. When he walked into the bar, all conversation stopped. He had that aura about him of the truly great player, and Viv Richards came to have it too. When you were walking around with him, people would stop and stare. Apart from anything else, he had this superb physique, built like a middle-weight boxer, with the sheen of the super-fit athlete. He carried himself like a man to be reckoned with, always looked you straight in the eye when he was talking to you, and on the pitch he had this fierce, penetrating stare, which you felt could almost turn

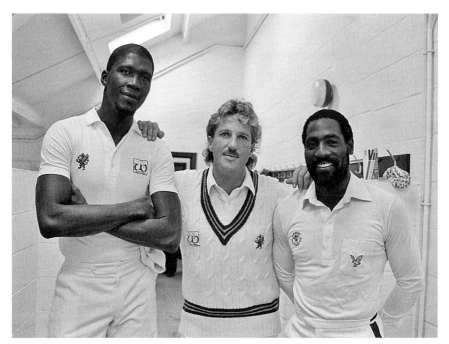

Joel, Ian and Viv

bowlers to stone like Medusa. He was a man completely confident in himself and his abilities, and that was reflected in the way he played his cricket.

For a young cricketer from a small island who had visited England only once before, Viv settled into life in Somerset remarkably well. A lot of that was down to Len Creed, who had spotted his talent in the Caribbean, brought him over and made him feel one of the family at his home in Bath, a kindness that Viv always remembered. When he moved to Taunton, his biggest danger was sharing the flat at the County Ground with Ian Botham and Dennis Breakwell, but he quickly learned how to handle them and the sort of stuff they got up to. The pair of them were hyper-active, Breakwell even more so than Beefy – hence his nickname, given to him by Botham, of 'the severed nerve'. He was like a spring escaped from a mattress, bouncing around, never still. When I tell you that he once almost got himself arrested for throwing spuds out of the Plough in Station Road in Taunton at the pub on the opposite side of the road, just as a police car came round the corner, you'll get the picture!

The three of them had a great time but, whilst Viv liked a drink, he was more interested in the girls. You didn't see many black men in Taunton in those days, certainly not black men as impressive physically as Viv, and he attracted girls like moths to a flame.

As a batsman, he had all the shots in the world and all the power in the world, but what really set him apart – his 'X factor', if you like – was the way he could intimidate the opposition bowlers. Very often, he would target a particular bowler, especially if he thought that they had questioned his ability or said something disrespectful. In the run-up to the Old Trafford Test in 1980, Bob Willis had been quoted as saying that he'd got the measure of Richards and knew how to get him out. Well, when Richards walked out to bat on the second morning, he had only one thing on his mind, and that was to show Willis who was boss. Beefy had me fielding at mid-on for Willis, from where I was able to watch ball after ball sailing over my head and out to the leg-side boundary. Viv's first 44 runs all came off Willis – 10 fours and two twos – and I don't think I've ever seen a top-class fast bowler treated with such a mixture of hostility and contempt. Something similar happened to Glamorgan's Greg Thomas in a game at Taunton. He'd had Richards playing and missing a couple of times, and at the end of the over he went up to him and said, sarcastically, "It's red and round, Viv, and you're supposed to hit it." The first four balls of the next Thomas over finished up in the river Tone, whereupon Viv went up to the bowler and said, "They're red and round, Greg, and they're in the river!"

He was probably at his best on bad wickets, and we had plenty of those. He loved the extra challenge of it, and he could take good bowlers apart, even on a difficult surface. His style of batting was based on three characteristics: first of all, the bowler could see almost nothing of the stumps as the ball was delivered. Viv took a middle-and-leg guard but then would shuffle across at the last minute. This left the bowler with three options: to bowl an inswinger, looking for an lbw, which would invariably end up going through or over mid-wicket; to bowl an off-stump line, which he could cope with easily; or to try to tempt him with a ball outside off, which he would usually whack through the covers! And if the bowler decided to drop it short, there was no better puller or hooker in world cricket. His record against the quicks was sensational, and he was equally good against spin. He used his feet well to smother the spin on a turning pitch, and anything loose would be dealt with mercilessly. If he felt threatened at all by a bowler, he would go after him. When Pakistan came to Taunton in 1982, the leg-spinner Abdul Qadir had us in all sorts of trouble until Viv came in. He hit his first two balls from Qadir for six and went on to make 181*. Like all great batsmen, he had fantastic hand-eye co-ordination, but it was the combination of that with his great strength which made him such an intimidating, dominant presence at the crease.

Batting with him was always an experience. If he had the strike at the start of an over, I knew that I might very well be in the firing line for his

Viv batting

on-drive at the non-striker's end, so I would usually keep out of the way by not backing up and standing close to the umpire. And if he was still on strike when it came to the fifth ball of the over, you knew you'd have to be on your toes for a quick single so that he could keep the strike!

I don't remember him ever giving less than his best. He was fiercely competitive, even in games of little consequence, and wasn't shy of having a pop at someone in the dressing room if he felt they weren't giving it their best shot. Once he had a go at me – for sending a message to ask what was happening in golf's Open Championship when I was batting in a Sunday League game!

People always remember the hundreds he scored in the one-day finals: 117 in the 1979 Gillette; 132* in the 1981 B&H. But some of his very best and most valuable innings were played when Somerset were fighting to avoid defeat. The obvious example of that would be when he batted for a day and a half to score 241* to save the game against Gloucestershire at Bristol in 1977, but there were ever so many 50s, 60s and 70s that he scored when we were up against it, often with Peter Roebuck battling away at the other end. We may not have won the county championship in those years but we didn't lose too many three-day games – just one in 1979, for example, and two in 1981 – and a lot of that was down to Viv Richards.

Viv was a more than useful bowler as well, especially in one-day cricket. He operated off a short run, mostly bowling seamers and off-cutters, with a good swing of the arm. Because he was such a strong man, he could vary his pace from the gentle to the alarming with no change in his run-up or action, and his quicker ball would often take batsmen by surprise. It was with that delivery that he took probably his most important wicket for Somerset, having Allan Lamb brilliantly stumped down the leg side by Derek Taylor just as he was threatening to take the game away from us in the 1979 Gillette Cup final. Viv took almost 100 wickets for us in limited-overs cricket, going at barely four runs an over, which was just what I needed from my third or fourth change bowler.

I suppose that things started to go wrong between Viv and Somerset over his relationship with Peter McCombe, whom everyone knew as Jock. Initially he was a sort of professional sporting hanger-on, who had arrived in Somerset from Scotland via Old Trafford, where he had been helping to look after several of the Manchester United footballers, including the great Denis Law. He attached himself initially to Viv Richards, as a sort of minder/personal organiser, although he came to do a lot for Beefy as well as time went on. I never had a problem with that because Viv was hopelessly disorganised in his personal life and needed someone like Jock to get him where he was supposed to be in good order at the right time, especially if it involved driving, which

Phil Slocombe, Joel, Viv, Jock McCombe

Viv hated and wasn't very good at either. Jock could be irritating at times, but he was well liked in the dressing room and a good man to have on your side if ever things started kicking off. At the end of the Old Trafford Test in 1980, I'd arranged for me and Beefy to meet up with Viv and Joel to go for a drink in the bar. Viv had Jock in tow as usual, and we were coming down the stairs from the visitors' dressing room when two blokes, obviously drunk, started having a go at Viv. Well, Jock wasn't having that. He got hold of one of them by the lapels and poleaxed him with a Glasgow kiss, sending him crashing to the bottom of the stairs!! Then there was the time, at a benefit dinner at Taunton Town football ground, when some drunks decided that they would climb through the rafters and perch above our table, which included Dasher, Beefy, Viv and, of course, Jock. I sensed trouble brewing and had just said to Dasher that I thought we ought to be heading off. When we got to the door, one of the idiots dropped onto the table. Jock thumped him into the middle of next week, and then all hell broke loose. It was the biggest punch-up you've seen outside a Wild West film. Jock was absolutely in his element. And not a word about it appeared in the papers!

There were plenty of people on the Somerset committee who saw Jock as a disruptive interloper, who had no business in the dressing room, but to us he was just part of the team and an important part at that. He looked after Viv's kit, so that it was always immaculate; he kept people away from him,

Ian

so that he didn't get bothered; and he organised his life for him, so that he could concentrate on his cricket. Jock was a big factor in Viv's success and therefore in Somerset's success.

The committee didn't see it like that. They didn't have much of a rapport with Roy Kerslake, the Chairman of Cricket. They had three superstar cricketers who appeared to be a law unto themselves. They had a group of independent-minded players who had shown up the club's lack of commercial expertise by setting up the marketing company. They resented the fact that they didn't have control, and the presence of Jock McCombe exacerbated that feeling – so were the seeds sown for what happened in 1986.

All I would say is that under my captaincy Viv Richards was the ideal overseas professional cricketer. You couldn't fault either his attitude or his achievements. He was the perfect team player, as well as one of the greatest batsmen the game has ever seen. And when Jock McCombe died suddenly of a heart attack in 1984, he was sincerely mourned by all the players, myself included.

Ian Botham was, and is, a very different type of character from Viv. The first time I saw him, he was 17 and bowling medium pace in the nets at Taunton. He had a game or two for the 2nds, then went off to join the Lord's ground staff. The coach at Lord's, Len Muncer, didn't think much of Beefy's bowling, seeing him very much as a batting all-rounder. But, when he came back to Taunton, he had a huge amount of help from Tom Cartwright. By the time he played his first game for Somerset – at Hove in the Sunday League – he was a very different bowler. He was bowling down the hill; he didn't take any wickets, but he was quick. Beefy was one of those rare cricketers that you only had to watch for a minute or so to know that they'd be worth signing. Marcus Trescothick was another, and so were Craig Kieswetter and Jos Buttler.

His two strongest influences as a young cricketer were Tom Cartwright, on his bowling technique, and Brian Close, on his cricketing attitude. Tom had recognised his potential right from the start and set about moulding the raw talent into the great bowler that Beefy became. He helped him with the way he held the ball, his wrist position, that great leap in his delivery stride, a terrific pull-back and getting side-on. But Closey was his real hero. He admired his strength, his bravery and, above all, his bull-at-a-gate style of captaincy. Closey, domineering, headstrong and entirely his own man, was exactly the type of cricketer and captain that Ian Botham wanted to become.

This didn't make him easy to captain. Even Closey never knew quite what might be coming when he put him on to bowl. He was the ultimate competitor, but he sometimes tried too hard to make things happen. If things weren't going well for him with the ball, he would tend to start experimenting, often quite early on. With the bat he was always looking to attack, but he didn't quite have Richards' tenacity, which meant that he lacked consistency. My attitude was, within reason, to give him his head. If he came off, as he often did, then great; if he didn't, well I had bowlers like Hallam, Dredgie, Joel and Vic Marks to call upon, and our batting strength was such that we could usually afford the odd failure from our star all-rounder.

It seems a strange thing to say about a cricketer who scored almost 20,000 first-class runs at an average of a shade under 34, but I don't think he ever quite fulfilled his potential as a batsman, because he had a wonderful eye, great strength, an indomitable spirit and all the shots. But too often he would get bored, or over-ambitious, try something outrageous and that would be that. What you have to remember in assessing him as a batsman is how much bowling he had to do. It began to take a toll on his body at around the end of the 1970s, when he started to complain of tiredness, and then he had a couple of knee problems and issues with his lower back. It was about that time as well that he started to put on weight, something to which his lifestyle undoubtedly contributed. His drinking and experimentation with soft drugs has been well documented and, when you look at his achievements as a cricketer, you can't say it exactly ruined him, but it's the sort of lifestyle that is always going to catch up with you in the end.

But that's how he was. Even as a young man, he sometimes didn't know when to stop. In 1976, he was in the Somerset side to play Lancashire at Weston in August. I was twelfth man but volunteered to put him up for the night in my mother's house, as he had nowhere else to stay. Beefy being Beefy, he decided to go out on the town with the Lancashire lads, who had a reputation for enjoying a beer or two. I had arranged to pick him up from the Royal Hotel at 10.30 but, when I got there, a sing-song, led by Barry Wood, was in full swing, and Beefy was completely plastered. I must have something to eat, he said, so I took him to the local Chinese, where he bought a meal for four which he ate back at my mother's house and then went to bed. The next thing I heard was the sound of someone chuntering. It was Ian. He'd brought up the entire contents of his stomach, all down my mother's smartly carpeted stairs. She went berserk. And, of course, it was me who had to clear it all up!

In the winter of 1978/79, I was out in Perth playing for Claremont Cottesloe, and Dasher was with Bassendean-Bayswater not far away. Beefy was also in Perth, playing in the second Test at the WACA. On the Saturday evening, I got a phone call from him: "Rest day tomorrow. Do you and Dasher fancy a few beers on the beach?" Oh God, I thought, knowing what a 'few beers' with Beefy would probably amount to, but he wasn't going to take no for an answer. So I rang Dasher up: "Beefy's been on the phone. Says he wants to go to the bloody beach. Wants me to pick him up."

"Grrrr," he said, in that famous growl, because we both knew what was in store. Anyway, Stevie and I and baby Stuart picked up Beefy the next morning from the hotel. He'd armed himself with one of those giant flagons of white wine, complete with a cooling bag. We collected Dasher, his wife Annie and baby Claire and headed for Scarborough beach. We were there, I suppose, from about 11 in the morning to five in the afternoon. The giant flagon of white was soon disposed of, and Beefy visited a couple of bars to get replacements as the day wore on. Eventually I decide it was time for us to go. After all, Beefy had a Test match to play on the following morning. We got as far as Dasher's place, where Beefy insisted that we stop for "a couple more" beers and a barbie. By the time I got him back to the hotel, he was spark out. I had to heave him over my shoulder in a sort of fireman's lift to get him up the steps to the main door. He was a big lad, of course, and I couldn't carry him any further, so I dropped him on the mat. It was one of those doors – which had only just been introduced – which was operated by pressure pads, pads that Beefy's almost unconscious body was evidently lying on. I say 'almost' because he was capable of just enough involuntary movement to activate the door, which started opening and closing like a mad thing. So there was I, outside this posh hotel in the centre of Perth at ten o'clock in the evening with England's star all-rounder out for the count at my feet and a door flashing to and fro. There was only one thing for it – I didn't want any England management suddenly appearing on the scene – so I legged it! As for Beefy, he scored a quick-fire 30 the next morning, showing no sign of any ill-effects, and England went on to win the Test by 166 runs!

Beefy loved the club, and he never gave less than 100 per cent. He could be a nightmare in the dressing room, playing practical jokes which usually involved somebody getting a soaking, although one of his favourite tricks was to hide Peter Roebuck's bat, just as Pete had to go out to bat. He was loud, boisterous and pretty free with his distinctly right-wing political opinions, and he loved to wind up the university boys, who were all, to a greater or less extent, left of centre in their politics. None of this bothered me particularly. I just let him get on with it. But on the field was a different matter. He wasn't at all a difficult cricketer to captain until he got bored, when he would start fooling around in the slips, or sometimes even when he was bowling. He would want to set strange fields or would bowl too many bouncers, and that could be frustrating. On the other hand, it was that element of unpredictability which got him so many wickets. He was always in the batsman's face, always trying something different. They say he got more wickets than anyone else with bad balls, but there was a lot of judgement about that as well as a fair amount of luck. It was almost as if he forced the wickets to come, through sheer strength of character.

At his best, he was as good a quick bowler as I've ever seen. I remember two overs that he bowled, in particular. The first was in the Gillette Cup semi-final against Middlesex at Lord's in 1979. At the start of the over, I had two slips. By the end of it, I had six. Mike Smith, the Middlesex opener couldn't lay bat on ball. It was an over of six perfect outswingers. At the end of it, Smudgie smashed his bat into the turf and threw his gloves away! The other over was in a B&H game against Hampshire at Bournemouth in 1983. Beefy took three wickets in that over– Mark Nicholas, Nigel Cowley and Nick Pocock – but he could have had a wicket every ball. When he got it right, swinging the ball both ways at pace, he could be devastating. Who could ever forget his 8/34 against Pakistan in the Lord's Test of 1978? I only watched it on the television, but he was beating the bat three or four times an over.

As a batsman he had immense power. The only player I've seen who has come close to hitting the ball as hard as Beefy is Jos Buttler. He played two innings for England, at Headingley and Old Trafford, that will live in the memory for as long as cricket is played. For Somerset he was often at his best when we were up against it, blasting a quick 50 or 60 on a dodgy pitch at some out-ground. No one who saw it will ever forget his partnership with Viv at Leicester in 1983, when he came in number nine and they added 172 in about an hour and a half. That was stunning. Even more thrilling was the partnership that I have already mentioned against Hampshire in the Sunday League in August 1981: 179 in 21 overs, Botham finishing with 106 not out and Richards with 93. Beefy went from 50 to 100 in nine minutes as the Hampshire bowling was destroyed. But those were the exceptions rather than the rule, when it came to partnerships between the pair of them. The desire to outdo each other was intense. Beefy would always say that Viv was far and away the better batsman, but neither liked to be eclipsed. Which is why I tended to bat Viv at three, and Beefy no higher than six!

I often wonder how Ian Botham and others in the team would have fared in the modern cricket environment, where there is so much more management of players, and he would have had to curb his natural instincts when it came to his lifestyle. He might have stayed fitter for longer, I suppose, but whether it would have made him a better cricketer, I'm not sure. He was a wonderfully exciting cricketer, playing for a strong and exciting team at Somerset, against some of the best players the cricket world has ever seen. I'm not sure you can really better that. The only real regret that I have, on his behalf, was that he was made captain. However much he wanted it, I thought the role of captain, especially in county cricket, didn't really suit him. I think he would have remained a great player for longer and achieved more, for England especially, without the extra burden of captaincy.

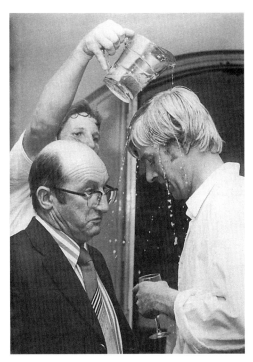

Ever the practical joker, Beefy gets in on the act while I am trying to be serious with Jock Livingston of Gray Nicolls

He and I got on pretty well, most of the time. I kept well away from all the post-match action, which wasn't difficult, as I was living in Weston and would go home every evening if we were playing in Taunton. I did have some idea of what he was getting up to, as the committee would sometimes get complaints from local members, and the Taunton Chief of Police had my telephone number if things got out of hand. He only rang me a couple of times, once when they were holding Beefy in the police station after he'd got involved in some sort of bust-up with the usual sort of drunken yobs who had no doubt done their best to provoke him. I said, "Hold him there for a couple of hours to let him cool off, and he'll be fine," and that was the end of it.

As far as the cricket was concerned, we only had a couple of set-tos. The first was at Edgbaston, when he was bowling poorly and I decided to take him off, a decision that he didn't agree with one bit, and said so. He was still fuming when he went out to bat and decided to take it out on the Warwickshire bowlers, whacking 126 in about an hour and a half. I look back on that as one of my more inspired pieces of captaincy!

The other was at Lord's in 1983 when he was captaining the side in the NatWest semi-final because I was out with the chronic back condition which eventually finished my career. He seemed to think that I was fit enough to play in such a big game, and we had words. In the end I said, "Look, let's put this to bed and sort it out at the end of the season." He said OK, and that was that.

Big Bird

If Viv was proud and Beefy was loud, then Joel Garner was about the most laid-back fast bowler you could ever meet. Many times, when I arrived at the County Ground for a day's cricket, I would find my great international fast bowler stretched out on the physio's bench, fast asleep. The chances are that he'd been up to Birmingham or even Manchester the evening before for a night out with his West Indian mates from his Littleborough days. They were certainly in attendance one night during our game against Lancashire in May 1981. I was staying at the Lord's Hotel, on the edge of Moss Side, an establishment which didn't really live up to its name when it came to comfort and style! I'd gone to bed at around 11, but sleep was impossible because of the racket which was coming from the room above, where it sounded like a herd of elephants were having a party. Eventually, at about two in the morning, I could take no more, and went downstairs in my pyjamas to complain to the night porter. I told him about the noise and explained that I was the captain of Somerset. "Oh, are you?" he replied, with a big grin on his face. "Well, in that case you'll be interested to know that the person in the room above yours is your fast bowler, Joel Garner!"

When I arrived at the ground the next morning, Joel was, as per usual, fast asleep on the physio's table. "Big day ahead today, Joel," I suggested, after he'd woken up. "You'll need to bowl fast. Hope you got plenty of sleep last night."

"Oh yes, skip; sure, skip," replied my bleary-eyed bowler, as if butter wouldn't melt. But he did bowl fast. Lancashire were skittled out in their second innings for 121, Garner 5/57, to leave us as winners by 33 runs!

Joel had apparently first been noticed in the West Indies as a young fast bowler with a rather slingy, round-arm action. All of that changed when he was coached in Barbados by Charlie Griffith, of Hall and Griffith fame, to produce that leaping, high, straight-arm action we knew so well. At 6'9", with incredibly long arms, it meant that he was delivering the ball from the best part of ten feet, which on many grounds around the world was, from the batsman's point of view, above the height of the sight screen. What with that, and the pace and bounce he could command, it made batting against him a nightmare, as I discovered in the Oval Test of 1980. I had made 41 and was playing pretty well, as we battled to avoid an innings defeat, when Joel had me lbw with a full toss that hit me smack on the knee. He was bowling from the pavilion end, and I never saw the ball that got me, as it merged with the red-brick of the pavilion wall and disappeared.

I suppose that, if there is one type of delivery for which the Big Bird will always be remembered, it was his toe-crunching yorker. It was the angle, from that great height, and the accuracy with which he bowled it, that made it so deadly. He could produce it seemingly at will and, besides the countless wickets that he took with it, it was an incredibly valuable weapon in one-day cricket because it was almost impossible to score off.

Most of the time, Joel bowled well within himself, concentrating on line and length, which was generally just short of a length on off-stump, with the yorker and an occasional bouncer as variations. It may seem an odd comparison to make, but in some ways he reminded me of Tom Cartwright, not just for his remorseless accuracy but also because, like Tom, he hated giving runs away. The only disagreements I ever had with him on the field were over whether or not to post a third slip, with me saying he ought to have one and he – remarkably for a fast bowler – disagreeing. His economical instincts also meant that I usually gave him a third man, set very fine, for the one that was nicked through or over the slips. Joel's meanness when it came to giving away runs was the perfect counter-balance to Beefy's more attacking, and sometimes more expensive, approach. I always reckoned that, in one-day cricket, Joel's accuracy would cost the opposition maybe five or six overs.

When he wanted to, he could be fearsomely fast, as Kent discovered in that Gillette quarter-final at Taunton in 1979 when, chasing a modest 191, they were bowled out for 60, Joel destroying their top order to take 5/11 in 9.4 overs. With Beefy steaming in from the other end, I don't think I've ever seen a set of batsmen look so frightened. In all our one-day finals at Lord's, he was immense. Even in the one we lost, against Sussex in 1978, he went for only 34 in his 12 overs and had the hugely dangerous Javed Miandad caught behind for 0.

In our winning finals, his figures were:

		O	M	R	W
1979	Gillette v Northants	10.3	3	29	6
1981	B&H v Surrey	11	5	14	5
1982	B&H v Notts	8.1	3	13	3
1983	NatWest v Kent	9	2	15	2

That gives him an economy rate of 1.84 runs per over and a strike rate of a wicket every 14.5 balls: this in big games, in front of big crowds, against teams featuring some of the best batsmen in the world!

His career stats make pretty interesting reading, as well:

	O	M	R	W	Ave	StR	EcR
West Indies Tests	2194.5	576	5433	259	20.97		
West Indies ODIs	888.2	141	2752	146	18.84	36.5	3.09
Somerset first-class	2646	752	6121	338	18.10		
Somerset one-day	1079.1	209	3122	206	15.15	31.4	2.89

Figures, however impressive, do not get near reflecting the immense contribution Joel made as a man and as a team-mate in our Somerset squad. He was as popular as he was competitive, and he gelled perfectly with the rest of the team, be they local boys, Oxbridge intellectuals or international superstars. In Hallam and Viv, he found kindred Caribbean spirits, not that any of us could understand a word they were saying when they got their heads together in a huddle! They also shared a huge ghetto-blaster, which would pump out Bob Marley and co at full volume whenever they had the chance.

Giants don't come much gentler, nor fast bowlers much nicer than Joel Garner, but just occasionally he would lose his rag and then, as Vic Marks used to say, watch out! Two occasions come to mind. One was against Northants, when we were expecting a declaration to set up a finish, and they batted on and on. I could see that Joel was getting angry, so called him up to give them the hurry-up. Nick Cook was batting and, as he saw Joel come charging in at full pace, he looked absolutely terrified – and with good reason. An over later, they declared!

The other time was against Glamorgan at Sophia Gardens when John Hopkins, one of their openers, said something uncomplimentary to him. The next two deliveries flashed past his nose. Blimey, I thought. Somebody's going to get hospitalised here, and by the end of the over I had two fly slips posted. I'm happy to be able to report that both Nick Cook and John Hopkins emerged unscathed.

For most of his time at Somerset, Joel gave it everything he'd got, whether bowling flat out in the biggest games, spearing in his yorkers in our one-day games, or mixing relentless accuracy with the occasional unplayable delivery in the county championship. He did, though – and I suppose this was inevitable for such a tall man putting such a huge strain on his body – suffer from knee problems, which he did his best to hide. Dennis Waight did a great job in keeping him reasonably fit but, as the seasons wore on, the number of games he was able to play fell away. After his great season in 1981, when he took 88 wickets at just over 15 runs apiece, he played only 10 championship games for us in 1982 and nine in 1983. With Beefy away for much of the time with England and Hallam nearing the end of his career, it meant that for many games we were short of bowling fire-power and that was inevitably reflected in our results.

We must not forget Joel's batting – or swiping, as he called it – in which he took great pride and which was never anything less than entertaining, even if he wasn't the best judge of a run who ever set foot on a cricket field. His highest score was a 90 against Gloucester at Bath in 1981, the game in which

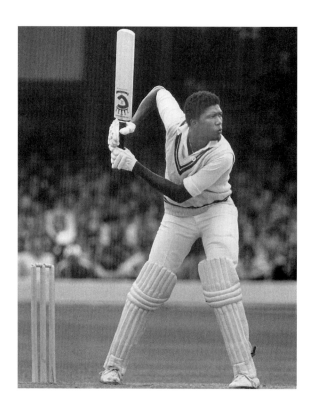

Joel batting

Peter Roebuck and I, on one leg apiece, batted out time. But undoubtedly the most valuable innings that he played for us was the spectacular 59 not out he blasted against Surrey at Bath in 1982. At 94/6 in 25 overs, needing 176 against Sylvester Clarke and co, we were staring defeat in the face. But Joel was having none of it. Whilst I dug in at one end, Joel gave it the long handle at the other. The ball was flying everywhere. He needed only 48 balls for his 59 and carried us to victory with four sixes in an over from the unfortunate Andrew Needham. A big crowd loved it.

People often ask me how I managed to captain so successfully with all of those big egos and strong characters in the dressing room. "How could you control that lot?" they say. Well, the answer is that, off the field, I didn't try to control them. What they got up to wasn't my concern unless it started affecting their cricket and invariably it didn't. But on the field was a different matter. Certainly, for the first five years, I had their complete confidence in me and my ability to control the game, in terms of tactics, bowling changes, fielding positions and so on. I like to think that I freed them to concentrate on what they did best, and they did it brilliantly. Whatever happened later on, no captain could have asked for more in terms of both attitude and performance than I got from Smokey, Beefy and Big Bird. They were at the heart of our success.

10

The road to Shepton Mallet

Peter Roebuck dates the gradual decline and eventual disintegration of my Somerset team to the game against Hampshire at Dean Park, Bournemouth, a few days after our B&H win in July 1982. Viv Richards turned up at the ground on the first morning but didn't play. 'Something happened on the morning of the match about which all save those most intimately involved remain in the dark,' he claimed in his autobiography *Sometimes I Forgot To Laugh*. Well, as captain, I would most certainly have been counted amongst those 'most intimately involved', and I can remember nothing untoward about that morning at all! I suspect that the reason for Viv's non-participation was the one that Roebuck quotes me as giving at the time: illness and a slight leg strain. My own feeling, both at the time and now, is that there was nothing wrong with relationships within the team during that 1982 season. Of course, you always get niggles and problems, especially in a dressing room containing so many strong characters, but I don't recall anything out of the ordinary.

Inspecting a wet outfield with Toby

One seed of future troubles that was sown that summer of 1982 was the appointment of Tony Brown as Secretary in succession to David Seward. If the club had had any sense, they would have appointed Roy Kerslake, who had the complete confidence of the players. I was not directly involved so can't say for sure what happened, but there's no doubt that the club made it very difficult, if not impossible, for Roy to apply for the job. I have nothing against Tony Brown and personally got on with him, but there was history between him and Somerset – and not all dating back to his playing days. He had been particularly outspoken in his criticism of the Worcester declaration, three years earlier, and cricketers don't forget that sort of thing, particularly if it emanated from Gloucestershire and was aimed at Somerset! I am sure that the club's thinking was that, by appointing a fairly recently retired player as Secretary, it might bring team and committee closer together. In the event it had precisely the opposite effect.

Something else which was changing that summer was Peter Roebuck's attitude. When he had first come into the side he had seemed rather shy and didn't say much, although he did offer lots of useful advice, to Viv Richards in particular. But once he had got himself established, he wasn't backward in coming forward with his opinions, even to the extent of having a go at people if he didn't think they were pulling their weight, which would certainly manifest itself in dressing room problems, with Beefy in particular.

I think that the truth of the matter is that, as a team, we had been together for a good many years and that familiarity, if not exactly breeding contempt, undoubtedly did breed a certain amount of irritation and tension. No team can stay the same for ever. As older players age, and younger ones come into the side, there is a process of evolution. Even during our years of success, when so much was going right, there were things going wrong from time to time. But the fact that we were winning soon papered over any cracks. It was when results started to go into decline that those cracks began to widen. Lifestyle issues didn't help, either. Beefy's off-field exploits were the talk of Taunton, and often of the tabloids, not to mention the dressing room, with some of the younger players unsure what to make of it all, and the more strong-minded among the team – Roebuck and Popplewell especially – openly disapproving. The pressure of having played so many big games over so many seasons was also beginning to take its toll, mentally as well as physically. More or less the same group of players had been in contention for one trophy or another for every season since 1977, and it is bloody difficult to sustain that level of intensity, without it creating tensions and difficulties between team-mates.

The other big factor in the equation at this relatively early stage in the saga was my own fitness. I had missed the last game of the 1982 season with my long-term calf injury, and my back was still giving me periodic trouble. Even so, there seemed no reason at the start of the next season why we should not be among the contenders in both the championship and the one-day competitions, with Joel fresh from a record breaking season with South Australia, and everyone else seemingly fit and well. My old mate Derek Taylor – who had been so central, in his own quiet way, to our run of successes – had retired at the end of the previous season, his place behind the stumps being taken by his patient long-term understudy, Trevor Gard. As usual in the early '80s, it rained for most of May, ruining our first three championship matches. Our defence of the B&H did not last long; we were eliminated at the group stage. We fared rather better in the Sunday League, winning four of our first six games, and it might have been even better if the other two hadn't been completely washed out.

On 4 June, we started a three-day match against Essex at Taunton. Keith Fletcher won the toss and decided to bat. When Brian Hardie was out early on to our promising young left-arm seamer Mark Davis, I decided to post myself at backward cover, to cut off what I knew was one of Fletcher's favourite shots. Sure enough, he soon shaped to play that little back cut, and I anticipated to my left, expecting it to go fine of me. Instead of which, it came more or less straight to me and, as I changed direction, my feet got stuck, and I could feel something go in my lower back. I knew straightaway that I'd done something nasty. There were pains all down the back of my legs, and I got carted off.

With the help of pain-killing injections, I managed to get myself fit enough to captain the side against Sussex at Hove, the New Zealand tourists in early July, and for the trip to Leicester which followed. That latter game will mostly be remembered for the spectacular partnership between Richards (216) and Botham (152). With Beefy batting at nine because of a stomach upset, they added 172 for the eighth wicket, a then Somerset record, to set up an innings victory. But I will always remember it as my last game as Somerset captain.

1983 was my benefit year, and the end of the season had always seemed an appropriate time to step down, as captain if not as player. The back injury turned a probability into a certainty. I could sense that there was unease in the dressing room, with some players evidently sceptical as to how serious this 'back injury' really was, given that I looked perfectly normal. It probably didn't help that I had always tried to keep a certain distance between myself and the rest of the team. When it came to providing leadership for a disparate and sometimes difficult bunch of players, it was fine. But when it came to inspiring sympathy and understanding for a mystery back condition, that degree of separation was not helpful.

A benefit evening at the Creech Castle Hotel
Colin Dredge, Peter Robinson, Trevor Gard, me and (kneeling) Dasher

It was during that Leicester game that a group of players tried to mount a coup to get me removed as captain. Peter Roebuck tells the story in his autobiography of how, on the evening of the first day, after I had apparently made myself unpopular by calling out rather testily "Come on, boys" in response to some poor fielding, a 'lackey' came to his room to summon him to the bar where 'some of the lads' were planning to 'tell Rosey to resign'. I knew nothing of this at the time and heard about it only later from Vic Marks who, like Roebuck, had wanted nothing to do with it. However, the feeling among most of the team at the time can be deduced from Roebuck's closing sentence in that particular paragraph: *'Complaining of an injury,* Rose did not play again that summer.'

All I can say now is that the injury was all too real. It was, as I say, my benefit year, and I tried desperately to play in one or two of the many benefit games that were laid on. But it was no good. The doctors even tried putting my torso into a plaster cast, which was agony, and eventually had to be ripped off, although it may at least have served to convince one or two of my critics that the injury was real, rather than imagined! In my enforced absence, the captaincy was shared between Botham, the official vice-captain, Richards and, when they were both on international duty, Roebuck. Roebuck handled his severely weakened side well enough, according to his own account, to be approached at the end of the Bath Festival by Somerset 'officials' and asked whether he would consider taking over the captaincy from me at the end of the season. Botham was evidently not being regarded as suitable!

Richards did not let captaincy inhibit his batting, averaging just under 90 in the five championship matches in which he took charge. But it was, entirely typically, Beefy who put an end to all the speculation, through sheer brilliance of performance. In the NatWest semi-final at Lord's, Somerset were struggling, at 52/5, needing 223 and a captain's innings. Botham provided it. Coolly and with calculated aggression, in stands of 104 with Popplewell and 62 with Marks, he carried his team to within touching distance of their target, and then played out the final over of the innings as a maiden, knowing that, with the scores level, Somerset would win by virtue of fewer wickets lost! It was the performance of a master and of a master showman.

No one but Botham was ever going to be appointed as captain after that, especially as he then went on to lead the team to yet another Lord's triumph in the final against Kent, a game which yours truly watched from the pavilion, chain-smoking small cigars, before having to leave early for yet more

Viv congratulates Vic as he goes up to collect the Man of the Match award at Lord's – our fifth trophy in five years

treatment on my back! I can't deny that I did have mixed feelings, watching someone else lift a trophy that 'my' team had won. But I also knew that I was standing down from the captaincy with my reputation intact, because in the run-up to that final, both Richards and Botham had tried to persuade me to play, even if only half fit, because my captaincy was so much respected. It was never going to happen, because there were times when I could barely walk, but it was a comforting thought.

If Botham's appointment as captain was inevitable, that didn't make it right. During the season, when I had told the chairman, Michael Hill, of my concerns for the future, he had asked me who I thought should take over. Vic Marks, I said, knowing that if there was anyone who could heal the growing rifts between the various factions in the team, then Vic was the man. He had led the team well back in 1980, when Beefy, Viv and myself were all involved in the Test matches; he was shrewd, much tougher than he appeared, and, crucially, he wasn't identified either with the superstars or with their arch-critics. But it didn't seem as if anyone was particularly interested in my opinion. No one consulted me after that. It wasn't that I had anything against Botham personally; we hardly ever had cross words. But I'd seen at first hand in the West Indies what captaincy might do to his form as a player, and I was only too well aware of what his well-publicised off-field activities were doing to the mood in the dressing room.

The only regret I had on stepping down as captain was that I wasn't fit enough to make my farewells on the field of play. I had done my bit. Under six years of my leadership we had won five trophies and come second in five others, having never won anything previously. The thought of retiring altogether and becoming a teacher did occur to me, especially as I spent some time that winter helping Bryan Lobb at Millfield Junior School. But somehow I couldn't see my long-term career as a teacher and, anyway, what I really wanted to do was to carry on playing cricket for Somerset – always provided I could get my fitness back, which at the time seemed anything but certain. Fortunately one of my closest and oldest friends, Frank Williams, with whom I had been at school in Weston, was now consultant radiologist at Nevill Hall Hospital near Abergavenny. Hearing about my back problems, he invited me over and got me to see the hospital's back specialist. The upshot was that he gave me an injection in my spine, which sufficiently eased the pain from what were effectively two prolapsed discs to enable me to carry on playing. It would still flare up from time to time, and it wasn't until a new treatment became available, some 14 painful years later, that the problem was, if not solved, then properly controlled, but at least my worst fears that autumn – that my cricket career might be over – went unrealised.

By the start of the 1984 season, I was fit enough to take my place in the side, batting at five, just below our new overseas batsman, Martin Crowe, who had been signed to replace Richards and Garner, who were with the touring West Indians. Crowe was immensely impressive, both on and off the field. Although he was only 21, it was immediately apparent that here we had one of the world's great batsmen in the making. Quite apart from his skill, what set him apart was his attitude. He was incredibly intense in the way he approached his cricket. In some ways, he was a forerunner of the modern professional cricketer, in terms of his training regime, diet and lifestyle. Unlike most cricketers of that era, he drank pretty sparingly, mainly in the context of the group of younger players which he convened every Thursday evening at the Nag's Head at Thornfalcon. The fact that he went out of his way to help the youngsters did not go unnoticed by the Somerset committee-men. Richards could often seem aloof and brooding, Garner too laid back. But in Martin Crowe they seemed to have found the ideal overseas player: hugely successful on the field, with 1,769 runs in the championship, including five centuries of the highest class, plus 750 runs in the one-day competitions; conscientious and enthusiastic off it. As ideal a role model for young cricketers as you could get.

Vic Marks had a great season in 1984 (1,197 championship runs and 78 wickets) and so did Peter Roebuck (1,535 championship runs, including six centuries) and Nigel Popplewell (1,056 championship runs plus any number of valuable contributions in one-day cricket). And, despite still being troubled by the calf strain and the back problem, I didn't do so badly myself, with 847 runs in 19 championship games at 31.37, plus 576 runs in one-day cricket, my second highest season's total. By and large, we were a pretty happy bunch, and there were some memorable moments. In the game against Leicestershire at Taunton in June, Peter Willey's declaration left us to score 341 in 87 overs, against an attack led by Andy Roberts and Jonathan Agnew. We lost two wickets in Agnew's first over, whereupon Roebuck and Martin Crowe put together one of the classiest partnerships I have ever witnessed – 319 in 80 overs – to carry us to a six-wicket victory!

In one-day cricket, we were too inconsistent to challenge in the John Player League, especially after the loss of Dasher to a knee injury after only a few games, and we lost in the quarter-finals of both the B&H and the NatWest, to Warwickshire and Kent respectively. I enjoyed mixed fortunes in those two games. At Edgbaston it was BC Rose b Small 0. Gladys, as we called him, was quite quick, and he bowled with that skiddy sort of trajectory to which, as a tall man, I was always slightly vulnerable, especially after my back injury when I made a conscious decision to stand even taller at the crease. In the game against Kent at Taunton, we needed 276 in our 60 overs, which was a daunting total in those days. After a good start from Roebuck and Nigel Felton, we lost three quick wickets, including Botham and Crowe, to be 177/4. I can't remember whether I consciously thought back to that game at Cardiff in 1978 when I had given it away instead of keeping my head and we missed out on the Sunday League. At any rate, after Roebuck was out for a typically determined 81 at 206/5, it was left to me and Vic Marks to take us over the line. We added 59 in seven overs, but came up ten runs short. For a long time afterwards I worried about whether the defeat was my fault, for having left it too late.

Our problems were all with the bowling. Joel was with the West Indies, Beefy missed more than half of our games through his England commitments, Hallam Moseley had turned down a 'subject to fitness' contract and Hugh Wilson, whom we had signed the previous year from Surrey, made little impact. In Botham's frequent absences, that meant that our opening attack consisted of Colin Dredge and our promising young left-armer from Kilve, Mark Davis, with Martin Crowe or maybe Gary Palmer as first change, leaving Vic Marks to do most of the donkey work. Vic bowled superbly all season, bowling half as many overs again as anyone else, and Mark Davis showed great promise, moving the ball both ways from a disciplined off-stump line, to take 59 wickets. It would have been more but for a back injury he picked up towards the end of the season, which turned out to be a sign of things to come. Even so, it was not an attack guaranteed to strike fear into the hearts of our opponents, and we struggled to bowl sides out twice in the championship or to contain in the one-day matches.

Given the resources at his disposal, I thought that Beefy captained the side pretty well – when he got the chance. But having to miss so many games (15 out of 26 in the championship) meant that he rather lost touch with his team and, when he was available, he would come back as a sort of cricketing superstar descending from on high, which could also cause problems. One of his weaknesses as a captain – and I did talk to him about this – was that he tended to have his favourites, and his not-so-favourites, players who had got the wrong side of him. An example of the former would be when he picked his great mate Dennis Breakwell, who had played only three games of any sort for Somerset in the previous two seasons, ahead of Hugh Wilson in the NatWest quarter-final against Kent. As for the not so favoured, Peter Roebuck and Nigel Popplewell were already making no bones about their disapproval of their captain's much-publicised off-field activities. But perhaps the saddest casualty was Jeremy Lloyds, who left us to join Gloucestershire at the end of that season. As an opening bat and as an off-spinner, Gloucestershire's gain was very much Somerset's loss, and the fact that it was the old enemy that he'd gone to rubbed salt into the wound.

Living your life in the way Beefy did is all very well if you're performing on the field. But it was bound to take its toll eventually, health-wise and fitness-wise, and that, in turn, inevitably raised questions among the team about his decision-making, especially when results started to go against us. Alongside his limited availability, that was one of the main reasons I thought he should never have been made captain in the first place. I wish the club had listened to me at the time.

Vic Marks captained in Beefy's frequent absences and again did the job well, in his understated way. People sometimes accused him of sitting on the fence and of failing to take radical decisions but, for my money, it was better to do that than to get into a confrontational situation with the many strong characters in that Somerset side. I was not in the least bit sorry not to be carrying the burden of captaincy. I might have wanted to carry on a bit longer if my back hadn't given way. But looking back now, I can see that six years in that job was enough. There were times during that 1984 season when I could sense the unease among some of the younger players at some of the things that were going on involving their captain, but I took a very conscious decision not to get involved. If Beefy got himself in trouble, that was the club's problem, not mine. I believe that Vic thought much the same.

Despite continuing problems with my back and both my knees, I started the 1985 season in good form. I scored 43 in the first innings against Notts, and then batted as well as I have ever done in our match at Taunton against the Australian tourists. By this stage in my career, just about every quick bowler I came up against would bowl short at me, knowing how strong I was on the front foot, so I developed a new shot – a sort of pull-hook slog, which worked particularly well if the ball was pitched short just outside off-stump. In this particular game we were 65/4, replying to Australia's 356 for 4 declared, when Beefy came out to join me, late on the first afternoon. We decided to have a bit of a whack and, when Jeff Thomson bowled one just short of a length outside off-stump, I flat-batted it back at him. It was the hardest I ever hit a cricket ball in my life. I honestly thought it was going to kill him! Fortunately, he managed to get out of the way and the next morning the Australians had their revenge when, with 81 to my name and looking forward to another century against them, Craig McDermott dug one in just short of a length on leg stump, which got up sharply and broke my right arm.

So that was ten weeks out, which meant that I missed Viv Richards' magnificent 322 against Warwickshire, as well as several barn-storming

Botham innings, including his 149 in 106 balls against a Hampshire attack led by Malcolm Marshall. Viv got 186 in the second innings of that game, yet we lost by five wickets. It was a performance, and a result, which typified that season for Somerset: loads of runs, from Richards and Botham especially, but not enough wickets. Joel took only 31 in 15 championship games, Beefy contributed just 11, Mark Davis was troubled with back injuries and Colin Dredge missed half the season through injury. Vic Marks did his level best, as usual, bowling more than twice as many overs as anyone else in our championship games and picking up 67 wickets but, without a fit and firing seam attack, Somerset were pretty much toothless in the field.

I played only four championship games, coming back from my broken arm for the Warwickshire match at the end of July, then having two knee cartilage operations, which kept me out until the final game of the season. But I was with the team enough to realise that the atmosphere in the dressing room was strained and getting worse. What really brought it home was Nigel Popplewell's decision to pack in his Somerset career. It was a shame, because he was a fine all-round cricketer, if anything still improving as a batsman, but he had an emotional, sometimes impulsive character and was more upset than most by the sort of things that were going on in the dressing room and off the field. In the end I think he decided that he wasn't enjoying playing for Somerset sufficiently to make it worthwhile delaying his legal career any longer.

The arrival on the scene that summer of Tim Hudson, the flamboyant 'manager' who was going to make Ian Botham a Hollywood star, did nothing at all for the Somerset captain's credibility with his team. The flashy jackets, the mane of dyed-blond hair, the hangers-on, it all seemed to be symptomatic of where Beefy was going in terms of his leadership.

It did not help that the senior officials did not seem to have any plan for where the club was going. Years later, when I took over as Director of Cricket under Richard Gould as Chief Executive, we sat down together and worked out a four-to-six-year plan, both commercially and where we wanted the club to be and who was going to be playing for us. That sort of thing did not happen in the mid-'80s. Part of the problem was Tony Brown. He had been brought in as an ex-player, presumably with the idea that he could act as a bridge between the dressing room and the committee. He ran the club efficiently but, in terms of his relationships with the players, especially the more experienced ones, he either couldn't handle it or did not want to handle it.

By the time I was fit enough to come back into the side, for the last championship game of 1985, at Canterbury, it was pretty clear that Beefy's days as captain were numbered. Somerset were bottom of the championship, having won only one game all season. We had lost three out of our four group games in the B&H, lost badly to Hampshire in the NatWest quarter-final (the game made famous for 'sun stopped play', after Beefy complained that he and his batting partner Vic Marks were being blinded by a low sun reflecting off a nearby office window) and come a lowly joint tenth in the John Player League. Yes, injuries played a big part in that dismal record, but the captain was clearly not getting the best out of the resources available. Add to that the tabloid headlines and controversies that seemed to accompany Beefy wherever he went, plus the fact that he let it be known that he was only prepared to sign a one-year extension to his contract, rather than the two years that the club wanted, and the writing was clearly on the wall. My working assumption was that Vic, as vice-captain, would take over, as he had led the team perfectly competently in Beefy's frequent absences and got on reasonably well with both the superstars and their main critic, Peter Roebuck.

I have always held Peter Roebuck in the highest regard as a cricketer. He was brilliant in that Somerset side because he would hang in there, allowing the stroke-makers like Viv, Beefy and me to play around him. You could not find a more determined, gritty, team-minded batsman, and I have always felt he was hugely unlucky never to have been picked for England, especially when you consider some of the batsmen they did pick during that era. He had a brilliant mind, almost in the Brearley class, and I guess that Tony Brown and Brian Langford, when they appointed him captain, were hoping that he might work as successfully with Beefy as Brearley had when he'd taken over the captaincy of England from him a few years before. I have to say that I was surprised when he was given the captaincy ahead of Vic, who would always have been my choice, and ahead of Viv, if it comes to that, whom Roy Kerslake always thought should have been given the job. It was certainly a surprise to Viv and Joel as well, and even more so to Beefy, who by this time had fallen out with Roebuck, who had never made any secret of his disapproval of Botham's extra-curricular activities and the effect which he believed they were having not just on his cricket but on what had been his team.

The trouble was that, whatever the intellectual comparison, Roebuck was no Brearley when it came to man-management. While he had always held strong opinions about how players should behave, his success as a journalist had given him the self-confidence to express them, often quite forcefully, rather than keeping them to himself and a few close friends. He could be abrupt, acid, self-centred and sometimes deliberately provocative. I think he

Vic Marks would have been my choice to succeed me as captain

saw himself as some sort of guru, to whom everyone ought to look up. There was nothing wrong with the way he read a game of cricket, or set the field, or picked the team. But I would never have made him captain because of that abrasive personality. Yes, he made a very successful captain of Devon later in his career, but there he was a seasoned professional, surrounded by part-timers and amateurs. At Somerset he was a county player, looking to impose his way of doing things, none too diplomatically, on international superstars. It was a car crash in the making.

1986 turned out to be probably the most traumatic season in Somerset cricketing history. It started off in suitably dramatic fashion at Taunton, when off the last ball of a championshup match against Yorkshire Colin Dredge was brilliantly caught at wide long-on, going for a second successive six. I was fit enough to play in that one, before more knee and back problems intervened to keep me out until the game against Kent at Bath in June.

Against an attack headed by Terry Alderman, and on a slow pitch, Viv was at his imperious best, stroking 128 from 144 balls. I came in at six and batted with him for a few overs before he was out, whereupon Vic Marks and I took the score on from 266/5 to 433/6 declared, BC Rose 107 not out! It was my first century for almost two years, and I surprised even myself. As for Viv, he couldn't believe it. He greeted me with 'Hey, skip, you still got it,' albeit with a distinct note of surprise in his voice, as I made it back to the dressing room. We won that game by an innings and 24 runs, thanks to a combination of Vic Marks and Joel Garner, who seemed back to something approaching his best.

The other innings I remember most vividly from that season was against Middlesex at Lord's in July. Expecting to bat at five or six, I'd been out the previous night, drinking with Dennis Waight and was suffering for it the next morning. I think Peter Roebuck may have sensed what I'd been up to, because as soon as I arrived, bleary-eyed, in the dressing room on the second morning he said, "Right, get your pads on, you're opening with me" – against Wayne Daniel and Norman Cowans! In the event I played what I have always thought of as one of the best innings of my first-class career. By that stage, conscious of my eyesight problems and the fact that I'd been hit a few times, the default option for quick bowlers was to bowl short at me. But I'd also learned a thing or two over the years, not least how to compensate for my poor eyesight and back and knee problems, by standing up straight and keeping quite still as the ball was delivered. It meant that I was in the perfect position to swat the ball, on either side of the wicket, if it was short. It also meant that I was a very different sort of batsman from the much more cautious, swaying out of the way BC Rose of my earlier career. When it came off, it could be spectacular – and it certainly came off that day. I hit 20 fours, mostly off the fast men, mostly behind square, in my 129, sharing a partnership of 225 with Roebuck, our second successive century opening partnership.

Any hopes that this might launch a lasting renaissance in my batting career were swiftly snuffed out. Quite early on it that innings, my front pad had slipped around my knee, so that it offered virtually no protection when I was hit smack on the knee-cap by Wayne Daniel. I batted on without a runner for the rest of that innings, but I already knew that I would be out for another spell. The injury had cleared up sufficiently to allow me to come back for the Weston Festival in early August, and that was quite a week. In the game against Worcestershire, on as good a wicket as I ever saw at Clarence Park, I took a quarter of my entire collection of first-class wickets in the Worcestershire second innings, removing both openers, Tim Curtis and Damian D'Oliveira (albeit after they'd put on 143 together!), and then, when we batted a second time, needing 341 in around four and a half hours, I contributed a hard-hitting 56 out of an opening partnership of 99 with Peter Roebuck, who went on to make a superb 147 not out, which, with Vic Marks' rapid 71, won us the game with four balls to spare. We couldn't quite force a win in the following game, against Warwickshire, but I made 76 not out in the first innings, and followed that with a not out 96 in the second, sharing a partnership of 164 with a slightly less astounded Viv. The usual big holiday crowd absolutely loved it. I was the hero of Weston that week, surrounded by old school friends, and it was a great way to bring down the curtain on what turned out to be my final Weston appearance.

The Worcestershire match was Beefy's first cricket since May. On May 29, he had been suspended from all first class cricket by the TCCB's Disciplinary Committee for two months, for having admitted – in a front page article in the *Mail on Sunday* designed presumably to pre-empt more serious charges – using cannabis as a younger man, having previously denied any such activities. I can't say that any of us involved with Somerset cricket were in the least bit surprised. Beefy's recreational activities were an open secret. But coming on top of a tour of the West Indies which was disappointing on the field, and full of lurid accusations off it, it did seem to vindicate the opinion of some in the team, Roebuck foremost among them, that our star all-rounder was becoming almost more trouble than he was worth. Mind you, if they ever put such thoughts into words, Beefy certainly made them eat them pretty quickly on his return. His century against Worcester came off 60 balls with seven sixes and six fours, and he followed that with a simply astounding 174 in the Sunday League against Northants at Wellingborough the following weekend!

But, drugs ban or no drugs ban, no one in the Somerset hierarchy was seriously thinking about getting rid of Ian Botham. The rumours that began to swirl around in June and July were all about Joel and Viv. Not that they weren't still doing it on the pitch when the mood took them, but Joel's knee problems and Viv's superstar status were coming increasingly to mean that, with Joel, he wasn't the consistent force that he had once been, and, with Viv, that something of a gulf was opening up between him and some of the younger players. To me, Vic Marks and Colin Dredge, who had grown up with them in the Somerset side, they were just our mates. But the younger players were rather in awe of them and perhaps didn't get the help and advice from the superstars that they might have expected.

What should have happened is that either Tony Brown, or Brian Langford as Chairman of Cricket, should have taken Viv and Joel aside, individually, to discuss how they saw their future with Somerset. I had already had a chat with Joel about his knee problems, because it was abundantly clear that, at the age of 33, he would have to manage his cricket if he was going to stay fit enough for what was his priority, bowling for the West Indies. Contracts to play just one-day cricket were rare in those days, but that would have been an obvious option, if only someone had bothered to discuss it with him.

As for Viv, he had been giving his all for Somerset for more than ten years, as well as being the West Indies' main man, and was entitled to feel a bit tired. But he loved Somerset County Cricket Club, he loved Somerset, he had many friends in the county and the emotional ties ran deep and strong. He too could have been asked how he saw the future. Instead of which, Brian Langford called him in to tell him that there would always be a place for him in the Somerset team. The next formal contact that the pair of them had was when Langford gave him the sack!

You can argue about whether the decision was the right one from a strictly cricketing point of view. Viv, and especially Joel, could be seen as fading forces, increasingly reluctant to give it all they'd got in routine county championship matches. Martin Crowe, on the other hand, was young, keen and had become a world-class batsman. He had impressed many on the committee – foremost among them the chairman, Michael Hill – with his attitude during the 1984 season. As far as I know, no one in Somerset was aware in the summer of 1986 of the psychological issues and back problems that would come to affect Martin's career and bring an early end to his time with Somerset. The Somerset powers-that-be must have suspected that Beefy might go as well if his two great mates were sacked, but again, they would have reasoned, first, that with his thickening waistline, he wasn't the player he had been on the pitch; and second, that his off-field activities were a bad influence on the younger players and a source of almost constant controversy which the club could very well do without.

I can honestly say that I knew nothing about the Cricket Committee decision in July to dispense with Viv and Joel and sign Martin Crowe instead until after the event. It was probably early August when Michael Hill and Brian Langford called me in to tell me what had been decided and to ask for my opinion as to how it would affect the future of the club. I said that, as things stood, I didn't see the future as being very bright!

It was not just the loss of two, or possibly three, of our star players. This was a conversation that should have happened two or three years previously. They should have realised that the team had played together more or less unchanged since the mid-1970s and that we were growing old together. The obvious thing to have done was to draw up a plan to introduce new younger players – from other counties, if necessary, given that our own youngsters were mostly not fulfilling their early promise – and new overseas signings. The club had completely failed to do that and were now faced with what was obviously going to be a huge and traumatic upheaval. With a bit of forethought, they could have planned a gradual evolution. That's what I told them, at any rate, although they did not seem terribly interested.

When the sackings were made and the news broke on August 23, my immediate feelings were ones of profound sadness. Not so much for Joel, as I knew he was coming to the end of his career because of persistent injuries. But Viv was a different matter. He had given himself, heart and soul, to Somerset, as one of the world's greatest ever players. It was a tragic way for his Somerset career to come to an end.

On the day after the announcement, we drove up to Edgbaston to play Warwickshire in a Sunday League game. That was one of the most uncomfortable experiences of my playing career. The atmosphere in the dressing room was strange. Viv and Joel were trying to make light of it, but I could tell that Viv especially was in a state of shock. No one said too much, but I could sense the emotional turmoil that would come to the surface in the following three-day match against Essex. I felt that we were completely rudderless. The irony was that we produced one of our best Sunday performances of the season. Quite what was going through Peter Roebuck's mind when he asked Joel and Viv to open the bowling together, I don't know. But it was a ploy that certainly worked; they took 2/14 and 2/19 respectively as Warwickshire were skittled out for 88, and we won comfortably, even if Viv was furious with himself for getting out for just one.

The real bitterness started when Beefy came back into the side for the Essex game at Taunton on the Wednesday. I wasn't playing, but I took Beefy aside before the start, to advise him not to do anything too impulsive. But it was no good. He had a furious show-down with Roebuck, and things went from bad to worse thereafter. By the end of the season Somerset cricket was a wreck.

I was genuinely torn between my loyalty to the club, which has always transcended whatever I might have thought of particular managements or decisions, and my sympathy for my friends Viv and Joel. I had been asked my opinion after the event, when it was too late to make any difference, and I didn't feel any responsibility for the mess that Somerset had got itself into. I just wanted out. So Stevie and I headed off to our apartment in Estepona in Spain and stayed there for a month, playing golf and enjoying ourselves. So I wasn't at the meeting at Shepton Mallet, and ended up being criticised for my absence – unfairly I thought – in the press. Had I been there and been asked for my opinion, I would have said that the fatal mistake was in not making either Vic Marks or Viv Richards captain when I had stood down at the end of 1983. With either of them in charge, none of this would have happened.

Peter Roebuck with friends at the Shepton Mallet meeting

11

Picking up the pieces

Towards the end of that 1986 season, with the club in disarray, Tony Brown and Brian Langford called me in to talk about my future. They knew that, with no sign of an end to my constantly recurring back and knee problems, retirement was very much on my mind. They also knew that, having lost Viv, Joel and probably Beefy as well, with only Martin Crowe lined up as a replacement, the playing squad desperately needed reinforcement. So they asked me if I would stay on for another year, to play when I could, to act as a bit of a mentor to Peter Roebuck as captain and, in the meantime, to sign some new players. They offered me the post of what they called Cricket Development Officer, although it was more like being Cricket Manager, a forerunner almost of the role of Director of Cricket that we see today.

Over my years as captain, I had built up good contacts with both players and players' agents around the country, and I had a clear idea of what we needed in the way of new players, which was mainly seam bowlers. With Joel and Beefy going, Colin Dredge suffering persistent shoulder problems and nearing the end of his career, Mark Davis injury-prone and Nick Taylor disappointing, Somerset's once-imposing seam attack had all but disappeared.

We also needed a wicket-keeper. After waiting so patiently to step into Derek Taylor's boots, Trevor Gard had struggled: not as a keeper, because he was one of the very best, but with the bat. With so much one-day cricket in the fixture list, you needed a keeper who could contribute quick runs in the lower middle order, whereas Trevor batted at ten and could barely get it off the square. It was a shame, because no one was more committed to Somerset cricket than Trevor, and I liked him enormously as an individual. At the time I didn't feel too bad at the thought of bringing in a new keeper over his head because I knew that he had been offered a job with a haulage company near Yeovil. I assumed he would take that and spend more time at home with his ferrets. In the event he decided to carry on playing for and captaining the 2nds and retired eventually at the end of the 1990 season. He may only have been a first-team regular for four of his 16 seasons with the club, but Trevor Gard was one of Somerset cricket's great characters.

I travelled to Chelmsford in early September, to watch Essex 2nds against Middlesex 2nds. My main target was the young Middlesex keeper Colin Metson, who went on to enjoy a long and successful career at Glamorgan, and I was hoping that Neil Burns, understudy to David East at Essex, might be playing as well. He wasn't, but I already knew enough about him to have decided that he, rather than Metson, was the man for Somerset. He was developing into a top-class keeper, but what I really liked about him was his attitude. He was dedicated, forceful and always up for it. Yes, he could be irritating, but he had that force of personality that I felt we needed behind the stumps in a team struggling desperately to rebuild. The other player I was interested in at that game was the young Middlesex all-rounder Graham Rose. Tall and strong, he bowled at a lively medium pace and hit the ball hard and cleanly. He was an Ian Botham type of player, if nowhere near in the same class, and I felt he could do a job for Somerset, particularly in one-day cricket.

As for opening bowlers, I had my eyes on Neil Mallender, whom I had got to know over the previous few seasons and who was unhappy with the set-up at Northampton. He was accurate, economical, a good team man and could move it both ways off the seam at a decent pace, rather in the Geoff Arnold mould. In trying to tempt him to come to Taunton, I promised him green wickets at the County Ground. I don't think he's forgiven me yet!

Getting the contracts of my new recruits signed proved to be more difficult than I had imagined. By the time all the details had been sorted out, Graham Rose was playing grade cricket in Western Australia and Neil Mallender was with Otago. So, rather than risk losing them, I flew out to Perth to tie things up with Rose, then on to New Zealand to seal the deal with Mallender.

Burns had already signed as our new wicket-keeper, so that just left another opening bowler to be procured. After much thought and not a few misgivings, I decided to approach the Sussex quick bowler Adrian Jones. He had the reputation of being injury prone and a slightly awkward character, but I had been impressed by his pace when we had played against him at Sussex, and genuinely quick, home-grown bowlers were thin on the ground. I knew that, with Imran Khan, Garth le Roux and Tony Pigott in the Sussex squad, Jones's chances there were limited. So I approached him, he agreed and in the next four seasons, despite recurring problems with his fitness and health, he took 245 wickets for Somerset. Yes, he could be eccentric, hot-headed and at times erratic, but he did a job for Somerset when it was most needed.

So we started the 1987 season with four new players in our ranks – five if you include Martin Crowe, and we almost had a sixth. Martin Crowe was expected to be in Sri Lanka until the middle of May, playing for New Zealand in a hastily arranged tour, so, come March, I was looking for a replacement for our early

The fruits of my travels as Cricket Development Manager – four new players for 1987: Adrian Jones, Neil Mallender, Graham Rose and Neil Burns

games. I knew about Steve Waugh from my Australian contacts and got in touch to see if he was interested. He was, but he was under contract to Nelson in the Lancashire League. With no time to be lost, I legged it up to Nelson to talk to their officials. The meeting was at the Secretary's house, complete with the entire Nelson committee, several of whose wives were in the kitchen, making tea and sandwiches for us all. I explained our situation and said how valuable it would be for Steve's career to play some county cricket. They tentatively agreed but said that they would mull it over and let me know. Three days later a draft contract, detailed and correct in every particular, arrived in the post! In the event, there wasn't quite that degree of urgency, as the New Zealand tour was abandoned because of terrorist incidents and Martin was with us for our first game, after flying through the night from Colombo. But I now had one of the most promising young cricketers in the world up my sleeve if anything did happen to Martin. Steve made his debut for Somerset in the game against the Pakistani tourists, then came back in August after Martin had broken his thumb. He scored two centuries in six innings; then the following year, when Martin's back gave way, he played almost a full season. He wasn't a bad signing.

Considering what we had been through, and the number of new faces in the team, the season started remarkably well. Martin Crowe was every bit as popular and influential with the younger generation of cricketers as he had been in 1984 and, when Steve Waugh arrived, he impressed everyone with his competitiveness and work ethic. Despite the battering he had taken the previous autumn, Peter Roebuck had gained in confidence as captain, and all of the newcomers, Adrian Jones included, fitted in really well. The difference in the mood of the dressing room, compared with the previous year, was palpable.

We qualified comfortably for the quarter-finals of the B&H, Neil Mallender marking his arrival with a hat-trick against the Combined Universities, and, although we lost our opening game in the championship against Lancashire, we had the better of a high-scoring draw against Surrey, then beat Gloucestershire by an innings on a beast of a pitch with a large wet patch at one end. It would have suited Mallender down to the ground, except that Roebuck lost the toss and David Graveney put us in!

By now, my knees were completely shot, my back was periodically playing up and my eyesight was continuing to deteriorate. I think I only played against Gloucestershire because injuries meant I was the last batsman standing. I like to think that my opening partnership of 60 with Nigel Felton was the key to our win. If we had been out early, we could easily have been five or six down at lunch against Syd Lawrence and Courtney Walsh. As it was, Jon Hardy made a gritty century, Crowe a typically stylish 61 and Neil Burns showed what a useful acquisition he was with a valuable 50 down the order. Roebuck was able to declare at 376/9, then Gloucestershire were bowled out twice by Mallender and Marks, with Adrian Jones and Graham Rose also picking up useful wickets. My winter recruitment efforts had not been in vain!

It was back down to earth with a bump in the B&H quarter-final against Northants: a 29-run defeat, BC Rose bowled Capel 0. Then it was up to Leicester for what turned out to be my last game for Somerset. Not that I knew that at the time, but I could sense that the end was coming, and the thought of giving up cricket honestly did not bother me. I stayed with the team for the rest of that season, helping out with bits of advice whenever I was asked and keeping an eye both on our own youngsters coming up through the seconds and on other promising cricketers around the country.

There was no big send-off at the County Ground, which was a bit of a shame, but I was given a retirement dinner at Millfield School, jointly with Tony Brown, who was moving to be a big wheel at the TCCB. The main speaker was Colin Atkinson, which I thought was a bit rich, given what he had said about me after the Worcester declaration. Apart from that, it was an enjoyable occasion!

12

Paper tiger

I had first come across St Regis Paper Company as one of our more prominent Somerset sponsors. Originally an American company, they had bought Wansbrough Paper Mill at Watchet in 1979 and set about raising its profile. Every summer they would take a marquee at the Weston Festival to entertain their customers, as well as having 'St Regis Paper' on boundary boards at the County Ground. As part of my duties as captain, and as one of the keenest promoters of sponsorship at the club, I made a point of visiting their marquee and got to know both the Sales Director, John Leahy, and the Managing Director, David Norman.

The possibility of my joining the company after my retirement from cricket was first suggested by John Leahy, who was, and is still, a huge Somerset cricket supporter. My contacts with him over sponsorship had shown him that I had a good commercial brain, and I think he liked the fact that I could talk easily to his customers, plus of course I had a reasonably good image as a successful captain well regarded in the cricket world.

My first match of the 1987 season, against Oxford University in the Parks, coincided with the St Regis company's managing director, Sandy Stratton, driving down the M4 in his Jaguar, and it was arranged that I should meet up with him at Membury Services, to talk through the possibilities. The meeting seemed to go well enough. Although he didn't offer me a job, there was a pretty clear understanding that, if I wanted to join St Regis for a trial period when I retired from cricket, the opportunity would be there.

The plan was that I should eventually take over as Sales Director for the Wansbrough Mill when John retired in a few years' time. But first, as a complete novice, I had to learn the ropes of the paper industry. So after I had retired in the autumn of 1987, they sent me first of all to UMIST, the University of Manchester Institute of Science and Technology, for an introductory course in paper-making. Then, in the new year, it was up to the Robert Gordon University in Aberdeen for a four-month diploma course in paper technology, which I somehow managed to pass. After that, I was installed as Commercial Manager at the Watchet Mill, a post I held for about five years.

At Wansborough we made lightweight glazed papers for sweetie bags and doilies and corrugated paper for cardboard boxes, although the bulk of our production went for envelopes, mostly at the John Dickinson factories at Sawston near Cambridge and Washington in the north-east. By this stage almost all of our production was from recycled paper and cardboard. Paper-making is only profitable if it is a continuous process, 24 hours a day, seven days a week. The only prolonged time the machines stopped running was over Christmas and the New Year, when the engineers would move in. The cardinal sin is to have to shut down a machine for lack of orders, and this put huge pressure on the sales side. As Commercial Manager, my job was to act as liaison between transport and incoming orders on the one side and engineering and production on the other. We had a huge board in the operations room on which incoming orders would be posted alongside the production schedule, and woe betide the Commercial Manager if he got it wrong! The great thing about that job was that it involved all sides of the business, from raw material in to finished product out. That did not make me a paper-making expert overnight – and some colleagues and customers would take great delight in testing me out on my technical knowledge in the early days – but it did show that I could handle a highly technical and responsible role. I was not just a retired cricketer looking for an easy ride.

In 1994 John Leahy finally retired, to head off to Australia for England's winter tour, and I took over as Sales Director. Unlike the role of Commercial Manager, in which I spent most of my time at the mill, this involved travel – and lots of it: not only the length and breadth of Britain but also, increasingly, overseas, as I worked hard to develop the export side of the business. This was where my experience as a cricketer really came in handy because, whilst I never much enjoyed being away from home for long periods, I was at least used to it. I also had a supremely efficient PA, Rita Backhurst, to make all the arrangements for me: booking hotels, buying air tickets, arranging meetings and so on. Every Monday morning I would be at the mill first thing for our management meeting. Then I would be on the road, often to either Bristol or Heathrow airports to fly out to meet existing or potential customers across Western Europe. We did a lot of business in Germany and Holland, and I was particularly successful in developing sales into Southern Ireland.

One of my first forays into Europe was when I was still Commercial Manager. Every year the big European paper-makers would get together at a conference somewhere, to discuss trade-related problems. That eventually got them into trouble with the competition authorities, and new regulations came in through the European Union. This particular conference was held at the Hotel du Lac, just outside Zurich, and was hosted by St Regis, in the person of John Leahy. As usual, a good time was had by all, including a slap-up dinner and drinks on the last night. When I came down the next morning, I discovered that John had already departed, leaving a note asking me to settle the bill, as he wanted it to appear on my expenses claim, rather than his! This came as something of a shock. I did have my rather battered Barclaycard, but I didn't think there was much more than £90 of credit left on it, and the bill was for £850. Still, there was nothing for it but to try, so I handed the card to the receptionist, fearing the worst. And do you know what? The card went through and the bill was paid!

I had two excellent sales managers working under me: Derek Jones for the north of the country and David Kirk for the south. They would usually make the first contact, then we would meet a customer together, often over lunch or dinner. I have always been a great believer in looking after your customers, whether they are our faithful members at the County Ground or a firm of Singaporean doily manufacturers. And again this was an area where my cricket connections certainly helped. When the Ondaatje Pavilion was built at the County Ground, we took out a lease on what I thought was the best of the hospitality suites, and every year we would organise a big day out for our customers: cricket with all the trimmings during the day, then a dinner in the evening, which some of the Somerset players would attend. It was the sort of occasion which none of our competitors could match. Quite apart from that, if there was a particular customer I wanted to impress, what better than to invite them for a day's cricket in our company box. It became a great business asset.

Thanks to John Leahy, St Regis had a high profile at the ground. Quite early in my time with the company, he asked me what they could most usefully do to help the club. This was just after the rule on fully covered pitches had come in, so I suggested he could get us a decent set of covers. Rather than buying them, he had them made by our engineers at the Watchet Mill and they did good service for many years, always with the 'St Regis Paper' logo on the top of them, and 'Wansbrough Paper Mill' on each end.

I like to think I did a pretty good job as Sales Director in what was a hugely competitive business. The technology of paper-making was evolving all the time, particularly on the health and safety front, where the industry's record was poor, and you had to keep running just to stand still. Rapidly rising energy costs, as compared with our overseas competitors, were another big challenge. The money was pretty good, certainly compared with what I had been earning as a cricketer. With St Regis, I earned twice the amount I was on at Somerset, plus a bonus based on profit margin. The most I had earned with Somerset was £15,000, even though that had

Some serious gardening at Ashtrees in East Brent, which I bought with the money from my benefit and where we lived from 1983 to 1991

made me, at least according to the *Daily Telegraph*, 'one of the highest paid cricketers in England'!

But all good things come to an end and, as we went through the 1990s, I became increasingly aware that big changes were afoot, driven from the very top of the St Regis business. Rather than having separate sales teams and work programming for each of the company's mills, the plan was to centralise sales from the group mills into a single, national operation. So for the last year or so of my time with the company, I had the job of running down my own sales force, knowing that, at the end of the process, I would be out of a job as well. I could see perfectly well why they were doing it, and that it was no reflection of the performance of myself and my sales team, so I didn't feel any great resentment. Even so, I was sad to be leaving an industry that I had very much enjoyed working in, and in which I reckoned I had made a worthwhile contribution.

I also learned a lot about future planning, a subject I implemented when I became Director of Cricket at Somereset. I was not going to make the same mistakes Somerset had made in the mid-'80s. Ironically, just about the first thing that I did after I left St Regis was to produce a report for our main competitors, the Scottish company Smith Anderson. They were struggling and, aware of my success in overseas markets, asked me to write a report on how they could develop the export side of the business. It didn't seem to do them much good, as a few years later the paper-making side of the business went into receivership. Sadly Wansbrough Mill was shut in 2015, and a lot of people in the area lost their living.

My next business venture was much closer to home. Whilst I had been with St Regis, my younger son Joey had attended Birmingham University, studying Geography, but had decided not to pursue an academic career but to make the most of his undoubted talent in carpentry. He had also inherited a lot of my and my father's horticultural skills. So, after he had taken a college course in Taunton, we decided to set up our own little business, BCR Services, doing landscape gardening and constructing wooden-framed buildings such as greenhouses and conservatories. We had a lot of help from my great friend Tony Jarvis, who ran what used to be The Goat House on the A38 at Brent Knoll and who had also, by coincidence, been in the paper industry as an agent for St Regis and other companies. A lot of new housing development was going on at the time, and we picked up plenty of work landscaping the new estates around Weston. We also did custom-built kitchens, one of many satisfied customers being David Graveney's son John at his house in Bristol. BCR Services is still going, although I can't really do anything with my hands these days because of arthritis, whilst Joey has been contracting out his carpentry skills. He has been doing very well refurbishing hotels in London and Bristol and National Trust properties in West Somerset.

It is interesting how the two boys have turned out: Joey having definitely inherited my practical, hands-on skills whilst his elder brother Stuart takes after his mother, having passed every exam in sight and done really well in the insurance business, currently as Managing Director of Birnbeck Insurance Services, based at Worle, a company owned by one of my best friends from school, Simon Wotton. I am equally proud of both of them!

Stevie, meanwhile, had not been idle whilst I was making my way in the paper industry. She had always been much the more academic of the two of us and decided to make up for missing out on university when she had married me by taking a four-year degree course as a mature student at Bristol in Spanish, with a subsidiary in the history of Spanish art, something which fitted in well with our regular trips to our apartment in Estepona. That was something else that made me very proud!

Stevie (right) graduating with a BA in Spanish
from the University of Bristol, 1993

13

Somerset cricket in the 1990s

I had resigned as Cricket Development Officer when I took the job with St Regis in 1988, but that didn't mean that I lost touch with Somerset cricket. I was still a member of the Cricket Committee, which by now was being chaired by that wonderful West Indian opening batsman Roy Marshall, who had retired from playing for Hampshire in 1972 and now kept the Westgate Inn in Taunton with his wife Shirley and three daughters. Roy was a quiet, gentle man who disliked controversy and was just the man to restore some calm to Somerset's cricketing waters after the storms of 1986. To help him in that task he soon had the services of my old friend Jackie Birkenshaw, who was appointed to succeed me as Cricket Manager (the role I had effectively played in everything but name) after handing in his umpire's white coat at the end of the 1988 season. Somerset also had a new Chief Executive, as the role of Secretary was redefined, with Peter Anderson, from Devon by way of the Hong Kong Police Service, taking over from Tony Brown that same summer.

It was Peter Anderson who called me in one day to ask if I could suggest an overseas batsman to replace Steve Waugh, who had followed on from Martin Crowe and, after a wonderful season for Somerset, would not be available for 1989. I said I would think about it, knowing that we would need someone pretty good to live up to Messrs Chappell, Richards, Crowe and Waugh, and was doing just that when I happened to watch a report on BBC television news about floodlit cricket, which included footage of a day-night game in South Africa. It reminded me of a game I had watched at Newlands when I was out in South Africa in the mid-1970s. Playing for Transvaal that day was a young right-handed batsman called Jimmy Cook, and I remembered having been seriously impressed with his batting: upright stance, head still, classic shots. Not having really kept track of South African cricket during their exclusion from Test cricket, I thought, "I wonder what happened to him."

The other South African batsman I had had in mind was rather older and better-known: Graeme Pollock, whom I had approached back in 1979, when we were looking for a replacement for Viv for the 1980 season. OK, so he'd said he was too heavily committed back then, he was into his forties by now and had announced his retirement from cricket in South Africa – but the man was genuine class, and you never know…!

I rang him up, first of all to ask about his own availability. He said he was flattered to be asked, but that his business interests now took priority, so he would not be able to come. "So who else could you suggest?" I asked, and the very first name he came up with was Jimmy Cook. "Fine," I said. "Here's my number. Perhaps you could ask him to give me a ring." – which he did, after about a week.

"Would you be interested in playing for Somerset?" I asked.

"Interested? Man, I'd swim over there to play for you guys!"

So I armed myself with some footage of Jimmy batting and went to see Peter Anderson again. He said to me, "If you think he's the right man, then I'm prepared to trust your judgement." The deal was done.

Signing Jimmy was a bit of a gamble, given that he was 36, had never played a Test match and had hardly played outside South Africa, but it was a gamble that paid off spectacularly. In his three seasons with Somerset, Jimmy scored 7,604 runs, at an average of 72.41, with 28 hundreds and a top score of 313 not out against Glamorgan, as well as any number of match-winning innings in one-day cricket. Yet, although he was one of the most classically correct batsmen I have ever seen, those figures say almost as much about the sort of pitches we were playing on at Taunton as they do about Jimmy Cook. In those three seasons Somerset could win only six county championship games at Taunton, a ground on which Jimmy Cook averaged over 81!

If Somerset were ever going to be in with a chance of winning a first county championship, they had to win more of their home games but, to do that, they needed bowlers who could take wickets on the immaculate pitches that Phil Frost was by now preparing. By the early 1990s there was such a bowler in prospect – Andy Caddick, born in New Zealand to English parents but having to be treated as an overseas cricketer until his four years' qualifying was up. So, for all his runs and his popularity with both team-mates and supporters, that meant Jimmy Cook giving way to Andy Caddick as Somerset's overseas player for the 1992 season.

Peter Anderson was mainly responsible for recruiting Andy, who had played a game or two for Middlesex 2nds after his arrival from New Zealand in 1988. My first encounter with him was in a match at Clevedon in which I had – unwisely as it turned out – agreed to play for Trevor Gard and Dennis Breakwell's benefit year. The Clevedon chairman had connections with Andy and had persuaded him to play for the club whilst he served his

Andy Caddick

qualification period. Anyway, Andy knew that I was Cricket Chairman, and he was determined to impress. My first ball from him was past my nose almost before I had lifted the bat; the second I somehow managed to fend off from my ribs. I called down the pitch to him: "Hang on, Andy. It's OK. You're signed!"

I had taken over as Chairman of Cricket in 1991, when Roy Marshall was sadly forced to stand down by the skin cancer which would kill him the following year. As for Jackie Birkenshaw, although he did a great job as Cricket Manager and was popular with players and spectators alike, life in Somerset didn't really suit him from a family point of view, and in 1992 he resigned, Bob Cottam taking over. After the riches of the '70s and early '80s, the supply of local talent, if not drying up entirely, had certainly slowed to a trickle. At one level, that meant that we could only really strengthen the side by bringing in players from other counties. Hence the arrival of good experienced players like Chris Tavaré, David Graveney, Andy Hayhurst and Peter Bowler. But it also showed that we had to do much more to nurture and develop our own young cricketers. As far as I was concerned, that meant investing in facilities better than the dark, dank indoor nets in the bowels of the old pavilion.

Fortunately I found a kindred spirit in Peter Anderson. I had liked him straightaway; he was forthright, spoke his mind and knew his cricket. We worked well together. When he asked me what he needed to do to produce good, local talent, I replied, "Build an indoor school of excellence," and he did, with the financial support of Sir Christopher Ondaatje. Opened in 1995, the new facilities were hugely important in developing home-grown talent such as Richard Harden, Marcus Trescothick, Keith Parsons, Jason Kerr and Rob Turner as well as being a valuable asset for the wider cricketing community.

I had first seen Trescothick in a schools match. But it was when he came to Taunton to play for our Under-15s and I saw him batting in the nets that I realised we had something special on our hands. He had – still has! – such a wonderful natural ability to hit a cricket ball. One or two technical issues held him back in his early years with Somerset, the same sort of technical flaws that held me back in the early 1970s: an issue with his head position and a tendency to plant the right leg on the line of leg stump and go after the ball outside the off. But I knew that he would sort those out in time, not least because – unlike me! – he absolutely loved batting in the nets – and still does!

In 1996, when the runs had dried up for our captain Andy Hayhurst, I got a call from Peter Anderson when I was in a board meeting at the

Watchet Mill. He said that there was a problem with the team selection for the game starting that morning against Hampshire, I knew exactly what to do. "Drop Hayhurst, make Peter Bowler captain and play Trescothick," I said straightaway, "and tell Hayhurst yourself, but not in front of the other players." Later that morning he called me back, wanting to know what time I would be arriving at the County Ground, so that he could meet me in the car park. When I got there, not knowing the score, he came up to me and said straight out, "You are an effing golden bollocks, you are, Rosey." Baffled, I asked what he meant. "Trescothick's 90 not out," he replied, and Marcus went on to get 178. But there was no luck about that decision. I knew class when I saw it.

Mark Lathwell

Marcus's opening partner that day was Mark Lathwell, an almost equally talented batsman but with a much less happy story. Like many other people, I felt that it was too early for him when he was picked for the third Test against Australia in 1993. It was not that he lacked the ability to play Test cricket, but mentally there was no way he was ready for it. To make things worse, the way he was handled by the England set-up was dreadful. Here you had a shy young man from North Devon, lacking in self-confidence, with a tendency to drift away into his own private world, suddenly dropped into the deep end of an international dressing room. He was in the squad for two one-day internationals against Australia but made twelfth man for both. Then, when he was included in the side for the Trent Bridge Test, instead of giving him the help and support which any of us could have told them he needed, he was left alone in a corner and generally made to feel even less adequate than he already believed himself to be. It broke my heart to see what happened to Mark. Probably he was not cut out mentally for top-level cricket, but to be treated like that and then dropped after just two games was shocking.

That was the year when another remarkable cricketer arrived at Somerset, Mushtaq Ahmed. Caddick had served out his qualification period by now, leaving a place for an overseas cricketer, and it was perfectly obvious that, if we were going to win matches at Taunton, we needed a top-class bowler, preferably a spinner, to complement Caddick's pace. I had been on tour to Pakistan and faced Abdul Qadir in his prime, so I had a good idea what quality leg-spinners could achieve on good pitches. So, when Mushtaq became available, Peter Anderson, Bob Cottam and I decided to sign him.

Mushtaq was another inspired choice. In his first season with us he took 85 wickets at 20.85, including several match-winning spells. Not only that, but his bubbly personality, infectious enthusiasm and willingness to bowl all day made him hugely popular with everyone at the club: supporters, team-mates, committee-men and, not least, the Cricket Chairman! I said at the time, "He has been the model overseas player; he wins matches for the club and adds members."

Sadly, towards the end of his time with us, he got himself mixed up with some dubious characters on the fringes of the Pakistan dressing room. There was talk of match-fixing, Mushtaq himself was clearly distracted, his bowling a shadow of its former self and, midway through the 1998 season, I decided that the best thing to do was to get him back to his family in Pakistan, out of harm's way. It was a sad way for his Somerset career to come to an end, after all the pleasure and success he had given us over the previous five years, but I was convinced it was in his best interests – and ours. Mushie evidently thought so, too. Years later, when I was Director of Cricket and we were playing Sussex at Horsham, I met up with him for the first time since we had put him on the plane to Karachi. He went down on his hands and knees in front of me, saying, over and over again, "Oh thank you, Mr. Rose. Thank you from the bottom of my heart. You saved my career." It was all a bit embarrassing, but in a good way!

After the triumphs and trauma of the 1980s, the 1990s was a relatively uneventful decade for Somerset cricket, at least until the arrival of Dermot Reeve as coach in 1997. Like many other people in cricket, I had been a huge admirer of what he had done at Warwickshire, where he had turned a fairly ordinary county side into multiple trophy winners, and I was delighted when Peter Anderson made the most of the Hong Kong connection to bring him to Somerset. He only played a handful of one-day games for us, but he made a big impact as Director of Cricket for three years, with his emphasis on fitness and the innovative tactics that he employed in one-day cricket. It was a shame that, after reaching the final of the NatWest in 1999, we failed to do ourselves justice and were comfortably beaten by Gloucestershire. That hurt, I can tell you! But it was an affable decade, in which the club was well run, the wounds caused by the 1986 controversy largely healed, and the task of chairing the Cricket Committee became easier, as more of our own young players came through.

I like to think that the culmination of all that was winning the Cheltenham & Gloucester in 2001. It remains, as I write, the only trophy that Somerset have won without my being either club captain or Director of Cricket, but the team that won at Lord's that day was very much the one that Peter Anderson and I had put together over the previous ten years. Vic Marks had taken over from me as Cricket Chairman and, as I followed the game from Munich, where I had the great good fortune to watch England beat Germany 5-1, I did feel a distinct sense of pride as the final Leicestershire wicket fell. Well done, Vic!

14

In sickness and in health

I think it would be fair to say that I have not had the best of luck with injuries over the years.

My first encounter with the surgeons was when I was still at Borough Road, playing the odd match for Somerset in the summer vacation. I started to develop lumps on my left hand and forearm. They turned out to be lesions on the arteries – non-malignant fortunately but nasty enough to have seriously affected my ability to hold a bat, so they were taken out immediately. That was followed by the usual crop of injuries to which a left-handed opening batsman was prone in those days, when the protective equipment, gloves especially, was so poor: broken fingers, cracked ribs courtesy of Sylvester Clarke, the arm broken by Craig McDermott and goodness knows what else.

Ribs cracked by Sylvester Clarke

Thigh pads, such as they were, offered very little protection, so that the insides of my thighs were often black and blue from the battering which they took from lifting balls on seaming pitches.

But my worst problems, then and now, were always to do with my teeth. Over the years I must have spent thousands of hours in dentists' chairs and thousands of pounds in dentists' fees! It had all started with that incident in Singapore when I was about 10, when I was hit smack in the mouth by a rock thrown by one of the locals who had decided to have a go at us. Two of my upper front teeth had been broken in half and, for some reason, they insisted that they could not be properly repaired, with crowns, until I was 18. So, for years and years, I was making regular visits to the dentist to have the pretty useless compact fillings replaced, until finally, when I was 18, the teeth were properly crowned.

The next episode was when I was hit just below my right eye in Perth in the winter of 1976/77. A huge abscess formed, which spread down through the inside of my cheek and eventually reached my lower jaw, resulting in the loss of my four middle teeth. For a time I made do with a plate, which was constantly falling out and was very far from ideal if you were a professional cricketer. Eventually, when new techniques were developed, I paid a lot of money to have implants put in at either side of the gap, with a bridge to hold the replacement teeth in place. But that was also a problem because, every three months or so, the bridge would fall off, and then the only way I could speak was with a pronounced lisp. Some of the players – notably Peter Trego, because it happened was when I was in the course of signing him – thought this was a great laugh, but it was not so funny for me when I was trying to make myself understood as Director of Cricket.

By this stage I was getting problems with my upper teeth as well. Eventually it got so bad that I became reluctant to leave the house. Fortunately, Peter Trego and Graham Masarik knew what was going on and had a word with Ian Thomas, who looks after player welfare issues for the Professional Cricketers' Association in Wales and the West. He got in touch with me straight away, and I was referred to David Houston, of the Houston Dental Group, who did a brilliant job, putting in two plates, top and bottom. They still come adrift from time to time, but it has given me my confidence back and the ability to live a normal life. And all thanks to the PCA.

If I had had to pay for my treatment myself, it would have cost me something like £7,500, which I simply could not have afforded. The PCA do a wonderful job, not just helping people like me, whose lives have been blighted by injuries suffered during our playing careers, but in providing counselling and support for the very many cricketers who suffer from mental problems of one sort or another. And the two are very often linked, because physical problems often lead on to mental problems, as you struggle to cope with whatever the issue may be.

In 2017, I was asked to appear in a promotional video for the PCA and was absolutely delighted to do so, not only because of the help they gave me, but because I know from long experience how many other cricketers they have helped over the years. Most cricketers do not make big money, as in some other sports, and the prospects can look pretty bleak when you retire, say in your mid-thirties. You may have injury problems or financial worries or family breakdown to cope with, because of the nature of a professional cricketer's life. That is why the PCA is so important, now as much as ever.

I have already written about the back problems that brought an end to my cricket career. For about 14 years after I'd had my first spinal injection at Nevill Hall Hospital, the problem would flare up from time, and I always had to be careful not to twist my back more than could possibly be avoided. It meant that I was wary of playing even charity and benefit cricket matches and led eventually to having to give up my golf at Burnham & Berrow. I was always on edge, half expecting my back to go into spasm, which didn't make life easy, given that I was having to travel all over Europe in my role with St Regis. The episode that brought matters to a head happened when I was flying back from a business trip into Heathrow. This time, my back spasmed so badly that I could not move. When the plane landed, they had to leave me in my seat, in absolute agony, until all the other passengers had got off and they could bring a stretcher to carry me off the plane. I finished that journey in a wheelchair in a train.

Fortunately, a consultant called Mr Webb had just arrived in the West Country from one of the London hospitals, bringing with him a new technique for dealing with prolapsed discs. Instead of the injections, or the more drastic operation to fuse the relevant vertebrae, he had developed a technique whereby the surgeon remodelled the troublesome discs, removing the sections causing the pressure. Equally fortunately, I had private health insurance, paid for by St Regis, which meant that I could be referred for this new operation at the Nuffield almost immediately. It worked a treat. Within two days of having the operation I was up and about, and within two weeks I was walking normally. I still have to be careful, and still get the occasional twinge, but in comparison with what I went through in the '80s and '90s, it has been a blessed relief. In fact, when I left St Regis to join my son Joey in the gardening and carpentry business, I was fitter physically than at any time since the peak of my playing career.

But that happy state of affairs did not last for long! One day, Joey and I were working on a staircase leading from a ground floor flat to a garden flat in Weston. I made the mistake of leaning on the spindles at the top, thinking they were secure. Well they weren't! They gave way, sending me crashing head-first down the stairs, finishing in a heap at the bottom with my head cut open. Joey rescued me and got me home to bed, and it wasn't until a couple of days later that I realised that my wrists, shoulders and knees had swollen up so badly that I couldn't get out of bed. I was taken to hospital on a stretcher, where they diagnosed polymyalgic rheumatica. I had swellings everywhere and could not move for about nine months, despite all of the medication I was on, including big doses of steroids. It then turned out that, apart from polymyalgic rheumatica, I had rheumatoid arthritis, something that is incurable at the present time. That was a blow, I can tell you, but over the last three years or so I've learned to live with it, coming to terms with what I can and cannot do. My walking is fine, which means that I can still take the dogs out, thank goodness, but I am very wary of going down a flight of stairs and I can't do much lifting or raising my arms above shoulder height, which makes dressing and undressing fairly tricky.

No, fortune has not been very kind to me in terms of illness and injuries, what with four knee operations, three back operations, thousands of painful visits to the dentist and now rheumatoid arthritis. At times, that has been hard to take; there are times when I think 'Why me?', especially when set against all the golden days I have enjoyed in my association with Somerset cricket. Some of the dark days have been very black indeed. What has kept me going and saved me from self-pity has been the tremendous support of my friends and family, Stevie in particular. She, like me, has a natural tenacity and determination, allied to great pride in her family, and that has seen us through some difficult times.

The other factor has been the overwhelming support that I have enjoyed from the general public and, in particular, the Somerset members and supporters, and that includes very many who weren't around in the glory years when we won all those trophies. They can see the development of the ground, recognise the success of the indoor cricket school, appreciate the fact that Somerset have been in the first division of the Championship for longer than any other county, and are kind enough to attribute some of the credit for those achievements to me. Nothing provides a better antidote to occasional gloom than that, and nothing has given me greater satisfaction.

But if I have so far managed to avoid succumbing to depression, many other cricketers have not been so lucky. All professional sport is stressful. I have been stressed at times throughout my cricket career, probably more so as Director of Cricket than when I was captain, because you can't directly influence events. They always knew when things were going wrong at the

County Ground when I would get my two dogs out of the car and set off for a walk down the river bank, because I couldn't bear to watch what was going on in the middle.

With cricket, what sometimes turns that stress into serious mental problems is time. Most team games are over within 90 minutes or so. With cricket, a game can last for up to five days – five days in which you've got almost too much time to think, to watch, to brood, and then suddenly you've got to perform, with not just your individual fate but that of the entire team resting on your shoulders. It's hardly surprising that some cricketers find it hard to cope.

I can't say I was very conscious of the mental side when I was playing. It was when I had the senior management role with St Regis, going on to be Director of Cricket for Somerset, that I began to recognise when stress was turning into something more serious. With Marcus Trescothick, for instance, I could tell that he was seriously stressed by playing for England, even before I spoke to him about it. I could see it in his eyes. The time when he flew out with me and Andy Nash for the Champions Trophy in Dubai, and we did everything possible to ease the pressure on him, even arranging for a chat with Sunny Gavaskar, whom I had bumped into in Dubai airport, I knew that he wasn't going to be able to make it. And what a credit it is to him that he has been so open and honest about his problems. That must have been a tremendous help to many other cricketers going through similar difficulties.

In my experience, two types of character are particularly susceptible to mental problems. The first are the jokers, who are almost too outgoing, too anxious to seek company and approval from their team-mates, as if almost to distract themselves from their inner thoughts. The other group are the quiet ones, who keep themselves to themselves and find it difficult to confide in team-mates, family or friends.

Travel is a big factor in the equation. You are away from home a lot, particularly if you are an international cricketer, and these days you usually don't even have the company of a room-mate, as cricketers tend to get given single rooms. When I went on my first tour, to Pakistan, I had Geoff Cope as my room-mate, and what a great bloke he was. It would be a bit different, of course, if you were rooming with Geoff Boycott, or with a serial snorer – but, by and large, room-sharing has got to be a good thing for cricketers on tour.

We were lucky in that Somerset dressing room of the late '70s and early '80s. We had a wonderful cross-section of different backgrounds and personalities, from the wurzels, through the university lads, to the West Indians and the good-time boys. We did not always get on, but everyone spoke their mind and nothing was allowed to fester. It was a brilliant mix.

15

Director of Cricket

After standing down as Chairman of Cricket in 1999, I had stayed involved on the fringes, watching the odd game and being asked for my opinion on various issues from time to time. Then in 2004, with Somerset languishing in mid-table in the second division of the Championship and not winning much in the one-day stuff, I was asked to join Roy Kerslake and Vic Marks on what was called the Cricket Review Committee, to make some recommendations for improving both the quality and the management of Somerset cricket. What we proposed was what I had been arguing for for years: the separation of the running of the club from the running of the cricket, which should be taken out of the hands of an unwieldy committee and become subject to professional management.

So it was not a complete a surprise when I got a call from the club the following year, asking if I'd be interested in applying for the job of Chief Executive, as successor to the retiring Peter Anderson. I didn't say yes straightaway, because I was very much involved with Joey and BCR Services but, after talking it over with Stevie and the boys, we decided yes, I would give it a go. I didn't really know the Chairman, Giles Clarke, but I reckoned that, with my cricket knowledge and the business skills I had learned with St Regis, I could do a good job.

The final interviews were due to be held at the Holiday Inn, out by the M5. Giles Clarke, Roy Kerslake and one or two others were there, plus, to my surprise, Richard Gould. I had known his father Bobby a bit, from my visits to Bristol City, but Richard only by reputation. Anyway, he and I were sat down together, and Giles came straight out with what he had in mind: "We've discussed all the points in your report, Brian, and we've talked it over with the committee. Our plan is to appoint a Chief Executive to take charge of membership, marketing, the development of the ground and the commercial side, and a Director of Cricket, to take charge of the cricketing side of things, including the pitch." He pointed at me and said, "We want you, Brian, to be Director of Cricket and you, Richard, to be Chief Executive."

I decided to accept, and I always had an excellent relationship with Richard Gould. He knows his own mind and is not a man to mess with, but he gave me complete freedom as to how to spend the cricketing budget we had been given by the ECB – just as long as I didn't overspend it! Continuity was provided by the stalwart Sally Donoghue, who had been Peter Anderson's right-hand person and who would perform the same invaluable role for Richard Gould. What a help and support she was to me through all my time as Cricket Chairman and Director of Cricket.

I got to grips with a strategy for our cricket straightaway, looking at the players who were coming towards the end of their careers, the home-grown talent coming through and the two or three players we needed to sign if we were going to start winning cricket matches.

Fortunately I had a great ally in Graeme 'Biff' Smith, who had been appointed captain earlier in that 2005 season. He and I saw eye to eye on what the priorities were and how our cricket should be managed. He was also, of course, a brilliant captain. He was almost Closey-like in the command he had of his players but much better at explaining to them what he wanted and how they were going to help him get it. For a man of only 24, he had remarkable presence and self-confidence, as well as being a great player in his own right.

We agreed that our first priority was to do something about Somerset's one-day cricket, which meant pensioning off one or two of the more senior players and bringing in some new blood, particularly on the bowling side. Mike Burns, who had captained the side the previous season, was already planning a career in umpiring and was happy enough to move on. But it was a different story with Rob Turner, who was still a top-class keeper in championship cricket but was no longer contributing the quick runs down the order that we needed in one-day cricket; I felt we needed Carl Gazzard's energy and vitality. It wasn't easy explaining to a cricketer who had given great service to Somerset and was desperate to carry on why I couldn't keep him, but it had to be done. So Burns, Turner and Aaron Laraman all played their last championship games for Somerset against Worcestershire at Bath in June that year, and I got the reputation of being a ruthless Director of Cricket, something which probably didn't do me much harm in the long run.

I used a matrix to help me plan ahead. It had four sections: first-team players, second-teamers, academy players and known Under-15s. Starting with the first team, I would make a judgement as to who would still be playing in five years' time, then what I would need to do to move academy players into the second team, and second-teamers into the firsts. If I found that I didn't have enough up-and-coming talent to fill what I reckoned would be the gaps in the first team, then I would look to sign one or more players from elsewhere.

I had not been in my new job for very long when Graeme Smith played one of the biggest and best innings I've ever seen: 311 in 255 balls against Leicestershire at Taunton. I was actually summarising for the BBC in the old commentary box on top of the Ridley Stand, and it felt very much like being in the line of fire, as big hit after big hit flew over our heads and out of the ground. Graeme sought me out at close of play to say that he had found the answer to our seam bowling problem; the man we needed to sign was none other than Charl Willoughby, the self-same bowler whose best efforts had been ending up in St James' churchyard! But it was, in fact, shrewd advice for Charl had taken 6/16 against us in the 50-over C&G earlier in the season and would go on to take 347 wickets for us in five seasons. His nagging accuracy and left-arm angle of attack were just what we needed, in limited overs as well as championship cricket.

It did not take me long to resume the winning habit. I can't in all honesty claim much of the credit for our T20 Cup win in 2005, but I did change the personnel very quickly, which gave Graeme Smith and our new coach, Mark Garaway, the opportunity to change the way we played – we became a very good fielding side, for instance. Arguably, the moment that turned the final against Lancashire at The Oval was when Wes Durston, an outstandingly good fielder, ran out Andrew Symonds. Of the side who won that game, only four had played in our last T20 game in the previous season. With Marcus at the top of the order, Andy Caddick and Richard Johnson still two of the best opening bowlers in the country, Ian Blackwell in the middle order at a time when he was a very threatening cricketer, Charl Langeveldt a real box of tricks in white-ball cricket and with Carl Gazzard's enthusiasm and vitality behind the stumps, we very quickly became a force to be reckoned with.

The really big change came when I signed Justin Langer. I had seen him get runs at Lord's and had been impressed, as much by his attitude as his skill so, when I heard that he was available for five weeks or so in the summer of 2006, I stepped in straightaway. It didn't take him long to make an impact. In his second championship game he amassed 342 against Surrey at Guildford, which was, and remains, the highest individual score by a Somerset batsman. After that innings he came up to me and said, "Do you know what, Rosey? This team is going places. You've got some great players and, in Sarge [Andy Hurry], just about the best coach in the world. I'd love to come back next year if I get the chance."

Langer and Hurry were indeed the perfect pairing. They got on like a house on fire: both fitness fanatics, both strict disciplinarians. When I got the chance to sign Justin as captain for the following season, I leapt at it. We had a few players at that time who might have been trouble if given enough rope. Justin and Sarge gave them no rope at all. With me to provide the overall strategy and sign new players, everything was in place for the team to go forward quickly, which is exactly what we did in 2007.

The contrast between those two seasons – 2006, when we finished bottom of Division 2, and 2007, when we won 10 championship matches and the Second Division title by the length of a street – could hardly have been more dramatic. Justin Langer, as both captain and batsman, was a big part of the explanation for that. But to win matches, you have to take wickets and the other absolutely vital ingredient in our success that year was our opening attack of Caddick and Willoughby. They were the perfect combination: Caddick, always so keen to bowl and always so accurate, swinging the ball away from the right-handers at pace; Willoughby swinging it into the right-handers from close to the stumps and every now and then getting one to go the other way. Perhaps their finest performance in tandem was at Bristol, where Caddick had match figures of 12/71 and Willoughby 7/121 to roll Gloucestershire over by an innings. Between them, they took 132 wickets that season and, with Pete Trego and Steffan Jones in support, we had the strongest seam attack since the days of Garner, Botham and Dredge.

Not that it looked as if was going to work out that way at the start of the season. The pitch at Taunton had been a concern for me from the moment I took over as Director of Cricket. Phil Frost was a perfectionist and also something of a law unto himself when it came to preparing his pitches. Yes, they were beautiful to bat on, manicured to a fault, but we were never going to win many matches if our home pitch was a batsman's paradise. Given that the strength of our attack was with seam, we tried leaving a bit more grass in the middle of the pitches so that they looked a lot greener. It did cause some consternation among visiting sides, who tended to go into a bit of a huddle when they first saw the playing surface, as if to say "This isn't the sort of pitch we expect at Taunton." But early on in that season, it did not seem to make much difference. We made 850/7 against Middlesex in the first home game, and Derby racked up 801 in the second, after which I gave an interview in which I compared the pitch to the M4 motorway! But what that extra greenness did provide, for Caddick and Willoughby especially, was a bit of extra bounce and carry, so that if a batsman got a nick, it would carry to wicket-keeper or slips.

Five of our batsmen scored over 1,000 championship runs that season: Trescothick (1,315), Langer (1,231), James Hildreth (1,147), Neil Edwards (1,039) and Cameron White, who ended up topping the averages with 1,083 runs at 72.2. He was another big factor in our success. It was in a conversation with Greg Chappell that I had first heard of him as a promising young all-rounder, and what an asset he proved to be. Two innings, which I particularly remember, are the 260 not out he scored when we were trying to save the game against Derbyshire in 2006 and his quite remarkable 141 not out in a T20 game at Worcester that same season, scored off 70 balls out of a total of 198/4 – and somehow we contrived to lose!

Our only championship defeat in 2007 was against Middlesex at Lord's, the game in which Langer declared our first innings at 50/8, to give our bowlers a crack at the Middlesex batsmen while there was still plenty in the wicket. It didn't work out in the end, but it was typical of Langer's combative captaincy and a tribute to his confidence in his bowlers. After that, we won six out of our next eight games, making sure of promotion by beating Glamorgan, the game in which Craig Kieswetter confirmed his infinite promise by making 93, batting at number eight, and taking eight catches. After that, we headed up to Chelmsford, knowing that a win there would give us the second division championship.

I did not get to the ground until the morning of the game, to be greeted with a volley of four-letter words by Peter Willey, one of the umpires, who was threatening to report Langer to Lord's. It turned out that, the day before, Justin had decided to start digging away with his spikes on a good length on one of the practice pitches. When asked by the groundsman what on earth he thought he was doing, he replied that he was just giving the practice pitch the same sort of treatment that the real thing had been given, the implication being that Essex had scratched and dusted the wicket for the benefit of their leg-spinner, the subsequently disgraced Danish Kaneria. Peter Willey calmed down eventually, after I had suggested that we wouldn't make a fuss about the match pitch, if he didn't over the practice pitch, but it showed that Justin Langer was not a captain to be messed with – as if anyone ever doubted it!

It was a nervous afternoon as we went in search of the 182 we needed to make certain of the Division Two Championship, against Kaneria and co on a dry, turning pitch. Tres was out early on, but Edwards and Trego, who was promoted to number three to get us some quick runs, put together a partnership of 76 to steady the ship, before Hildreth and Neil McKenzie, whom I had recruited to fill the gap left by the recalled Cameron White, calmly knocked off the remaining runs. I have to confess that at one stage I did take myself off for a walk around Chelmsford town centre, such was the tension, but I was there for the finish, and a great feeling it was. It reminded me almost of 1979, when we had won those two trophies in a weekend. I knew how important it was for the club to be in Division One, and so did the players. We had come so far from bottom of the heap the previous season and played so well, but you can't actually keep the emotion of victory going for very long before your mind says, "You've done it – it's time to move on." So after a few drinks in the dressing room and in our hotel, it was back to Taunton for the final game against Notts. That was one I really badly wanted to win, for the sake of our supporters. Thanks to centuries from Tres, Blackie and Tregs, and ten wickets for our leg-spinner Michael Munday, we gave our home crowd exactly the crunching victory that they wanted, and the celebrations could begin. Justin Langer was presented with the Second Division trophy in front of the pavilion and there was an ovation for Roy Palmer, standing in his final match after 29 years as a first-class umpire. He had been in the Somerset side in my very first game, back in 1969.

Justin Langer holds up the Division Two trophy

For our home town celebrations we (and a good many of our supporters) chose the Dellers Wharf night club next to the bridge in Taunton town centre. It turned out to be a fairly eventful evening! First, Justin Langer got himself thrown out for getting involved in some sort of fracas with an individual who had obviously over-indulged. Then, when I came to pay the team's £1,200 bar bill with my Somerset CCC American Express Card, the barman said he wouldn't accept it. It had to be cash. Now I can't say that I was entirely sober myself so, when he told me that and then refused to give me an invoice to be paid by the club, saying that I would have to go to a cashpoint, I'm afraid I rather lost it. So the Director of Cricket followed the club captain in being escorted from the premises! Fortunately, Marcus Trescothick came to the rescue and managed to put together enough cash to settle the bill. I'll always be grateful to him for that!

Andy Nash took over as Chairman of the club from Giles Clarke at the end of that season. I had got on exceptionally well with Giles, not just because he had appointed me, although I was grateful enough for that, but because he understood right from the start how I wanted the club to be run, with the Director of Cricket responsible for everything to do with the playing side of things – and no committees involved! He had a famously short fuse, and I once overheard him giving Geoffrey Boycott the mother and father of a bollocking over something that Geoff had said in the press or on the radio, but he and I and Richard Gould formed a sort of triumvirate and got on really well together. I was sorry to see him go. Andy Nash, on the other hand, was much more hands off. He left me to it to run the cricket while he concentrated on developing the ground, on which he did a great job.

The other big change at Taunton in those years was the arrival in a big way of women's international cricket. I had known Clare Connor reasonably well from having served with her on the ECB Cricket Committee, and I was delighted when, in 2006, I got a call from the ICC, asking if I would go to their offices at Dubai to discuss the possibility of the County Ground becoming the headquarters of English Women's Cricket. Richard Gould and Giles Clarke were as enthusiastic as I was, and in August that year the deal was done. In many ways Taunton was the ideal choice. Crowds for women's games had been bigger there than anywhere else except Lord's, the playing area is not too enormous, and the fact that it is a small ground means that there is plenty of atmosphere even without a huge crowd. I take real pride in the way that Somerset has helped nurture the women's game and transform its profile and popularity. And we've produced some pretty useful women cricketers as well, Bath's Anya Shrubsole foremost among them.

16

So near, and yet ...

At the end of that 2007 season, I sat down with Langer and Sarge to work out what sort of players we needed to bring in to be sure not just of surviving in Division One but prospering. We focused on the bowlers. Caddick was as willing and committed as ever but would be 39 by the start of the season, and Charl Willoughby was no spring chicken either. Another spin bowler would come in handy as well, and any new bowlers needed to be experienced performers, able to contribute from day one, rather than up-and-coming youngsters.

So I went for cricketers who had impressed me: Alfonso Thomas, whom I had seen just briefly in South Africa that winter but for long enough to convince me that he was the right bowler for us; Zander de Bruyn, a quality batting all-rounder, who had played a season for Worcester and came highly recommended by Jimmy Cook; Ben Phillips, who'd had his injury problems with Notts, but whom I had always rated as a second or third-change seamer; and Omari Banks, a left-arm spinner from Anguilla, who could smash it down the order. Yes, four out of the five were Kolpaks, and I got criticised for that, but the young home-grown players were not quite ready yet and our short-term priority had to be staying in the first division.

In the event, we very nearly won the thing. In a wet summer, in which well over half the championship games were drawn, we were at or near the top of the table for virtually the entire season, thanks not least to the runs, and therefore batting points, contributed by Trescothick, now back to his best, Blackwell, de Bruyn and, of course, captain Langer. At the start of the final round of matches, on September 24, we were second, eight points behind the leaders Notts, with Durham and Hampshire not far behind. If Notts faltered against Hampshire at Trent Bridge, a win against struggling Lancashire would secure us a historic first County Championship.

What happened turned out to be the first of all too many bitter disappointments. Our opening pair, Trescothick and Langer, so prolific all season, failed twice, and our innings of 202 and 227 left Lancashire needing 182 in the fourth innings, on a pitch which had got flatter as the match went on. By the end of the third day, Paul Horton and Mark Chilton had reduced the target to just 60 without being separated and, although Langer was heavily criticised for not bowling Caddick and Willoughby in harness at the start of the fourth day (not least by Caddick himself), the match – and with it our Championship hopes – had already gone.

Some harsh things were said afterwards, but the truth of the matter was that we had not won enough games earlier in the season, because we didn't have the spinners to bowl sides out in the fourth innings, especially on our home pitch at Taunton. I suppose the classic example of that was in May when, with all the time in the world in which to bowl Sussex out for a second time for an innings win, we could take only three wickets. I was so frustrated, I took the dogs for a walk along the Tone because I couldn't bear to watch!

That autumn we took the difficult decision to part company with Ian Blackwell. The Langer-Hurry regime was one of intensity and fitness. Any player who did not appear to be subscribing to that was very quickly singled out. It had a big effect on players like Peter Trego, whose approach to fitness previously had often amounted to not more than seven pints a night! He soon got the hang of what was expected of him and eventually became just about the keenest gym bunny in the squad. Unfortunately, there were two players that this emphasis on fitness and self-discipline really did not suit, and they were Ian Blackwell and Wes Durston, who just happened to be two of our spectators' favourite players. By 2008 Wes was on the fringes of the team, even in T20, where he had performed so well in earlier years, and he would leave us at the end of the 2009 season.

As for Blackie, he had had a good season with the bat in championship cricket in 2008, but he didn't take many wickets and, as the pounds piled on, he was not the force he had been in white-ball cricket. It was decided that Blackie had to go. JL didn't think I would have the balls to go through with it, given how popular Blackie was with the spectators, but I had a chat with him and we agreed that it would be for the best all round if he moved on. Durham snapped him up almost immediately, and rightly so, because he was a tremendously talented cricketer, one of the hardest-hitting batsmen I have ever seen, with a wonderful eye, and a more than useful slow left-arm bowler. Sacking both Wes and Blackie gave me the reputation of being a pretty ruthless Director of Cricket. I can't say that bothered me much. Nothing bothered me much after Worcester in 1979!

The next big decision I had to make was over Justin Langer himself. We had a roller-coaster start to the season in 2009: a triple century for Hildreth in a typical Taunton high-scoring draw against Warwickshire; bowled out humiliatingly for 69 by Durham, followed by a magnificent second innings recovery; and then the match of the season, if not of the century, when we chased down 476 in 85 overs to beat Yorkshire. Tres and Arul Suppiah led the charge, David Stiff contributed a rapid 49 and Pete Trego finished the second highest successful championship run chase in history by blasting 103 in 54 balls. But that was it, in terms of championship wins, despite the mountain of runs contributed by a rejuvenated Marcus Trescothick. Our remaining nine games all finished in draws, as testimony partly to the weather, partly to our lack of a top-class spinner and partly, of course, to that road of a pitch at Taunton.

We could, perhaps should, have won both of the white ball trophies, and I had to face the fact that a big factor in those failures was the captain himself. In white-ball cricket, he was becoming almost more of a liability than an asset, averaging only 20 in the T20 at a disappointing strike rate, which piled the pressure on the other batters to make up for the loss of momentum. In the T20 final against Sussex, when we needed 173 at nearly eight an over, he scratched around for 15, was cleaned up by Yasir Arafat, and, Pete Trego apart, the middle order panicked as they tried to make up for lost ground.

In the final game of the Pro40 League against Durham, needing a win to take the trophy, he proved even more of an obstacle, taking 36 balls to score just 13, when we badly needed some momentum, having lost Tres and Kieswetter early on. That rather limp defeat was not just down to Langer, of course, because once again our big guns failed to fire when it really mattered. But he didn't get many runs in the Championship either and, as his performances deteriorated, so did his demeanour, making him irritable and short-tempered without him necessarily realising it. In the end, towards the end of the season, I decided that I would have to talk to him about the future. It was a very difficult conversation, because Justin was a proud man, he loved Somerset and he deeply resented the suggestion that he was past his best. Not long after that, we went up to Chester-le-Street to play championship leaders Durham. Justin, who was once so well organised and in control against the quicks, was completely duffed up by Graham Onions, struggling to put bat to ball for the best part of an hour, then being clean bowled. Rather as in the old Closey days, the dressing room cleared as he came back in, leaving just me, sitting in a corner. To this day, I'm not sure if Justin knew I was there or not, but he slammed his bat down in rage and humiliation and started swearing: "Effing Rosey, effing Rosey, he's effing right, he's effing right."

It made for a difficult few weeks between then and the end of the season when, as runners-up in the T20, we flew out to India for the Champions League. It was not a great tournament, either for Somerset or its captain, as we lost three out of our four games, and Justin could hardly get it off the square. But on the last day, as we were coming back in the coach to our hotel in Hyderabad, he came up to sit next to me and apologised for the way he had reacted. "You were quite right," he said, "I was losing it. I just couldn't bear to admit it to myself." We are now the best of friends again.

The other big decision which I had to make at the end of that 2009 season was about the Taunton pitch and the Taunton groundsman. As Director of Cricket, I was nominally in charge of pitch preparation. In practice, the policy began and ended with Phil Frost and, after drawing so many home games in our first two seasons in Division One, often from potentially winning positions, I decided it was time to act. It was a tough call to have to make, for Phil had been head groundsman since 1983 and was respected throughout the cricketing world for the excellence of his pitches. But in terms of my and the club's burning ambition to win a first county championship, his approach stood in the way, and in the winter of 2009/10 we made him redundant.

One of the first things I did with our new groundsman, Simon Lee, was to take core samples of our pitches, on a good length. What we found was that the wicket had grown up in layers over the years, each layer representing a top dressing of either Surrey loam or Ongar loam. When a ball was bowled into the pitch, its energy would be absorbed by the top layer, or plate, but because there was, despite the use of the roller, a sort of dead zone between that plate and the one beneath, it killed the pace and bounce. You can get the same effect by banging a ball into a piece of cardboard on a hard floor.

Simon Lee

The following winter, we took the top layers off the three pitches in the centre of the square to get down to the original surface. Those are the pitches that we play a lot of our one-day cricket on these days, and they offer bounce and carry for the bowlers and get the ball coming nicely onto the bat for the batsmen. For top dressing, we switched to Mendip loam, which is lighter and has some coarse grit in it. The other thing that I did with Simon, on the pitches that could not be relaid, was to get a big screwdriver, push it into the pitch on a spinner's length at the Old Pavilion end of the square and lift the soil underneath. Simon would then roll the pitch to leave a smooth surface, but the fact that the soil underneath had been loosened meant that there was something for our spinners: Murali Kartik in the first instance, Jack Leach and Dom Bess more recently, to work with.

At the other end, to give our seamers more of a chance, Simon and I let the grass grow a little longer on a length to suit Willoughby, Trego and Alfonso Thomas. This didn't mean that it was always spin from the River End and seam from the Old Pavilion End, because if the prevailing wind was blowing from the west, that would negate Caddy's away swing. But it worked pretty well, especially when you had Willoughby kicking up some rough outside a right-hander's off-stump, so widening the 'sweet spot' that a spinner from the River End had to aim at.

At the end of that 2009 season, I was quoted, by David Foot in his *Wisden* summary, as saying ,"We've had enough of being cricket's nearly men." Little did I know how those words would come back to haunt me!

I had decided, not without some misgivings, to give the captaincy to Marcus Trescothick. He had had a magnificent season with the bat, his mental problems seemed to be under control, he was hugely popular with both his team-mates and our supporters, and I knew he wanted to do it. In any case, there was no obvious alternative within the club and, although I did consider bringing someone in from outside, I felt Tres had earned his chance. Yes, he had had to come home early from our Champions League campaign in India, but he seemed happy enough back in Somerset, and I would be there to give him support on the away trips. In the event, after a few wobbles when we lost our two opening Championship fixtures, away to Yorkshire and Notts, he settled into the role well enough. The only slight frustration was that his approach to captaincy was the opposite to his bold, attacking approach to his batting. He tended always to take the conservative option, maybe because he over-thought things, possibly because he subconsciously feared the mental consequences of making a bold move and getting it wrong.

But that did not stop us having a tremendous season. James Hildreth led the way amongst the batsmen, scoring seven centuries in the championship and topping the averages in all three forms of the game. Tres was not quite the force that he had been in 2009 but still contributed four centuries, including an unbeaten 228 against Essex. Craig Kieswetter was maturing fast, as both wicket-keeper and attacking batsmen, to the extent that he and Trescothick formed just about the most potent opening partnership in the country in white-ball cricket. And when Kieswetter was away on international duty with

England, we had one of the most exciting young cricketers in the country, in Jos Buttler, to take over the gloves.

Of the two new players I had signed that winter, Nick Compton took time to settle in, but eventually he became a rock and forced his way into the England side, and Murali Kartik took full advantage of the new pitch regime at Taunton to take 45 championship wickets, including 6/61 as he bowled us to victory against Warwickshire at the end of May. We won six of our last 11 championship games and might have converted more of the five draws into victories but for the wretched weather.

In the T20, strengthened by the arrival of Kieron Pollard, we won 11 out of our 16 qualifying games, to top the South Division, with Alfonso Thomas delivering any number of matching-winning performances to top the national T20 bowling averages. It was a similar story in the newly introduced CB 40 – comfortably top of the group, with 10 wins out of 12, Thomas once again the leading wicket-taker and Hildreth leading the way with the bat. No one who saw the game against Glamorgan at Taunton will ever forget it: Pete Trego smashed 147 off 89 balls, with 19 fours and five sixes, one of which went crashing through the commentary box window to lay out poor Eddie Bevan, while Jos Buttler missed out on breaking Graham Rose's record for the fastest ever limited over century when, on 90, with two balls in hand, he lost the strike. In reply to our mammoth 368/4 in 40 overs, Glamorgan were bowled out for 119, to leave us winners by the almost unbelievable margin of 249 runs! It was a performance which typified the dominance of our white-ball cricket – right up to the final hurdle.

On Finals Day at the Rose Bowl, we were brilliant in the semi-final against Notts. Tres played one of his best ever T20 innings at the top of the order, and Jos finished things off with some astoundingly unconventional hitting. Then, with rain threatening and Duckworth-Lewis in the mix, Keiron Pollard took one of the greatest catches I have ever seen: one-handed, leaping high in the air, on the long-on boundary, not only to dismiss Samit Patel but to deny Notts the victory which a six would have given them.

Triumph one moment, disaster the next. Such is cricket. At 170/4 after 19 overs in the final against Hampshire, with our two biggest hitters, Pollard and Buttler, at the crease, Somerset were in the box seat. Dominic Cork was the bowler, and he produced the over of his life. Off the third ball, Buttler was caught – 173/5; off the fourth, Pollard went to hook a short ball, missed and took a nasty blow above the eye as the ball squeezed between visor and grille – retired hurt; Arul Suppiah was caught behind off the fifth ball, and Ben Phillips could do nothing with Cork's final delivery: 173/6. But there was worse to come, even if I wasn't there to see it.

I was in the local hospital with Pollard. There was no television, so I had to listen to the closing overs of the Hampshire innings on BBC local radio.

It was excruciating. First Hampshire were coasting home, thanks to Ervine and McKenzie; then Phillips got McKenzie and Carberry, and suddenly we were back in it. Hampshire needed eight off the last over, to be bowled by Zander de Bruyn. Off the fifth ball, Dan Christian pulled a hamstring, and there was an agonising hiatus as a runner was summoned and a parallel set of creases marked out by the groundsman. The final ball hit Christian on the pad, the appeal was turned down, all three batsmen set off for what they assumed was the winning run, to level the scores with Hampshire having lost one fewer wicket. Despair.

It was not until I got back to the ground an hour or so later that I realised the full horror of what had happened. In running that final leg-bye, Christian was out of his ground. If any of the Somerset players had had the wit to throw down the wicket at the striker's end, he would have been run out, and Somerset would have won. The umpires knew the laws; in fact they waited before calling time, just to see if a run out might be claimed. I also knew the laws, having experienced exactly this situation when I was at school. But I was in a very small Somerset minority.

It was hard to take – beaten on yet another technicality with the scores level. But there was still the championship to win, and the CB 40. We resumed our winning ways in the four-day game with a thumping win over Essex at Chelmsford, a rain-affected draw with Durham at Taunton, followed by a solid all-round performance against Lancashire for our sixth win of the Championship season. By the start of the last round of matches, on September 13, we were two points behind the leaders Notts, both of us with away games to finish, Somerset up at Chester-le-Street, Notts at Old Trafford. Both games were badly affected by the weather and, despite a valiant effort on the last afternoon, we could not quite force the win that would have guaranteed the championship. Even so, by taking maximum points from both batting and bowling, we had opened up a six-point lead over Notts by the start of the fourth day.

On that fourth day at Old Trafford, strange things began to happen. It was on the television, and I watched with growing concern in the pavilion at Durham. Somehow or other, against some fairly tepid bowling, Notts managed to scrape their way to the 400 mark for the maximum batting points they needed. Then, when they came out to try to take the three wickets in 18 overs for the single bowling point that would give them the championship, Messrs Brown, Chilton and Chanderpaul were despatched without putting up much of a fight, to leave Notts as the champions by virtue of having won one more game than us.

I was absolutely gutted. I felt almost traumatised. It maybe was not quite as bad as 1978, when we had lost the Gillette Cup and the John Player in a single weekend, but this was the championship. We were on the verge of making history. To have come so close to the biggest prize of all, and then to have had it snatched away from us, on yet another bloody technicality ... it took me probably two seasons to get over that moment.

But cricketing life goes on. This was on a Thursday. Less than 48 hours later we were due at Lord's for our CB40 final against Warwickshire. So, while the team headed off in the coach for the long, miserable drive back to Somerset, I was taken to Newcastle Airport with Giles Clarke, to fly down to London in preparation for the final. We had a bottle of wine on the plane to start the process of drowning our sorrows. We carried on in the evening, first over dinner at Wilton's, later back at the East India Club where I was staying. I woke the next morning with a bad headache, but at least I had been able to blot out what had happened for a few hours.

The final was another bitter disappointment, and not just on the field. By scheduling a 3pm start time, meaning a finish after the last train would have left Paddington for Taunton, the ECB made it just about as difficult as they could for our faithful supporters to attend. Yes, they eventually agreed to subsidise some coaches, but the attendance was by a long way the lowest ever for a Lord's final, and that certainly affected us more than Warwickshire. Even so, we should still have won the game. At 176/3 in the 31st over, with Hildreth and Compton in full flow and a batting powerplay still to come, we were looking at a score of over 250. But then Compton ran out Hildreth, and our middle order were completely bamboozled by Imran Tahir, so that we were bowled out for 199. I never thought it would be enough but, when Phillips and Thomas nipped out Trott, Carter and Barker with only 39 on the board, hope briefly resurfaced, only to be snuffed out once and for all by a brilliant century from Ian Bell, who demonstrated exactly why at one stage I had been so keen to bring him to Taunton. By the end, we looked what we were: a tired, dispirited team who had yet again fallen short when it mattered most.

How do you explain those three last-gasp failures (and the three more that would follow in the next two seasons)? Was I, as Director of Cricket, in some way responsible? I have asked myself those questions many times but, in the final analysis, there is only so much that you can do from off the field, whether as Director of Cricket, coach or whatever. I sometimes think that the outcome in 2010 might have been different if I had been successful in signing Steve Kirby from Gloucestershire, when I'd first approached him in 2008. His pace, aggression and enthusiasm, which we enjoyed so much when he did join us in 2011, might have made that crucial difference. But, whoever your players are, they have got to rock up and perform when the chips are down. When I was captain, that is what they did. It was almost as if we made things happen through sheer force of personality: not just mine, but of the other key players in the side, like Viv and Both. It was a similar story when Graeme Smith captained us to the T20 Cup in 2005; he had that dominant, not-to-be-denied personality. The teams that came so close from 2008 to 2012 maybe did not quite have that force of personality to get us over the line.

Sadly, that proved to be the case again in 2011. On T20 Finals day at Edgbaston, it needed a 'super-over' to get us past Hampshire in the semi-final, although I never had the slightest doubt that Alfonso Thomas would do the business. As ours was the second of the two semis, that meant that time was short for Andy Hurry and me to get the team into the right frame of mind for the final against unfancied Leicestershire. We were just getting going in the dressing room when I looked around and said, "Where's Tres?" Of the captain there was no sign. It turned out that he had been nabbed by Sky television to go out for the toss and do a pre-match interview without even discussing with us what he would do if he won the toss! It was not ideal. In the event, he won the toss and put Leicester in, which was fair enough. This time, I didn't have much doubt that we would chase down the relatively modest 147 that we needed, with Tres, Kieswetter, Pollard, Buttler and Hildreth in our batting line-up. And that was very much how it looked, when we were 84/2 in the 13th, needing another 64 from 45 balls. Then Hildreth was caught by the Leicestershire 'specialist fielding sub', Matthew Boyce – one of four that he took that evening – Pollard was brilliantly caught by Nixon, and our remaining batters could hardly get it off the square.

There was some consolation at the end of the season when we went to India for the Champions League. We played superbly to beat the Kolkata Knight Riders and the South African team the Warriors, complete with Jacques Kallis, and qualified for the semis as top of our group. At one stage, it even looked as if we might get the better of Mumbai Indians and reach the final. That was certainly what Sachin Tendulkar thought when he gave me the thumbs up midway through our innings, with Mumbai's 160 very much in our sights. In the end, thanks mainly to a brilliant final over from Malinga, we didn't quite get there, but I felt very proud of my team, given that they had held their own against some of the strongest T20 outfits in world cricket.

In the meantime, we had lost yet another 40-over final at Lord's, this time against Surrey. Once again, hopes were high, after winning nine out of 12 games in qualifying – Buttler and Trego outstanding – and seeing off Durham comfortably in the semi-final, even with an injury-weakened side. Surrey were as full of themselves as usual and were well on top when they had us 79/5 in the 18th over, but then Jos Buttler played superbly to take us past 200 and give us just a sniff, only for the weather and Duckworth-Lewis to take a hand. In the end, Surrey reached their adjusted target easily enough. Yet again, we had failed to do ourselves justice on the biggest stage.

If we had underperformed as probably the best side in the country in 2010 and 2011, the reverse was true in 2012. The worst run of injuries I have ever experienced in all my time at Somerset, plus international calls, plus the appalling weather, meant that we did not really get going until towards the end of the season. On Jimmy Cook's recommendation – again! – I had signed Vernon Philander to bolster our new-ball attack in the first two months of the season, and he showed plenty of potential, though the South African Cricket Board did not allow him to bowl flat out. We showed what might have been with two championship wins in September, to climb up to second place behind Warwickshire, so that was yet another runners-up medal: my eighth as Director of Cricket to go with seven as captain. I have got an entire drawer-full of the wretched things at home!

Those injuries dashed our chances in the 40-over competition, but we yet again qualified for T20 Finals Day, only to come badly unstuck in the semi-final against Hampshire. By this time, I had as good as decided that the 2012 season would be my last. I had thoroughly enjoyed my time as Director of Cricket. I had been instrumental in building the strongest county side in the country; I had brought on some wonderfully talented youngsters in Craig Kieswetter, George Dockrell, Jos Buttler, Lewis Gregory, the Overton twins and Jack Leach; our success on the field had helped the club to transform the County Ground, and in a good way; and I had been part of a happy bunch of cricketers who had played masses of good, entertaining, Somerset-style cricket. Even if we had not actually won anything, we had been in contention for virtually every competition every season I had been in charge. I remember bumping into Gus Fraser at Lord's one day, bemoaning the number of second-place finishes we'd had. "You should count yourself lucky, Rosey," he said. "A lot of us would give our eye teeth to have a problem like yours."

So my departure was genuinely, and despite all the press speculation at the time, by mutual consent. Whether as player, captain or Director of Cricket, you know when your time has come and, for me, that was at the end of that 2012 season. What did surprise me was the club's choice of a successor. To give him his due, Dave Nosworthy did ring me up and ask to come and see me for a chat, but he was a totally different animal from what I had been expecting. He didn't seem to have any real idea of what he had taken on, of what Somerset cricket was all about. Besides, as one of the most successful clubs in the country, we were expected to have a big name, with a high profile, as Director of Cricket. Within two years he was replaced by Matthew Maynard.

One thing I can say is that, if I had carried on for another season, Somerset would never have got itself into the ridiculous position of having to choose between two hugely talented home-grown players in Kieswetter and Buttler, in both of whom they had invested so much whilst they were growing up. I was incensed. If I had still been in charge, I would have made Kieswetter captain, batted him at four or five, which he was more than capable of doing, and given Jos the gloves and batted him at six. It would have meant Craig easing up in some of his attitudes and opinions but, with the right advice, there was no reason why he could not have been a perfectly capable and popular captain. Yes, he had attitude, but I like that in a cricketer.

Somerset asked me to carry on for the 2013 season as a consultant, but by that time I'd had a telephone call from Glamorgan, asking me to write a report about the structure and development of cricket in Glamorgan and in Wales more generally. My main recommendations were, first, that Glamorgan should place much greater emphasis on developing its own talent, while also working more closely with Cricket Wales to oversee the development of the most talented 11-to-15 year-old cricketers; and second that, as we had done eight years before at Somerset, the role of Director of Cricket should be completely separated from that of Chief Executive, especially at a Test match ground like Sophia Gardens. The first recommendation was accepted; the second went by the board when, midway through that season, Glamorgan sacked the Chief Executive who had commissioned my report and appointed Hugh Morris – as Director of Cricket *and* Chief Executive!

The opening of The Brian Rose Gates, June 2013
(from left) Joey, Anne and Tony Jarvis, Stevie, me,
Andy Nash, Stuart, Dee and Simon Wotton

Later in the day
Roy Kerslake, me, Stevie, Andy Nash and Guy Lavender

17

Into the future

In early 2007, in the wake of the Ashes whitewash in Australia and a dismal performance in the World Cup, the ECB asked Ken Schofield, the highly-respected former director of golf's European Tour, to produce a report on improving the structure of English cricket to give the national team a better chance of success in the future. Schofield recruited six former county captains to help him in his task: Micky Stewart, Nasser Hussain, Nick Knight, Hugh Morris, Angus Fraser and me. I worked most closely with Micky Stewart, whom I had known and respected for many years and who is very much a kindred spirit in his thoughts on the future of the game. Four months or so later, we came up with 19 recommendations, mostly non-controversial (to the extent that some critics dismissed the report as an 'ECB PR exercise'), designed to give greater support to existing and potential England cricketers, slim down the fixture list and change the ECB management structure.

Most of what we recommended on player support and ECB structure has been implemented, and the Pro 40 League was indeed scrapped in favour first of the group/knock-out format of the CB40 and YB40 and, eventually, the 50-over one-day Cup, to mirror the format of one-day Internationals and the World Cup. But what Micky Stewart and I, in particular, were looking for in terms of the fixture list has not happened – a higher priority for four-day county championship cricket, to give current and future England cricketers more and better opportunities to prepare for Test cricket. The championship fixture list was a mess in 2007, and it remains a mess as I write, 12 years later. The consequences of that, in terms of top-order batting techniques around the counties and in the England side, are all too apparent.

For at least those last 12 years, the ECB's priority has been limited-over cricket, the T20 in particular. I can understand that, because it is T20 cricket that generates the most revenue, and cricket has to have revenue to survive. But the consequence has been that the county championship has been, almost literally, marginalised to the beginning and end of the season, to allow T20 and 50-over cricket to dominate the prime months of high summer. It is not easy scoring runs on green seamers in April or, for that matter, on dusty turners in September, and that makes it very hard indeed for front-line batsmen to groove their techniques and build their confidence.

The other consequence of the prioritisation of T20 cricket – and I include international T20 competitions like the IPL and the Big Bash in this – has been its impact on batsmanship. Because of the proliferation of T20 cricket, the first instinct of many batsmen in a Test match is to go for their shots and score runs quickly. On good pitches, the sort of pitches that T20 cricket tends to be played on, that is fine and provides for high entertainment. But you can come badly unstuck on pitches that are offering the bowlers something, be that lateral movement or uneven bounce, as England's top-order performances in the 2019 Test series in the West Indies demonstrated all too clearly.

Then, on top of all that, we have the prospect of the ECB's 100-ball competition, from the 2020 season onwards. I find it astounding that, as it stands, the ECB should have effectively cut out counties like Somerset, Essex, Sussex and Gloucestershire, where T20 cricket has been most successful and drawn the biggest crowds, in deciding on the format of their new competition. Nor can I see how, again as it stands, 'The 100' can be fitted into the fixture list without turning either the 50-over cup or the county T20 into a second-class competition, contested by teams lacking their best players who will be away in The 100.

If I was asked to produce a report for the ECB on the future of English cricket as of now, among my recommendations would be:

1   Start the season later, maybe in the last week in April, and, if necessary, carry on longer into the autumn, using floodlights to maintain hours of play, as it appears more of a risk to me to be playing in early April than at the end of September. Somerset now has a great set of floodlights, and we can make more use of that investment.

2   Think very hard about the situation where some of the weaker counties in the second division of the county championship are locked in a downward spiral. Having invested heavily in their own young home-grown players, they invariably lose the best of them to the first-division counties, so perpetuating what is in danger of becoming not so much second-division status as second-class status. This is a nettle that will have to be grasped sooner or later.

3   Revive a knock-out competition on the lines of the old Gillette/ NatWest cups that some of the Minor Counties can qualify for. The knock-outs were great to play in, drew huge crowds, you got a full house at Lord's for the final, and every game mattered.

4   Whilst it is difficult to be too specific about 'The 100', given that many of the details have yet to be settled, I would urge the ECB to work with

the counties to ensure that it is integrated into the season in a way that does not undermine or cut across the county basis of our domestic cricket.

Looking at the future of cricket more widely, my biggest concern is for Test match cricket. Really the only countries now which attract decent crowds for Test matches are England and Australia. Even in India, the stadiums are only half full, if that. I am not sure what the answer to that is. Maybe it would be worth dropping a day, playing Tests over four days rather than five. It would, after all, match the four-day format for most first-class cricket, and the way batsmen approach their task these days, very few Tests go into the fifth day in any case. Another possibility would be to give Test matches more significance by playing them in the context of two 'world Test leagues', with promotion and relegation, rather than as stand-alone Test series. It might mean playing either one-off Tests, or mini-series, which would involve a lot of travelling, but then a lot of top cricketers are well used to travelling all over the world to play T20 cricket, so I don't see that as being a big obstacle.

But with the best will in the world, it is hard to see big crowds flocking to Test cricket in future, except in England, Australia and maybe India, partly because a four or five-day sporting event, with the possibility of no definite conclusion at the end of it, is so out of tune with the modern desire for instant gratification and partly because of sheer economics. For an overseas tour which consists of, say, three Test matches, followed by a one-day series and finishing with two or three T20 games, the cricket public in poorer countries, like the West Indies, are almost bound to save their money for the guaranteed excitement of the white-ball stuff, rather than spending it on days at a Test match.

However, for all the popularity and financial success of white-ball cricket, I still believe that the longer form of the game, whether at county or Test match level, does have a future, indeed must have a future if the game itself is to be sustained. That is because it is linked so strongly to the development of cricketing skills from a young age. When young players are coached only to play one-day cricket, you see all sorts of technical flaws. The principles of getting behind the ball, keeping your head still and waiting for the ball to come to you are the foundation stones for batting in all forms of cricket, but they won't be coached if long-form cricket goes by the board. The other thing you have to learn as a batsman is when to leave the ball, and you will never learn that playing white-ball cricket because not playing a shot at every ball is regarded as a cardinal sin!

I produced a report for the ECB a year or two back on second eleven cricket, and one of the main themes of that was how important it is to have a development structure in place that can provide counties with cricketers well coached in the basic skills. Having got those skills, there will be those, like Alex Hales or Tymal Mills, who decide that they want to specialise in white-ball cricket, and I can see more players taking that option in future. But without the right coaching at school, club and county academy level, skill levels overall are bound to decline, and cricket as a whole will lose from that. What you always have to remember is that cricket is a bloody difficult game, in which a complex range of skills is required, plus you have got that element of danger. Coaching in the basic skills remains absolutely vital.

One of the biggest changes from my era is the bats. I wil go into the nets sometimes and pick up one of the bats being used by the current generation of Somerset players and think, blimey, just imagine how many more runs I would have scored if I'd had one of these! In my playing days I used a 2lb 10oz bat, but even that was a lot heavier than some. I remember once picking up Geoffrey Boycott's bat when we were playing together for England, and I couldn't believe how light it was. These days, a 3lb 3 or even 4oz bat doesn't feel any heavier or more difficult to handle than my old bats, due to their thickness and weight distribution.

The progress in bat-making technology is making life ever more difficult for bowlers, especially in white ball cricket. I sometimes wonder how the really tight, run-saving bowlers of my era – Don Shepherd or Tom Cartwright or even Derek Underwood, for instance – would have fared in modern one-day cricket. They relied on keeping an immaculate line and length, as much as anything, but these days, if you bowl length, you are asking for it. I don't know how that vital balance between bat and ball is going to be restored in white-ball cricket, but at the moment it's tilted too much in the direction of the batsmen.

One very positive development in the last few years has been the growing popularity of women's cricket with both spectators and participants. There is a lot to be said for their concept of international series combining a Test match with 50-over games and T20s, with points for each to decide the overall winner. It would not completely surprise me if something similar happened in the men's game, looking perhaps ten or fifteen years down the line. It does feel to me as if the dynamics of the game are changing very quickly.

But not necessarily for the worse! Cricketers and cricket followers are great ones for nostalgia, for saying that the game "isn't what it was in my day" etc. That is one thing that I have always tried to avoid since my playing days ended. When I was Director of Cricket, I made a very conscious effort not to say things like "Call that fast bowling! You should have faced Holding and Marshall", or "Yes, he's a useful batsman, but you should have seen Viv Richards. The most I would say when people ask me how cricket and cricketers compare, now with then, is that playing alongside the likes of Garner, Botham and Richards was a fantastic experience, which it was.

And I did play through a golden era in English cricket, when you had the best players in the world playing entire seasons for their counties. Just imagine going to Southampton to play Hampshire, knowing that the batting would be opened by Barry Richards and Gordon Greenidge, with Andy Roberts to lead the attack; or to Bristol, coming up against Zaheer and Procter. For myself, I feel genuinely privileged to have played alongside some truly great players. They gave you a wonderful insight into what you needed to do to survive as a batsman or take wickets as a bowler. Someone like Colin Dredge, for example, learned a huge amount from bowling with Joel Garner.

They said at the time that English cricket was suffering because there were too many overseas players. I am not sure about that. We have still got a lot of overseas players on the books of county sides today. The difference is that many of them are nothing like the same calibre as those we used to have back in the '70s and '80s. There are reasons for that, which go beyond finance. When I was Director of Cricket, I signed Chris Gayle for the T20 in 2012, only for him to pull out at the last minute because he had settled his difference with the West Indies Board, and there was nothing we could do about it. What with the various money-spinning T20 leagues around the world, and the restrictions which boards of control place on their Test players, it is getting more and more difficult to sign genuinely world-class players for any length of time.

Looking ahead over the next ten to fifteen years, the key will be maintaining the coaching and development structure from the ground up. With that structure, cricket in all its forms can continue to flourish. Without it, I would genuinely fear for the future of the first-class game as we have come to know it.

In the meantime, here at Somerset we've still got the county championship to win. I was hugely honoured to be elected President of Somerset County Cricket Club in January 2019 and, after almost fifty years of being involved with Somerset cricket, as player, captain, manager, cricket chairman, Director of Cricket and now President, the championship remains for me the Holy Grail just as I know it does for all of our thousands of loyal and devoted followers. This time there will be no more coming second!

18

Some of my favourite Somerset cricketers

I have already written about Somerset's Big Three, and the inimitable Brian Close, without whom no list of either my favourite cricketers or Somerset's greatest cricketers would be complete. So, taking those four giants as read, I have chosen two squads of thirteen, one drawn from locally grown cricketers and the other from the international cricketers who have represented Somerset down the years. And if some readers object that one or two of the locals have a slightly international flavour about them, and vice versa, well, I may have used a certain amount of author's licence to balance each squad. They are all cricketers I have played alongside or have been responsible for in my various roles at Somerset. Here are my two squads. I leave it to readers to pick their own.

The Locals	The Internationals
Harold Gimblett	Sunil Gavaskar
Marcus Trescothick	Graeme Smith (capt)
Peter Roebuck	Jimmy Cook
James Hildreth	Greg Chappell
Peter Denning	Martin Crowe
Jos Buttler	Justin Langer
Nigel Popplewell	Steve Waugh
Graham Burgess	Kieron Pollard
Peter Trego	Craig Kieswetter (wkt)
Derek Taylor (wkt)	Andrew Caddick
Vic Marks (capt)	Hallam Moseley
Colin Dredge	Mushtaq Ahmed
Charl Willoughby	Alfonso Thomas

Harold Gimblett

I met Harold Gimblett when I was a young cricketer, in the mid-1960s. He was coaching at Millfield, where I played a few games, and he was still playing fairly regularly for the MCC, even though he was well into his 50s. To me, he was one of the Somerset cricket legends, alongside Bill Andrews and Maurice Tremlett, yet when I met him at Millfield he spoke to me perfectly naturally, without a hint of arrogance or superiority. He seemed to epitomise all that was best about Somerset cricket with his wonderfully free-flowing approach to batting and, of course, that remarkable debut at Frome, after he'd got the call at the last minute. He missed his bus

from Bicknoller, had to hitch a lift on a lorry to Bridgwater, where he was picked up by the wicket-keeper, Wally Luckes, and then, with Somerset on 110 for 6 against Essex, proceeded to score 123 in 80 minutes with three sixes and 17 fours! You wouldn't believe it if it hadn't happened. He remains Somerset's leading run-scorer in first-class cricket, and goodness knows how many more he might have scored but for losing the best years of his career to the Second World War. Whenever I met him, he seemed cheerful and generous of spirit. There was no hint of the tragedy to come.

Marcus Trescothick

I first saw Marcus batting when he was about 13, and it was obvious even then that he had an exceptional talent. He has an innate ability to strike a cricket ball. As a left-handed batsman he had his early problems, just as I did, against balls angled across him. There is an obvious temptation to go after the ball, but that brings the slip cordon into play. My problem was compounded by getting my head too far across; with Marcus, it was more that he would put his right leg down the line of middle and leg, which made him vulnerable to nicking off or getting bowled. He sorted that out by tremendous technical application, very much helped in international cricket by Duncan Fletcher, who taught him how to get his feet into the right position, and everything else flowed from there. Another of his great strengths is the way he leaves balls outside the off-stump by playing deliberately inside the line, which is so important against genuinely fast bowling. He became, of course, a magnificent batsman, with a wonderful Test record, and it's a shame that his mental problems didn't allow him to continue an international career. As for how long he ought to carry on playing for Somerset, I did suggest to him a couple of years back, tongue in cheek, that it was time to retire, but he doesn't seem to have taken any notice, I'm glad to say! The thing about Tres is that he loves playing cricket, and if you love something, and are still one of the best in the country at it, why give it up?

Peter Denning

To me, Dasher was the epitome of Somerset cricket. If you play cricket around the towns and villages of Somerset, you get growled at, and Dasher was born with a permanent growl! They are a lovely family, the Dennings of Chewton Mendip: his father Tom, mother Maxine and Uncle Willie, who had the butcher's shop and pub in Radstock. I first got to know Dasher in my early teens when we were both playing for Somerset Under-15s. Bill Andrews would pick me up from home, then drive over to Chewton to collect Dasher, and away we'd go. We made our Somerset debuts within a few weeks of each other in 1969, and there was a lot of comment about the two blond-haired left-handers who put on 63 together in 80 minutes against Warwickshire at the Weston Festival in 1969. Later, he moved to Mead Vale, on the outskirts of Weston, and we always travelled together for away games, Dasher armed with his bottle of tomato ketchup. We made an interesting contrast, as batsmen and as characters. Dasher was always very intense, belligerent almost, to the extent that he'd growl at the bowlers, which used to make me laugh, but his aggression did show the opposition bowlers that, unlike Somerset in days gone by, we really meant business. The fact that we were so different also made life very difficult for the bowlers, because a ball that I might drive through mid-off, Dasher would lay back and carve past cover point with that famous 'Chewton chop'. And the other thing, of course, was the remarkable understanding we had when it came to running between the wickets. It dated back to our earliest days together, it meant that we hardly ever had to call, and it used to drive the fielding side half-crazy. As a batsman, he got better and better, not just in one-day cricket, but in championship cricket as well. He was at the heart of my team and was one of Somerset cricket's great characters.

Peter Roebuck

Peter had a tremendous influence on Somerset cricket throughout his career, and in my time as captain he was exactly the right bloke to go in at number four. Surrounded by all those stroke-makers, he did a brilliant job in closing up one end, getting heaps of runs and batting a long time. The present England team could do with one or two like Peter! He wasn't a pretty batsman to watch, but he had great mental strength and he would frustrate the life out of bowlers because they couldn't work out how they hadn't managed to get him out! His technique was built around waiting for the ball. He didn't try to force the issue by putting his hands out towards the ball. He covered his stumps, closing off everything, so that you would think that he was an obvious candidate for leg before. But he was good enough to get his bat down at the last second. In my time he was a great team player. It was only later in his career, when he started to be very forthright in criticising some other players, that it started to cause problems in the dressing room. But he would be in any Somerset team of mine, every time.

James Hildreth

Hildy's batting record speaks for itself. In first-class cricket, he averages 43, which is a good bit higher than most of the batsmen who have played for England in recent years. As a cricketer, and an all-round sportsman, he is obviously an outstanding natural talent. His batting reminds me a lot of Ian Bell, who went on to play 118 Test matches for England. Hildy has yet to play even one. Now that is clearly wrong, but I wonder sometimes how badly he really wanted to play Test cricket; whether, subconsciously, he wasn't happier in his comfort zone, scoring centuries for Somerset. It was maybe the same sort of mind-set which caused him to turn down the captaincy when I was lining him up to take over from Justin Langer. He just didn't want to do it, and he clearly didn't enjoy it much when he got to captain the England Lions. He is happy playing for Somerset, and who is to say that he's got it wrong in not being more ambitious? I've met some pretty miserable international cricketers in my time. But what a player! The century he scored against Notts in the last game of the 2016 season, after he'd broken his foot, was one of the most remarkable innings I've seen. To be able to compensate for an almost total lack of mobility, on a turning pitch, in pain, against good bowlers, showed quite extraordinary hand-eye co-ordination and guts. And it won us the game, and very nearly the championship!

Jos Buttler

The first time I saw Jos Buttler bat, when he was just 13 or 14 years old, I said to his coach that this boy would be playing first-class cricket by the time he was 18. Like Botham or Trescothick, he had a gift for hitting a cricket ball. In one way he has been very fortunate to have come into cricket just as T20 was taking off around the world, with big money to be made. On the other hand, the amount of white-ball cricket he has played has made it difficult for him to adapt to the demands of Test cricket. I spoke to him about it a few years back and said then that what he really needed to do was to change his mentality; to be content, if he batted for two hours in a Test match, to have scored 30 or 40, rather than 80 or 100. Jos is

good enough to be able to earn pots of money playing T20 around the world *and* captain England in Test matches, provided he adjusts his technique to the different forms. It's all about foot movement. In T20, you need to clear the left side, which means planting your front foot on or outside leg; in Test matches, all the great players look to get their front foot moving towards the line of the ball, on middle to off-stump, so that they are in an ideal position to play straight or through the off-side, or simply to leave the ball. And if the bowler strays towards middle and leg, looking for an lbw, then you can whip him away through the on-side, as Viv Richards and Greg Chappell used to do. If Jos can make that change, then he's got everything it takes to be a fine England captain. He talks a good game, he thinks a good game, and he's a thoroughly nice bloke with it.

Nigel Popplewell

Pops may have been one of the scruffiest first-class cricketers to take the field, but he was a terrific all-rounder who got better as his career went on. When he came into the Somerset side after Cambridge, he was batting down the order at seven or eight and was probably trying to bowl too fast. We got him to concentrate less on pace and more on accuracy, and he became a much better bowler, whilst his batting really blossomed towards the end of his career, when he was opening the innings with Peter Roebuck. He was, and is, obviously highly intelligent, but he has also got a strong emotional streak, which came to the fore later in his Somerset career when

he made no secret of his distaste for some of the goings-on – and, of course, he spoke very powerfully at the Shepton Mallet meeting in 1986. I was sad when he decided to retire because it seemed to me that his cricket was still improving. Maybe the atmosphere in the dressing room in his last season, 1985, had something to do with it, although I think it was more down to the fact that he felt it was time to concentrate on his legal career. He was a great team player, with a cool head in a crisis, and an integral part of my Somerset side.

Graham Burgess

Budgie was a one-off. He was a bit of a throwback to the Somerset side of the 1960s and, when I first came into the side alongside him, he could be a bit languid in his approach. But when Tom Cartwright came to Somerset, it made all the difference. You could see that he felt he needed to measure up to Tom, and his bowling improved steadily from then on. As for his batting, well, he played many important innings, but he was erratic. You never knew quite what you were going to get. What I'll always be grateful to Budgie for was the way he stood up to be counted in that 1979 Gillette Cup Final. We'd picked up two early wickets, but Allan Lamb and Geoff Cook were putting together a threatening partnership, and I needed to stem the tide. Budgie came up to me and said, "It's OK, Skip. I'll bowl." His nine overs went for just 37 and, when Viv Richards had Lamb brilliantly stumped by Derek Taylor at the other end, the game was as good as won. The other absolutely vital contribution that he made to that campaign was with the bat in the quarter-final against Kent. At one stage we were 110/7 and in real trouble but, playing calmly and intelligently, Budgie added 80 priceless runs with the tail, finishing with 50 not out. Winning the Gillette on the Saturday at the end of that season and the John Player on the Sunday made for the perfect send-off for another of Somerset cricket's great characters. He hung out his boots on the balcony at Trent Bridge that Sunday evening, and if anyone then deserved one of his most characteristic expressions – "That's alright you" – it was Graham 'Budgie' Burgess.

Peter Trego

It would be fair to say that Pete Trego is a bit of a one-off. I've known him since he and his brother Sam were playing for Weston as young lads. They were both good cricketers, but it was Pete who went on to play, very successfully, for England Under-19s and to join Somerset in 2000. The trouble was that, whilst he was clearly a very talented cricketer, his personal life was firing off in all directions. So he left us at the end of the 2002 season and played all over the place – Hereford, Worcester, Kent, Middlesex – while he tried to forge a career. It was in a conversation with Pete Robinson, shortly after I had become Director of Cricket, when we were talking about the need to sign some bowlers, that his name came up. "He's a bit of a prat," said Pete, "but you could do a lot worse." So I took myself off to Lord's, incognito (except that the gateman recognised me straightaway), and sat in the Compton stand to watch him bowling. He looked more than useful, so I came back the following day to watch him bat. He struck me as what he is: an exciting cricketer, who could change games and was just what we needed. So I brought him back, and he thrived under the Langer/Hurry regime and, of course, became hugely popular with our supporters. He reminds me a bit of Dennis Breakwell. You know that he's always going to be chirping away in the dressing room, and some of it will be rubbish, but he's the life and soul of the party and genuinely a very funny bloke. He should, of course, have played one-day cricket for England. Why he was never given the chance, given how many games he won for us, I'll never know. Maybe his earlier reputation went before him. But he has been an absolutely key member of the Somerset side of the last 12 or 13 years, as one of the most entertaining cricketers in the country.

Derek Taylor

I first met Derek when I played for Somerset 2nds against Surrey 2nds at The Oval in 1969. There was quite a party afterwards, at which I got to know the Surrey lads pretty well, and Derek and his wife Lyn have been very good friends of ours ever since. His arrival at Somerset in 1970 made a huge difference to the club. He was a steadying influence, very much in the know about players from

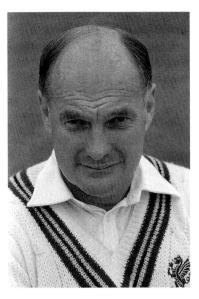

other counties and with a wonderful pair of hands. He had a tremendous rapport with Tom Cartwright, to whom he stood up to the stumps all the time. The batters were terrified to move, because Derek was so good. Tom used to say that he would have got hundreds more wickets if he'd had Derek keeping wicket throughout his career. Bob Taylor was probably a better keeper, and Alan Knott was ahead of both of them as an all-rounder, but Derek was up there with him as a batsman. When I came back into the Somerset side after Borough Road, and offered to open the batting, my opening partner was Derek and we carried on like that, very successfully, for the best part of two seasons. He was another one who could bat time, and we complemented each other really well. When I became captain, it was Derek I turned to most often for a word of advice. At the end of each over, we'd have a quiet word about which batsman was doing what, and I would adjust the field or have a word with the bowler accordingly. Derek and Lyn have lived and worked in Australia for many years now, but he still comes back from time to time and Stevie and I always meet up with them. I suppose his golden moment for Somerset was when he stumped Allan Lamb off Viv Richards in the 1979 Gillette final. It was a brilliant piece of work that snuffed out their main threat. Over all his years with Somerset he hardly put a foot, or a glove, wrong.

Vic Marks

I have just loved Vic from the first time I met him. Right from the start, he always had a twinkle in his eye and a chuckle in his voice. When he first started with Somerset, I sometimess used to wonder whether he wasn't almost too affable; whether he would be tough enough to survive. But I soon discovered that underneath that genial exterior lurked a very competitive and very shrewd cricketer. As an off-spinner, he was different from so many in that era, in that he didn't try and push it through. He bowled it slowly, with a good loop and great control of line and length, to the extent that in one-day cricket I would often put him on first change. That would baffle the opposition batsmen, because in those days it was almost unknown to bowl a spinner so early in a one-day innings. Bear in mind that we didn't have fielding restrictions in those days, so

I would put myself at short mid-wicket, have a straighter mid-wicket halfway back, and a long on, and it was remarkable how difficult batsmen found it to score against that sort of field. They couldn't get him away square of the wicket on the off-side either because there wasn't the pace on the ball that they could use. He started as more of a bowler than a batsman, but his batting got better and better as his career went on, and he played any number of valuable innings for us, in both one-day and championship cricket. He could cut and pull with the best of them, although none of us, least of all the bowler, could ever be quite sure what shot he would play or where the ball might end up!

Colin Dredge

Dredgie was brilliant. His would be one of the first names I would put on any Somerset team-sheet. He was always ready to bowl, he'd never let you down, he was a wonderful fielder and, when you needed some runs from the lower order, he could usually get you some. He also had a wonderful knack of being able to remove really top-class batsmen, people like Procter, Zaheer and Imran. In his very first game for Somerset, I was at second slip when Dredgie came in to bowl at the New Zealand run-machine, Glenn Turner, and I remember seeing the ball emerge from this whirl of arms and legs, to shoot back between bat and pad and send the stumps flying. I knew then that this was a serious bowler. Yes, he had an awkward-looking action, but that was part of the threat, because the batsman couldn't see the ball until the last moment. His nip-backer was a great weapon. He was a vital component in the Somerset side of the Glory Years. And he was, above all, a great team player.

Charl Willoughby

Charl is another of my favourite cricketers, and he was another Jimmy Cook/Graeme Smith recommendation, despite Biff carting him all over Taunton in that 2005 innings! The partnership that he formed with Caddick in 2007 and afterwards was quite outstanding. He could bowl the left-armer's stock delivery, putting his fingers across the seam or holding it straight up, to angle it across a right-handed batsman, or he could swing or seam it back, sometimes quite devastatingly. I hardly ever saw him collared, and in one-day cricket he could be relied upon to bowl his eight overs for virtually nothing. It was only when the umpires started forcing him to go wider on the crease because of his footmarks that he started to lose some impact, because it restricted his ability to bring the ball back and made him vulnerable to being hit through the off-side. Charl was a highly intelligent cricketer who made a big contribution to our success during the six seasons that he played for Somerset. He was also quite the worst batsman I've ever seen in first-class cricket!

Sunil Gavaskar

As team-mates and opening partners, Sunny and I hit it off immediately. I have already written about the then record opening partnership that we put together at Canterbury, and it is to my eternal regret that an attack of bronchitis prevented me from seeing his follow-up innings – 123 against Middlesex at Taunton, again in the B&H, which people who saw it tell me was one of the great Somerset innings of that era. He didn't have the best of luck, in that 1980 was a particularly wet summer, and he found it hard work against the seamers

on green-tops. But it was a privilege for me to be able to bat with another of the world's great batsmen, and I learned a lot from him – particularly his judgement of line, always playing late and using his hands and wrists to manoeuvre the ball into the gaps. He was a great influence on the rest of the side as well, and I think he enjoyed his time in Somerset every bit as much as we enjoyed having him here.

Graeme Smith

Peter Anderson's decision to sign Graeme Smith as captain for the 2005 season was a master-stroke. I have written already about his presence and tactical awareness as a captain. It wasn't that he was particularly aggressive. In the dressing room he was friendly, gave good team talks and was an excellent judge of character; out in the middle he led by example. He

was a dominant figure, who commanded the attention of his players and got the very best out of his two experienced bowlers Andy Caddick and Richard Johnson. His influence in the T20 Cup was crucial to Somerset reaching the final and then, when it mattered most, he delivered a magnificent innings of 64 not out to win us the Trophy. As a batsman he was obviously powerful, but he also understood his own strengths and weaknesses very well and played to them. Like all the great players, he covered his stumps and made life as difficult as possible for the bowlers. He may not have played for Somerset for long, but his influence lasted for many years, first of all in demonstrating what a difference a good captain can make, which was what led me to sign Justin Langer; and secondly, in that together with Jimmy Cook, he opened the door to my being able to recruit all those top-class South African bowlers over the next few years.

Jimmy Cook

Jimmy Cook's record for Somerset is phenomenal. In the space of just three seasons, he scored 7,604 first-class runs for the county, with 28 centuries and 27 fifties, at an average of 72.41, which is far and away the highest of any regular Somerset batsman. By comparison, Viv Richards averaged a whisker under 50, and Ian Botham just over 36. Add in the 3,048 runs Jimmy scored in one-day cricket, and his total for Somerset in the three seasons 1989, 1990 and

1991 was 10,652. But his runs were only part of the story, because he was a very positive influence on the entire team. You could not have asked for more. And then I sacked him! It was one of the most difficult decisions I have ever had to make, but I decided to be upfront about it, and he took it really well. At that time we were scoring mountains of runs but not winning many matches. To do that, we needed to sign bowlers and Andy Caddick was waiting in the wings. In a way, the timing worked out quite well, because Jimmy was developing his coaching business back in South Africa, his sons were growing up and

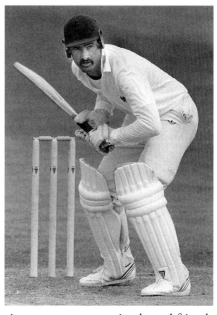

it probably suited him to be back home. At any rate, we remained good friends and he was instrumental in bringing many good South Africans to come and play for Somerset, from Graeme Smith onwards. When I was Director of Cricket, I persuaded him to come over to Taunton for spells as an additional batting coach, in which he did great work, focusing on the younger players, Jos Buttler included. As a batsman Jimmy had no obvious weakness, and I am sure he would have been one of the great Test players, given the chance.

Greg Chappell

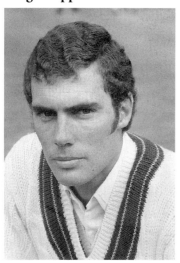

Greg was in his second season with Somerset when I made my debut for the county. He was only 20 and still developing as a cricketer, but you could already tell that here was one of the great Test batsmen in the making. He was a lovely player to watch, whether he was clipping the ball off his legs through the on-side, or playing those beautiful flowing off-drives which became his signature. There were times when he looked as if he had been coached by God! In the dressing room, he was by no means the typical abrasive Aussie. He had a great sense of humour, respected the senior players and he and I, as young batsmen together, got on really well. It was thanks to a combination of Greg Chappell and Graham McKenzie that I got the chance to play Grade cricket at Claremont-Cottesloe a few years later, and he was shrewd enough to see that, as a much better player of seam than spin, I would be better off opening the innings than coming in down the order.

Martin Crowe

Martin was another prolific run-scorer: 3,984 in first-class cricket in the two-and-a-half seasons that he spent at Somerset, at an average of just under 60. He was also, like so many of Somerset's overseas players down the years, a real force for good off as well as on the field, particularly in his case with the younger players. He set up a group called the 'Young Nags', after the Nag's Head at Thornfalcon, just south of Taunton, where they would meet every week to talk cricket. He maybe didn't quite live-up to the saintly image that some Somerset committee-men had of him at the time, but he was certainly a forerunner of the modern cricketer in terms of constantly working on his technique,  his diet, exercise regime and meticulous preparation – mental as well as physical – for each match. To that extent, he was a big influence on Peter Roebuck, although you could also say that there were times when both of them were almost too intense for their own and their team's good. After all the controversy over the sackings of Richards and Garner, it was sad and slightly ironic that his career at Somerset was cut short by a back injury. He told me about his stress fractures when I found him hanging by his arms from a beam in the dressing room at Bath one day, and I told him it was just about the worst thing that he could possibly be doing. But a great player.

Justin Langer

JL has to get into this list because of his outstanding contribution to Somerset's success from 2007 to 2009. The partnership of Hurry, Kerr and Langer laid a platform down that set the highest standards of training, behaviour and competitiveness and was an inspiration for many of the young players currently playing for Somerset. The word I would use to describe his batting is stoic; he fought hard and never gave an inch. He was not maybe the most naturally talented batsman in the world, but through application and determination he made absolutely the most of his ability. As a captain he set and expected high standards and liked to work to a plan. He took Somerset to his  heart, to the extent of bringing his family over and sending his two girls to local schools, and he was hugely popular with both team-mates and supporters. His elevation to coach of Australia has not surprised me in the least; he is just the man to lay down a set of standards others can follow.

Steve Waugh

 I was a tremendous admirer of Steve Waugh, both for his outgoing personality and his very competitive, almost aggressive approach to his cricket. He had a good cricket brain, and he understood his own game, overcoming an early weakness against the short stuff, for example. He learned a lot in a short time in England, both at Nelson in the Lancashire League and here at Somerset, where he could play on good pitches without the pressures of being in a big city. It is what has made Taunton such an attractive proposition to overseas players over the years. No Somerset batsman has a better record than Steve Waugh, admittedly over just a season and a bit: 1,654 runs in 19 first-class games, at 78.76 with eight

hundreds and five 50s By the time he left Somerset, his batting was pretty much the finished article: flashing cuts, square drives, powerful pull shots and very strong off his legs, and he was a more than useful bowler as well. Even as a young man, he was tough, shrewd and hard-bitten. You could see very clearly that here was a captain of Australia in the making.

Kieron Pollard

I have included Kieron because he had such an effect on our T20 cricket. He was a great character, who reminded me a bit of Joel in his sort of laid-back affability and the fact that he loved playing cricket – in his case, T20 cricket. And couldn't he hit a cricket ball! Two sixes stick in the memory: the first when he hit Shaun Udal onto the roof of the Lord's pavilion, coming as close as anyone has done to emulating Albert Trott in clearing the thing; the other when he hit the top deck of the new stand at Trent Bridge. I have never seen anyone hit the ball further. Kieron played a big part in Somerset reaching two successive finals days and suffered the most appalling luck. At the Rose Bowl he took that amazing catch in the semi-final, then ended up in hospital with that eye injury – while at Edgbaston the following year, he was the victim of

a quite astonishing catch by Paul Nixon. Yes, he could sometimes seem a bit lackadaisical, but he was a great competitor and a thoroughly nice guy.

Craig Kieswetter

I have often thought that Craig Kieswetter would have fitted well into the Somerset side that I captained. He had loads of self-confidence, he could be abrasive and you never knew whether what he came out with would make you laugh or make you cry. I first saw him batting at Millfield and decided within about three balls, two of which were driven fiercely for four through extra-cover, that this was a cricketer we needed to sign. That first impression was confirmed when he turned out for Somerset 2nds against Middlesex 2nds soon afterwards. I was watching him batting, when this bloke came up to me and asked me what I thought. I said that I was going to sign him straight after the game. It was the right response, as it turned out that my questioner was Wayne Kieswetter, Craig's father! As a batsman, he could hit the ball incredibly hard, his signature shot being a bullet-like drive over mid-off which once almost took out the Worcestershire Chief Executive sitting in his office at New Road! He and Tres formed quite the most devastating opening partnership in white-ball cricket. As a keeper, he practised hard

and got better as his career went on although, as I have said already, I would have given the gloves to Buttler and made Craig captain, batting at four or five, if I had still been in charge. The eye injury that eventually ended his career was not that dissimilar to mine, in the effect that it had on his eyesight, and I sometimes wonder if he might have been sensible to have given it a bit more time before calling it a day. But if that was the medical advice he received, then so be it. He was a big loss to Somerset cricket.

Andrew Caddick

Andy Caddick is one of my all-time favourite Somerset cricketers. 'Uncompromising' is the word that comes to mind whenever I think of him, in terms of how he wanted to bowl and how long he wanted to bowl for. It was difficult sometimes for the captain to get the ball off him. If I'd had him in my side, alongside Garner and Botham, we would have won the championship, simple as that, although I am not sure if any of them would have appreciated being first change! He could be uncompromising in his opinions as well, and he still makes me laugh when he starts sounding off like he does. But what a bowler! A bit like Joel, he made great use of his height and could bowl ball after ball, hitting the top of off, usually swinging away, with the occasional one that cut back. Considering that his home ground had one of the best batting pitches in the country, his record is remarkable, as was his longevity as a fast bowler. In 2007, when he played a huge part in winning us promotion, he was one of the leading wicket-takers in the country at the age of 38. Even though his last couple of seasons were plagued by injury, it was a very difficult conversation when I had to tell him towards the end of the 2009 season that his time was up. But he came to accept it in time, and I hope we are still good friends.

Hallam Moseley

Hallam was one of the most enthusiastic, cheerful, popular and hard-working players in my or any other era of Somerset cricket. It was when he was playing for the International Cavaliers in the summer of 1969 that he was picked out by my old coach Bill Andrews as just the sort of opening bowler that Somerset needed to replace Fred Rumsey and Ken Palmer, both then nearing the end of their careers. Bill's assessment of Hallam's potential was confirmed by none other than his fellow Barbadian Garry Sobers but, before he was actually signed by Somerset, I was given the task of batting against him in the nets, just  to be quite sure. It turned out I'd drawn the short straw! The nets in those days were in what is now the St James' Street car park, backing up against the outer wall. Eager to impress, Hallam fired the ball down at the best part of 90 mph on a dreadful surface, and I was soon ducking and weaving all over the place. There was no roof to the net, and two or three deliveries took off so sharply that they cleared the back wall and ended up in the road! He turned out to be a wonderful acquisition: ever-willing, ever-smiling – even when he lost his place to Joel – and hugely popular with spectators, not least for his brilliant fielding and spectacular Caribbean-style batting. His eyesight was never great and got worse as his career went on, so that by the end he couldn't see much, even if his glasses hadn't fallen off, as they so often did. Everyone in Somerset was delighted when he finally got a winner's medal at the 1982 Benson & Hedges Cup Final against Surrey. As a bowler, he maybe was not quite in the highest class, but as a county professional you could not fault him, and he's gone on to provide great service to cricket as a coach in the MCC academy.

Mushtaq Ahmed

Mushtaq is far and away the best spinner to have played for Somerset in my time. In 62 first-class matches for Somerset, he took 289 wickets, almost half of them on Phil Frost's shirt-front pitches at Taunton, including 22 five-wicket hauls, and he was just as effective in one-day cricket. He had a lovely bubbly personality and was a real favourite, with spectators and in the dressing room alike. As a leg-spinner, he had a beautiful loop, which could extract some useful bounce, even from a Taunton pitch, and he could turn it sharply both ways. He wasn't a bad batter down the order, either. It was a shame that he left Somerset under a bit of a cloud, but I am glad that things worked out so well for him in the end, even if it was a bit galling when he won those three championships for Sussex! What wouldn't I give for a home-grown leg spinner even half as good as Mushtaq?

Alfonso Thomas

After winning promotion to Division One at the end of the 2007 season, I set out to find a top-class seam bowler, to complement Caddick and Willoughby. South Africa seemed an obvious place to start, given my connections with Jimmy Cook and Graeme Smith, so I flew out to meet up with them. It was over dinner in Johannesburg that Jimmy suggested Fonzi. He had been playing for Warwickshire the previous season, but that arrangement had come to an end, and he was available as a Kolpak signing. I had to get home in a hurry, because my father had just died, so I met up with him at the airport and agreed a contract on the spot. When I got back, Richard Gould was happy enough, but Justin Langer had his doubts. "Jeez," he said. "You do realise he's only 5 foot 9?!" Anyway, at the start of the 2008 season, I went up to Durham to watch him in a 2nd XI match. It was not quite a 'Joel Garner at Bath in 1977' moment, but it was not far off it. He had pace, natural outswing, great control, and he was exactly what I had signed him to be – the perfect first change after Caddick and Willoughby. He also proved to be what Jimmy Cook had promised – a brilliant white-ball bowler, who virtually redefined 'death bowling' with his mixture of slower balls, slower-ball bouncers and spearing yorkers. He was a hugely committed, quite emotional cricketer, and I was genuinely sad when Somerset decided to let him go at the end of the 2015 season. Great bloke and a bloody good bowler.

Young lions

As I write, Somerset is blessed with some outstanding young cricketers. I first saw **Tom Abell** when he was still at Taunton School, and marked him down straight away as a future first-class cricketer. He has not fulfilled his potential yet. I would like to see him opening the innings because, if he is going to play for England, that is where it will be, but he has grown into a fine captain, who has shown great character in overcoming his loss of form when he was first given the job. As a batsman, he has all the attributes to be a top-class

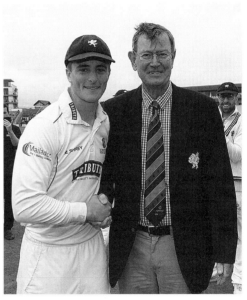

Presenting Tom Abell with his county cap

player, but he does need to convert that into runs – ideally, over 1,000 runs in two consecutive seasons – if he is to put himself in contention for an England place.

Craig and Jamie Overton

The **Overton twins** were also on my radar from a very young age. They have got the perfect physique to be fast bowlers, even if they have both been held back by injuries. Interestingly for twins, they have very different personalities. Craig is more contained and thoughtful. Jamie, on the other hand, is more emotional, prone to the red mist coming down when he gets hit. As I have explained to him, that is not helpful in any way because, if you lose your temper, your muscles tighten up, and that will make you less effective as a bowler, not more. For the time being, I would like to see him concentrating on bowling really well, more than on bowling really fast. The pace will come naturally, anyway, as his confidence builds from consistently good returns. But they have both got the potential, as counter-attacking batsmen and brilliant fielders, as well as fast bowlers, to play loads of international cricket for England, provided they can stay relatively injury-free.

Add in the likes of **Jack Leach, Lewis Gregory** and **Dom Bess** and, provided they are not all playing for England, all the ingredients are in place to achieve the one thing that every Somerset cricket follower craves: that elusive first county championship!

19

Gratefully onwards

I have never been a great fan of sports books in which the author looks back over his or her career in the final chapter. I prefer to look forward, especially as I've still got a lot to look forward to.

Being elected as President of Somerset County Cricket Club in January 2019 was a great honour and will keep me involved with the cricketing side at Somerset for at least the next three years – not that I have the slightest intention of interfering with the Director of Cricket, coaches or captain. If they ask for my advice on anything, or want to draw upon my experience in the game, then I'll be only too happy to oblige. But for the most part I'll just feel happy and privileged to be able to sit in on meetings, spend time with cricketing friends, old and new, and watch as much Somerset cricket as my nerves can take!

Being congratulated on my election as President
by Somerset CCC Chief Executive Andrew Cornish

Somerset CCC has a hugely talented squad of players, most of them home-grown, a highly professional team of coaches and administrators, a brilliant academy system, a sound financial base, one of the finest grounds in the country and, exactly as in my days as a player, the most passionate bunch of members and supporters you could wish for. All the ingredients are there to give us a great chance in all three competitions. To win the county championship would, of course, be a dream come true; it's something I hardly dare even hope for, it would mean so much. But after all the close-run things when I was Director of Cricket, I reckon the gods of sport owe me one, so you never know!

But cricket is only part of what I've got to look forward to. My family and, in particular, my two wonderful grandsons, Jack and Toby, are even more important to me. Jack is the son of Stuart and Claire; Toby of Joey and Jill. It's a bit early to say whether they'll turn out to be cricketers, but they are both fine boys who certainly enjoy their visits to the County Ground and all the fun and games in Maz Masarik's box! Watching them grow up is one of my life's greatest pleasures.

Joey, Jill & Toby

Stuart, Claire & Jack

When I do allow myself the luxury of looking back, it is the good guys that I think of: people who have helped me through my career and my life. In cricket, the names that spring immediately to mind include Bill Andrews, Peter Robinson, Roy Kerslake, Tom Cartwright, Brian Close and Peter Anderson, all of whom deserve my most profound thanks for their guidance and help. But there are many more, including all of those who have been kind enough to write nice things about me for the introduction to this book. There is no finer fellowship than the fellowship of cricket.

It goes without saying that the person I owe most to is my wife Stevie, who has stuck with me through thick and thin for over 50 years now. I'm never quite sure how much she knows about the technical side of cricket – although it's probably a lot more than I think! What she does understand is that it is a bloody difficult career for family life. With a lot of sports, you're on the field for 90 minutes, then into a coach and back home in the evening. With cricket, you can be away for days, weeks, sometimes even months at a time. All this at a time in your life when you're growing up, having children, with your wife back at home trying to cope with it all, on her own, and probably worried about what her husband may be up to. When I think of cricketers' wives, I often think of Vivienne Close and the way she stood by Brian through all of his triumphs and disasters. What a treasure she was and is. Mind you, she had to be to put up with Brian!

I have always had a tendency to be a bit lackadaisical (in everything but cricket). Stevie is the complete opposite. She is tenacious. The one thing that she cares about more than anything else is her family. She keeps going, for her family, no matter what. And she has kept me going as well, through some very rough times with injury, illness and financial misfortune. No man could wish for a better wife. So thank you, Stevie, for everything you've done, for me and for the family. You've been our rock.

Thanks

Finally, a special word of thanks to Graham 'Maz' Masarik and his company Eurocams for their very generous support for this book. Eurocams was founded by Maz's father Frank in Weston-super-Mare in 1999 and has since gone from strength to strength to become Europe's largest supplier of aftermarket engine components. Many young Somerset sportsmen have been helped by the Masarik family, including Peter Trego, on his return to Somerset, and Jos Buttler and Tom Abell at the start of their careers.

My first encounter with Maz was distinctly unconventional. I was batting at the Town end in one Weston Festival when play was interrupted after a young lad had fallen out of a tree at the far end, onto a sponsor's tent. It turned out to be Maz – fortunately a good bit lighter than he is today, so no harm was done, either to him or the sponsor's tent!

More recently, the Masarik family and Eurocams have been prominent sponsors of Somerset County Cricket Club, and I have been fortunate enough to visit their box at the County Ground on many occasions, sometimes with my two grandsons Jack and Toby. It is always a lively gathering and the two lads have both learned some interesting new expressions, like Maz's favourite "Ump, get your finger up!!" I'm not sure quite what they made of that at Jack's nursery school!

Maz has been a great friend for many years and never more so than when I was suffering from illness and tooth problems a few years back. It was a combination of Maz and Peter Trego who arranged specialist help through the Professional Cricketers' Association, for which I shall always be profoundly grateful. The PCA does great work helping former cricketers who may have encountered illness, mental health issues, financial problems or other difficulties, and the sponsorship that they receive from Eurocams and others is money well and wisely spent.

So thank you, Maz, for all that you and your family do, for me and for cricket.

I first remember seeing Brian Rose at the Weston festival in 1977. Straightaway I enjoyed watching his batting style, complemented by his mop of blond hair. His partnership with Peter 'Dasher' Denning was legendary, and I loved it.

A couple of years later I started sticking up skittles in the Albany bar at the Cabot Hotel on Weston seafront, and to see my idols close up was fantastic. You had the studious ones like Marks and Roebuck, you had Captain Sensible (Rosey), you had the lad from the village (Dasher) and Big Bird (Joel) who spent the night bent over, due to the low ceilings. And upstairs were the two rock stars, Botham and Richards, smoking fat cigars and drinking copious amounts of drink.

Little did I know that 28 years later Rosey would become my drinking partner at the Windsor Castle.

It has been a pleasure and a privilege to sit with him and chew the cud about life and cricket. I would like to thank Brian for bringing me into the Somerset family from a young age. I wish him well for the future and as Somerset President.

Graham Masarik

FIRST-CLASS CRICKET

BATTING AND FIELDING

HOME	M	I	NO	Runs	HS	Ave	100	50	Ct
1969	16	27	3	357	49	14.87	-	-	4
1970	6	10	-	73	16	7.30	-	-	4
1972	3	5	-	252	125	50.40	1	-	4
1973	11	16	1	240	34	16.00	-	-	4
1974	1	2	-	21	14	10.50	-	-	-
1975	22	41	4	1060	115*	28.64	1	6	9
1976	20	39	4	1624	177	46.40	4	8	11
1977	20	35	3	1193	205	37.28	3	3	6
1978	24	41	5	1263	122	35.08	4	3	12
1979	21	33	1	1317	133	41.15	2	8	11
1980	17	26	4	1084	150*	49.27	2	5	6
1981	23	39	4	1005	107	28.71	1	5	21
1982	21	32	8	1090	173*	45.41	2	5	10
1983	8	9	-	184	52	20.44	-	1	2
1984	20	33	4	856	123	29.51	1	4	5
1985	5	9	1	196	81*	24.50	-	1	2
1986	14	23	5	784	129	43.55	2	3	3
1987	3	4	-	60	31	15.00	-	-	1
Total	**255**	**424**	**47**	**12659**	**205**	**33.57**	**23**	**52**	**115**
OVERSEAS									
1977/78 *(P)*	7	10	2	281	110*	35.12	1	1	5
1977/78 *(NZ)*	5	9	1	227	107	28.37	1	-	3
1980/81 *(WI)*	3	5	-	69	43	13.80	-	-	-
Total	**15**	**24**	**3**	**577**	**110***	**27.47**	**2**	**1**	**8**
Total	**270**	**448**	**50**	**13236**	**205**	**33.25**	**25**	**53**	**123**

BOWLING

Overs	Mdns	Runs	Wkts	Best	Ave
74.1	6	289	8	3-9	36.12

SCORES OF 150+

205	Somerset v Northamptonshire	Weston-super-Mare	1977
177	Somerset v Leicestershire	Taunton	1976
173*	Somerset v Gloucestershire	Bristol	1982
150*	Somerset v Worcestershire	Worcester	1980

TWO CENTURIES IN A MATCH

124 & 150*	Somerset v Worcestershire	Worcester	1980

TEST CRICKET

BATTING AND FIELDING

	M	I	NO	Runs	HS	Ave	100	50	Ct
1977/78 *(P)*	3	4	-	56	27	14.00	-	-	1
1977/78 *(NZ)*	2	4	1	44	21	14.66	-	-	1
1980 *(WI)*	3	6	1	243	70	48.60	-	2	2
1980/81 *(WI)*	1	2	-	15	10	7.50	-	-	-
Total	**9**	**16**	**2**	**358**	**70**	**25.57**	**-**	**2**	**4**

FIFTIES

70	England v West Indies	Old Trafford	1980
50	England v West Indies	The Oval	1980

LIMITED-OVER CRICKET

BATTING AND FIELDING

	M	I	NO	Runs	HS	Ave	100	50	Ct
Home	251	237	33	5708	137*	27.98	3	28	63
Overseas	7	7	-	138	54	19.71	-	1	2
Total	**258**	**244**	**33**	**5846**	**137***	**27.70**	**3**	**29**	**65**

BOWLING

Overs	Mdns	Runs	Wkts	Best	Ave
34	-	152	7	3-25	21.71

CENTURIES

137*	Somerset v Kent *(B&H)*	Canterbury	1980
128	Somerset v Derbyshire *(Gillette)*	Ilkeston	1977
112*	Somerset v Essex *(John Player)*	Ilford	1980

LIMITED-OVER INTERNATIONALS

BATTING AND FIELDING

	M	I	NO	Runs	HS	Ave	100	50	Ct
1977/78 *(P)*	2	2	-	99	54	49.50	-	1	1
Total	**2**	**2**	**-**	**99**	**54**	**49.50**	**-**	**1**	**1**

FIFTIES

54	England v Pakistan	Sahiwal	1977/78

INDEX

221